The Yankees

The Yankees

The Four Fabulous Eras
of Baseball's Most Famous Team

Dave Anderson

Murray Chass

Robert Creamer

Harold Rosenthal

Revised and Updated

Random House  New York

Library of Congress Cataloging in Publication Data

Main entry under title:

The Yankees.

1. New York (City). Baseball club (American
League)—History.   I. Anderson, Dave.
GV875.N4Y28   1980   796.357′64′097471   79–3802
ISBN 0–394–51133–6

Manufactured in the United States of America
24689753
First Edition

Designed by Robert Aulicino

Introduction
by Dave Anderson

The New York Yankees

Introduction

The history of the New York Yankees is virtually the history of baseball.

Over the last six decades, the Yankees have dominated the game—from the glory of Babe Ruth and Lou Gehrig to the grace of Joe DiMaggio to the reign of Mickey Mantle and Casey Stengel to the turmoil of the 1977–78 World Series championship teams of "money" players—Reggie Jackson, Ron Guidry, the late Thurman Munson and the now-retired Catfish Hunter, to name four.

For the current team the word "money" is a double entendre. They are "money" players in the finest tradition of athletes who produce under pressure. They also are "money" players in the sense that George Steinbrenner, the Yankees' principal owner, has spent millions to obtain them or pay them, or both.

The Yankees have ruled baseball as no other major league team ever has. Consider that:

—The Yankees have won twenty-two World Series championships and thirty-two American League pennants; the St. Louis Cardinals are next in World Series titles with only eight, and the New York–San Francisco Giants are next in pennants with fourteen in the National League.

—The Yankees have won five consecutive World Series (1949–1953) and also four in a row (1936–1939); only two other teams have won three in a row even once—the Oakland A's (1972–1974) and the Chicago Cubs (1906–1908).

—The Yankees have won five consecutive American League pennants twice (1949–1953 and 1960–1964) and four in a row twice (1936–1939 and 1955–1958); the Giants are the only other team to have won four consecutive pennants even once (1921–1924).

Yankee players, meanwhile, have established some of baseball's most memorable records:

    —Roger Maris' sixty-one home runs in 1961.
    —Babe Ruth's sixty home runs in 1927.
    —Joe DiMaggio's fifty-six-game hitting streak in 1941.
    —Ron Guidry's 25-3 season in 1978.

In the Hall of Fame at Cooperstown, New York, bronze plaques commemorate the accomplishments of nineteen players, managers and executives who were with the Yankees during the most important years of their careers—Babe Ruth, Lou Gehrig, Jack Chesbro, Herb Pennock, Ed Barrow, Bill Dickey, Joe DiMaggio, Joe McCarthy, Miller Huggins, Casey Stengel, Red Ruffing, Waite Hoyt, Earle Combs, George Weiss, Yogi Berra, Lefty Gomez, Mickey Mantle and Whitey

Ford. Five other Hall of Famers also were with the Yankees, some for several seasons, some briefly—Willie Keeler, Clark Griffith, Frank (Home Run) Baker, Bucky Harris, Joe Sewell and Larry MacPhail.

Perhaps the primary reason for the Yankees' success is that, more than any other team, they have adapted to baseball's methods and rules.

When it was fashionable to purchase players from financially troubled teams, the Yankees obtained Babe Ruth and several other stars from the Boston Red Sox—the start of the Yankee–Red Sox rivalry that still flourishes. When farm systems were popular, the Yankees had one of the best. When the free agent era began not long ago, the Yankees invested heavily and wisely, restoring the prestige that had nearly disintegrated during the previous decade.

Because of their reign, the Yankees have even turned inanimate objects into symbols of success.

The club's most famous inanimate object, Yankee Stadium itself, is baseball's most famous ballpark. And their pin-striped white double-knits, which the players wear at home games, are baseball's most famous uniform.

From any viewpoint the Yankees are baseball's most famous team. That is their reputation and their tradition. And this is their history.

Dave Anderson

The Yankees

The New York Yankees

Babe Ruth and Lou Gehrig
by Robert Creamer

EVERYTHING THE NEW YORK YANKEES are now began with Babe Ruth. They had *existed* before Ruth, had for almost twenty years, but they were not the Yankees as we know them: traditionally, historically and currently the best of all baseball teams. Those primeval Yankees never won a pennant, and they finished higher than fourth only four times—including a third-place finish in 1919, the year before the Babe joined them, when they were finally beginning to jell.

Ruth descended on New York like an enveloping flame. The whole city seemed to light up under his presence. He reached people who had never been baseball fans, and who at first were more interested in the home runs he hit than the game he played. One of his most famous nicknames, the Bambino, almost certainly had its origin among the millions of more or less recently arrived Italian immigrants in and near New York who asked one another, Did the *bambino* (the baby, the babe) hit one today?

He could show petulance and even anger at times with fans both inside and outside the ballpark, but for the most part he was cheerful and accessible, at home in mobs of people.

He was quickly caught up in New York's social swim and found himself hobnobbing with celebrities from society and the theater and films, often without knowing precisely who the glittering people were. He once went to dinner at a fashionable home where Douglas Fairbanks and Mary Pickford, the most famous couple in motion pictures, were guests of honor. The next day a teammate asked about the evening. Babe said he had been to a swell party with "some movie people." What movie people? Babe couldn't remember.

He was never unduly impressed by other celebrities. He was introduced to Marshal Foch when the French hero of World War I was touring the United States in the 1920's and said amiably, making conversation, "I suppose you were in the war?" When he met President Warren Harding at the Washington Senators' ballpark on a blazing summer day, he said, "Hot as hell, ain't it, Prez?" (On such hot days he would put big cabbage leaves in the dugout water cooler and wear one, dripping wet, under his cap when he went out onto the field.)

In the 1928 Presidential election, when Herbert Hoover was running against Al Smith, Hoover's campaign managers brought their candidate to the ballpark to get a publicity photograph of him with Ruth. Babe refused, saying nothing doing, he wasn't going to get involved with politics. But to show he had nothing against the man personally he said graciously that if Hoover wanted to meet him he would be glad to talk to him under the grandstand. This innocent impudence was picked up by the newspapers, which ran banner headlines saying Ruth had snubbed Herbert Hoover. The Babe's agent, Christy Walsh, could see Ruth's off-field income dropping in half as the Republicans of the country turned against him en masse. He explained this to the Babe and hurriedly arranged for the picture to be taken. It was all a "misunderstanding," Walsh explained.

Ruth's appetite was famous, and stories about what he ate began to multiply and exaggerate to the point of impossibility. Still, there is no denying that he once ate an omelet made of eighteen eggs and three big slices of ham, and he certainly did eat voraciously. His belly was obvious and ample, although it occasionally shrank like the polar icecap on Mars when he was reforming. Then it would balloon again. The Babe tended to go to extremes.

He drove around town in flashy cars, usually at speeds far above what the law allowed. Often the law smiled and looked the other way, but now and then the police would crack down on him. In June 1921 a motorcycle cop nabbed him for speeding on Riverside Drive in New York, and he was taken to court, fined $100 and sentenced to a day in jail. The "day" ended in midafternoon, and as soon as he was released the Babe roared away, this time with a police escort, and raced north through Manhattan to the Polo Grounds, arriving in time to play the last few innings.

The previous year, in another car, he was driving back to New York after a series of games in Washington, D.C., when he skidded and turned over just south of Philadelphia. No one was seriously hurt, but the car was demolished and the rumor spread quickly that he had been killed in the crash. One newspaper ran a headline to that effect. It wasn't until Ruth showed up in New York that the Yankees breathed easily again.

He made bundles of money and spent bundles, until Christy Walsh took him in hand and made him plan for the future. He was always a lavish tipper. When a chambermaid in a hotel found and returned a treasured watch fob he had left behind in his room, the Babe gave her a $100 tip. He was as generous with his time as he was with his money and frequently visited hospitals, particularly children's wards. While many of his visits were initiated by publicity-minded friends or business associates, the Babe went willingly and was invariably a source of delight for the patients. And he would often go on unpublicized visits

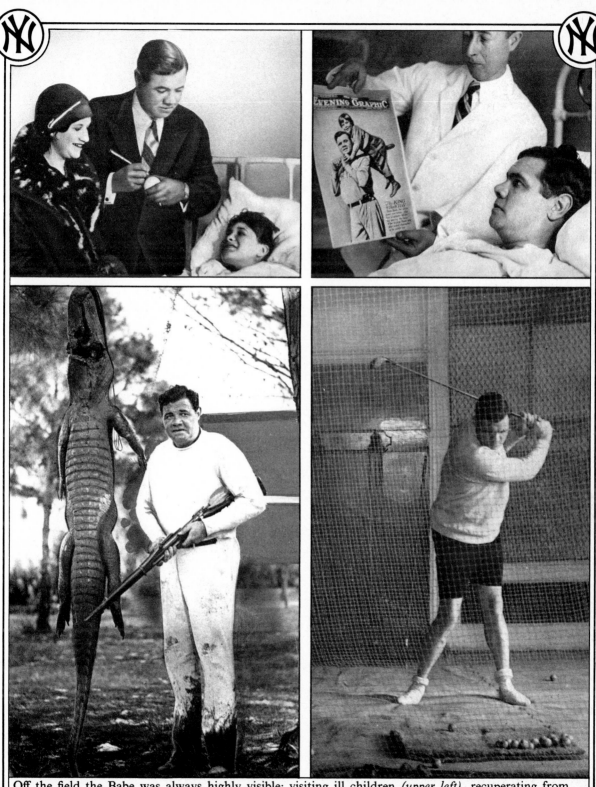

Off the field the Babe was always highly visible: visiting ill children *(upper left)*, recuperating from overindulgence *(upper right)*, hunting alligators *(lower left)*, and grooving his golf swing.

to sick people on spur-of-the-moment invitations with no publicity in sight.

His most famous, or at least most publicized, hospital visit came in the 1920's when the uncle of a seriously injured youngster named Johnny Sylvester arranged for Ruth to autograph a baseball for the boy. Ruth later visited the hospital, and the papers were soon filled with sob-sister stories about the Babe promising to hit a home run for a dying boy and then saving his life by actually hitting one, the excitement of the fulfilled promise having brought new life to the poor sick kid. Ruth apparently did say he would try to hit a homer, something he said often, and he did come through. But while Johnny Sylvester's injury was serious, he was not dying. In any case, he recovered, and his name became embroidered in Ruth's legend.

There is an engaging afterword. Some months later the boy's uncle ran into Ruth, introduced himself and said, "I just want to thank you again for what you did for Johnny." Ruth waved his hand magnanimously, said it was nothing, he was glad to do it, and asked, "How is Johnny?"

"He's fine," the uncle said. "He's home and everything looks okay."

"That's good," Ruth said. "Glad to hear it." After the uncle walked away he said wonderingly, "Who the hell is Johnny Sylvester?"

The Babe wasn't stupid. He had simply forgotten. The incident had not made nearly the impression on him that it had on the press and public. He wasn't interested in all the folderol that surrounded him. He *enjoyed* it, but he wasn't impressed by it. When he met Max Schmeling, then the world heavyweight boxing champion, he had a pleasant enough chat with the fighter, but a friend who was there felt he should have done more. He should have asked Schmeling for his autograph. Ruth, who gave out thousands of autographs himself in his thirty years in the public eye, said inelegantly, "Oh, hell, who wants to collect that crap?"

Despite his generally friendly nature and his widespread popularity, both in and out of baseball, Ruth often got into fights, or at least disputes, although they usually never amounted to much. His temper was mercurial and usually came down rapidly after a momentary tantrum. Sometimes he was lucky it did: if he had been a more aggressively angry man, he might not have survived a couple of tiffs.

One morning an angry woman waving a knife chased him through a Yankee train as it was leaving the station. Whatever the reason for her anger, the chastened Ruth had no desire to confront it. He escaped by jumping off the front car of the slowly moving train, racing to the rear of the platform and hopping back on the last car, leaving the pursuing knife wielder confused on the platform.

He once went into the bleachers after an abusive fan and found himself facing another knife; intervention by a teammate got him away from danger. In Louisiana, during spring training, a customer at an after-hours joint got mad at something Ruth said, followed him away from the place in his car, forced him off the road and was holding a gun on him when Ruth's teammates came along in another auto and rescued him.

He was loud, raucous, vulgar, often obscene, sometimes fairly witty, more often obvious and coarse in his humor. Men wore hard, flat straw hats in the summer then, but tradition said they were put away after Labor Day. Ruth thought it the height of subtlety to grab a straw hat lingering on an unsuspecting head a day or two after Labor Day and punch a hole through it.

Things kept happening to him. He signed to make a fast, cheap baseball-and-melodrama silent film called *The Babe Comes Home* in the late summer of 1920. The film was being shot near New York, and he would drive out in the morning, emote before the cameras and drive back in time for the day's game, which would not start until 3 or 3:30 in the afternoon. One morning on the set he was stung by a bee or some other insect, and his right arm swelled alarmingly. He needed medical treatment and missed several games, while the papers had fun writing about the savage insect that had attacked the immortal Babe and brought him low.

He was eternally restless, constantly moving, from woman to woman, from party to party, from nightclub to speakeasy to all-night restaurant. Ping Bodie, a glib, funny outfielder who was playing for the Yankees when the Babe joined them, roomed with the hero for a time. Except that the hero practically never used his room, finding fun and companionship elsewhere. Bodie once was asked what it was like rooming with the famous Babe Ruth.

"I don't room with the Babe," he said. "I room with his suitcase."

The Babe came to the Yankees from the Boston Red Sox in January 1920, in what remains the most stunning and significant switch of a player from one club to another in all of baseball's long history. The Babe had been with the Red Sox since July 1914, when the Red Sox bought him from the minor league Baltimore Orioles, then in the International League. He appeared in a couple of games in July, was farmed out for a couple of months to Providence, which was also in the International League, and returned to the Red Sox for good at the very end of the 1914 season.

He was a pitcher at that time, a tall, powerfully built lefthander— but lithe, not fat. He was six feet two inches tall and weighed about 190 pounds. The 1914 season was his first as a professional. In February, a few days after his twentieth birthday (a birth certificate unearthed years later indicated he was actually only nineteen, but Ruth himself always went with the older age), he had come out of St. Mary's Industrial School for Boys, a combination orphanage, house of refuge and reform school in Baltimore, to sign a contract with Jack Dunn, the Orioles' owner-manager. At St. Mary's he was plain George Ruth, the overgrown, troublemaking son of a Baltimore saloon keeper. He had first been sent to St. Mary's when he was eight, and while several times he had been in and out of the Home, as it was called in Baltimore, he had spent most of his life between the ages of eight and twenty behind the grim iron fences of St. Mary's. The prime recreation for the boys there was baseball, and George Ruth quickly demonstrated a genius for the game.

When he was released from the Home to join the Orioles, Dunn agreed to act as something of a guardian for him. Ruth was enormously talented as an athlete but woefully naive about the ways of the world —so much so that veteran players at the Orioles' spring training camp in Fayetteville, North Carolina, took to calling him "Dunn's babe." By the end of spring training everybody was calling him Babe Ruth.

Ruth was an immediate and overwhelming success as a pitcher. He had won fourteen games by the first week of July to help Dunn's powerful club open up a commanding lead in the International League race. Dunn, however, was having financial problems because of the presence in Baltimore of a team in the brief-lived Federal League, a third major league that lasted only two seasons. He sold Babe and his other prize players to big-league teams in midseason; the Orioles slumped and fell out of first place. Ruth spent a month with Boston, won one game and lost another, then went down to Providence, where he helped pitch that team to the International League pennant he had earlier all but clinched for the Orioles.

All in all, it was a fabulous year for a twenty-year-old kid. Counting his separate stints with Baltimore and Providence, as well as his brief appearances with the Red Sox, he won twenty-five games and lost only nine, even though he did not pitch at all for twenty-six days in midsummer when he was sitting on the Red Sox bench. He also hit his first professional home run, a blast in Toronto that was the only homer he ever hit in the minor leagues.

Ruth's prowess with the bat was apparent early, but he was thought of primarily as a pitcher—and with good reason. With the Red Sox in 1915 he won eighteen games, seventeen of them after June 1. In 1916 he won twenty-three, including nine shutouts (an American League record for lefthanders that stood alone for sixty-two years until the Yankees' Ron Guidry tied it in 1978) and had a 1.75 earned-run average, the best in the league. He also went all the way in a fourteen-inning game in the 1916 World Series, which is still the longest World Series game ever played and which Ruth won, 2–1. He was not just good; he was a *great* pitcher.

In 1917 he won twenty-four games, but in 1918, with many of the Red Sox hitters gone off to the war (the Babe was married and exempt from military service), he began the transition to the outfield and pitched only part-time. He would not have pitched at all that year if he had had his own way. He had fallen in love with hitting and wanted to give up pitching entirely and move to the outfield so he could play every day. But beetle-browed Ed Barrow, the Red Sox manager, who is usually given credit for changing Babe from pitcher to hitter, was in fact adamantly opposed to the idea. Barrow was fighting for a pennant, and he wanted Ruth's arm on the mound.

The two squabbled and fought, and at one point Ruth jumped the club and threatened to play for a wartime shipyard team. Late in July the two worked out a compromise. Ruth would play the outfield and bat cleanup, but he would also pitch every fourth day. That solution gave the Red Sox the pennant. The Babe's pitching record was thirteen victories and seven defeats, but seven of his triumphs came in the last month of the war-shortened season. He won two more games as Boston took the World Series and extended his streak of scoreless innings pitched in the Series to twenty-nine, breaking the record of twenty-eight set years earlier by the immortal Christy Mathewson. His record lasted more than forty years, until Whitey Ford broke it in 1961.

Ruth batted .300 in 1918, was third in the league in runs batted in and tied for first in home runs—with eleven. But most of his eleven homers were such impressive wallops that he was referred to for the first time as the Home Run King, prompting the development of a livelier ball. More significantly, even though he came to bat far fewer times than the big-name hitters in the league—Ty Cobb, Tris Speaker, George Sisler, Home Run Baker and the like—he had more extra-base hits (doubles, triples and home runs) than any of them. He was utterly spectacular, and he had become the most talked-about player in the game.

In 1919 he was even better as a hitter, banging out twenty-nine home runs, a fantastic figure for that day and age. He pitched a little—his record shows nine wins and five losses—but his hitting now almost totally obscured his pitching. He broke every home-run record in the book that year, including an obscure and freakish mark of twenty-seven set back in 1884 by a player named Ed Williamson, who had only two the year before his big season and three the year after. (Williamson's secret was that in 1884 his team played in a park where part of the outfield fence was only two hundred feet from home plate.) As Ruth swept past all the old records, he drove the excited postwar baseball crowds to a frenzy. He had been the best lefthanded pitcher in the game.

Now he was the best hitter, the best ballplayer, the purveyor of home
runs, the biggest drawing card, the one and only Babe Ruth.

Suddenly, stunningly, he was sold to the New York Yankees.

Harry Frazee, the owner of the Red Sox, was a theatrical producer
and seriously in debt. He needed money, and he got $100,000 from the
Yankees for Ruth's contract, as well as a $300,000 loan. In selling Ruth,
Frazee was destroying the Red Sox—he continued to sell his stars to
the Yankees over the next few years, and the Red Sox finished last nine
times in eleven seasons—but he made the Yankees.

In New York, the Babe found the ideal stage for his outsize personality. In his first season there, the no-win Yankees finished a close,
challenging third and then won three consecutive pennants. They won
six pennants in his first nine years, one of them by nineteen games,
another by sixteen. Ruth won the home run championship ten times in
twelve years. He hit fifty-four in 1920, his first season in New York, to
shatter his remarkable record of the year before, and in 1921 he broke
that record by hitting fifty-nine. Off the field he ate, drank, caroused,
chased women, got into trouble and made headlines. His huge moon
face was known everywhere. Almost certainly, he was the most famous
person in the country during the 1920's. Jack Dempsey, Charlie Chap-
lin, Charles Lindbergh and one or two others (Calvin Coolidge, possibly) were as well *known* by name as Ruth, but not so well known in
public, where Ruth seemed always to be. Ruth dominated his team, his
league, his sport, his environment; wherever Babe Ruth was, he was the
center of attention.

Through all those years of acclaim the Yankees were his base of
operations. His great years with the Red Sox receded into dim past
history; his later fitful appearances as a player with the Boston Braves
and as a coach with the Brooklyn Dodgers were passing aberrations.
Ruth was a Yankee, and the Yankees were Ruth.

When he joined the club, the Yankees were on the rise. For years they
had been a hangdog team, also-rans, failures. The club had come into
existence in 1903 when Byron Bancroft Johnson, the energetic founder
and president of the American League, arranged the transfer of a
moribund last-place Baltimore franchise to New York. It was a direct
challenge to the older, more established National League and the New
York Giants of John McGraw, a man Johnson despised. Not only did
Ban Johnson put an American League team in New York, he saw to
it that it was stocked with good ballplayers. Only a handful of the
last-place Orioles joined the new team, which was managed by Clark
Griffith and owned by two classic New York wheeler-dealers: Big Bill
Devery, a former chief of police with important political connections,

American League Park, the original home of the Highlanders

Miller Huggins and Colonel Jacob Ruppert

and Frank Farrell, a big-time gambler and racehorse owner, also with political pull.

Devery and Farrell gave Ban Johnson the owners he needed, men with ready cash and valuable influence. The National League had been fighting off the upstart American, but now it gave in and worked out a peace treaty, accepting the American League team in New York on the condition that the new league would no longer raid National League teams for players. Johnson agreed, having already skimmed five outstanding players, including pitcher Jack Chesbro, from Pittsburgh, the 1902 National League champions, as well as Wee Willie Keeler from Brooklyn and a few others. Most of them, notably Chesbro and Keeler, were assigned to the new New York team.

Farrell and Devery had made a man named Joseph Gordon the nominal president, and somebody, aware that the team's home field, American League Park, was on top of Washington Heights, the highest part of Manhattan Island, and that Gordon's Highlanders was the name of one of the most famous regiments in the British army, decided that Highlanders was a perfect name for the new club. There was immediate dissent, however, from sports editors, who hated the prospect of trying to squeeze an eleven-letter nickname into a one-column headline and from anti-British elements in the heavily Irish population. Almost at once, the staunchly American name Yankees was introduced as a countermeasure, and from 1904 on it was used interchangeably with the more formal Highlanders. By World War I it had taken over completely, and the old name quietly disappeared.

In 1903 the new team was also occasionally referred to as the New York All Stars, a sarcastic reference to the collection of outstanding players Johnson had diverted to the roster, but the team never really got together and finished a fairly sedate fourth. Then, in 1904, with Keeler batting .343 and Chesbro winning forty-one games, the Yankees battled for the pennant down to the last day of the season. That afternoon, one and a half games behind, they had a doubleheader with the league leaders—none other than the Boston Red Sox (known then as the Pilgrims). The Yankees had to take both games to win the pennant, but in the ninth inning of the first game, with the score tied 2–2, a runner on third and two out, Chesbro unloosed a wild pitch and let in the run that lost the game and the pennant.

Until the Babe arrived, the Yankees never got that close to the championship again. They fell to sixth place in 1905 and, after a respectable second-place finish in 1906, to fifth in 1907 and to last in 1908. Keeler was about washed up by then, and the only player of real note on the roster was Hal Chase, who broke in with them in 1905. Chase was a tall, rawboned first baseman who threw left and batted right, a rare combination in major league baseball but one that fitted his odd nature. Old-timers maintained that Chase was the best fielding first baseman who ever lived but that he was as crooked as a three-dollar bill; they charged that he consorted with gamblers and threw games for money long before the Chicago Black Sox dumped the 1919 World Series.

Curiously, Chase's fielding statistics do not bear out the high acclaim for his fielding. According to the old-timers, this was because he deliberately made errors or bad plays in key situations, but he could not have made *that* many bad plays on purpose. In nine full seasons in the American League, eight of them with the Yankees, he ranked last or next to last in fielding averages among first basemen in every year but one.

Ah, say the experts, fielding averages don't tell the complete story. A first baseman who plays on a dime won't have as many fielding chances as one who tries for every ball, and therefore he won't make as many errors. But Chase, who supposedly had great range, never led the league in assists and was second only twice, despite claims by old fans that he would often race across the infield to handle a bunt on the third-base side of the mound. In total chances handled per game, which includes errors (even deliberate ones), he finished better than third only once.

Nonetheless, Chase had a reputation as a genius in the field, if an evil genius, and he was also a good, if not scintillating hitter who later on once led the National League in batting. In any case, after Keeler and Chesbro, he was the most famous player the Yankees had before Ruth.

In 1908 Clark Griffith left as manager in midseason and was replaced by the splendidly named Norman Arthur Elberfeld, known as the Tobasco Kid. The next year the Tobasco Kid was replaced by George Stallings, who later gained undying baseball fame when he guided the miracle Boston Braves of 1914 from last place in July to the National League pennant in October and then to a four-game sweep of the powerful Philadelphia Athletics in the World Series. Stallings lifted the Yankees from last place to fifth in 1909 and to second, albeit fourteen and a half games behind, in 1910. But, badgered by front-office interference, he departed just before that season ended, and the evil genius Chase took over. The team fell to sixth place in 1911 under Chase's guidance and he went back to playing first base and footsie with the gamblers. Harry Wolverton—surely you remember Harry Wolverton? —was named manager in 1912, watched the team descend into last place again and was gone, one of many big-league managers whose careers opened and closed in one year. American League Park also closed that year, with the Yankees moving to the Polo Grounds as the Giants' tenants.

Owners Farrell and Devery were extremely unhappy. Their ball club,

The New York Yankees

Clark Griffith

begun with such promise a decade earlier, was stumbling along while the hated Giants of McGraw were either winning pennants or finishing a strong second almost every year. The owners therefore hired as manager McGraw's most redoubtable rival, Frank Chance, who from 1906 through 1910 had led the Chicago Cubs to four pennants in five seasons. Chance's teams finished seventh in 1913 and seventh in 1914 before his departure in mid-September as the sixth Yankee manager in seven seasons to get it in the neck. The Peerless Leader, as Chance had been called when he managed the Cubs, did one memorable thing in his brief tenure. He told Heywood Broun, one of the writers covering the club for New York newspapers, that Chase was throwing ball games. Broun's paper was afraid to print the story, so Broun reworded it to say that Chance did not think Chase was "playing up to his ability." Even watered down, the story caused a furor, and two days later Chase's career as a Yankee ended when he was traded away to Chicago.

These were dismal days for Yankee fans, but something good was brewing. Farrell was broke, and he and Devery were quarreling openly. They no longer had their own ballpark, and crowds were small at the Polo Grounds as the Yankees continued to fail. They began looking around for a buyer.

Among the regular fans of the more prosperous Giants was Colonel Jacob Ruppert, an impeccably dressed, impeccably mannered New York socialite whose wealth came from his family's prosperous brewery, and Captain Tillinghast L'Hommedieu Huston, a big, cheerful, sloppily dressed Ohioan who had been a U.S. Army engineering officer and had made a fortune in construction in Cuba after the Spanish-American War. (Later Huston would serve as a colonel in World War I to achieve equal rank with Ruppert, who won his title at the age of twenty-two when he was made an honorary colonel on the staff of the governor of New York.)

Ruppert and Huston had nothing in common except money and an interest in baseball. Separately, they had approached John McGraw to see if they could buy his team. McGraw said no, but late in 1914, aware of the situation with Farrell and Devery, he suggested that Ruppert and Huston get together and buy the Yankees. They agreed, and in January 1915 the deal was consummated. Ruppert and Huston paid Farrell and Devery $460,000 and took command of the ball club—Ruppert as president, Huston as vice president. They picked Wild Bill Donovan, a former American League pitcher who had been a successful minor league manager, to guide the team.

At first the new regime had little effect on the team's performance. The Yankees moved up to fifth in 1915 but played about as badly as they had in 1914. In 1916 they finished fourth but in 1917 were back down to sixth. Ruppert and Huston were frustrated. They had put

Home Run Baker

Wally Pipp

money into the club. They had hired a new manager. They had obtained Home Run Baker, the great star of Connie Mack's pennant-winning Philadelphia Athletics. They had inherited a good shortstop in Roger Peckinpaugh, and they had found a fine young first baseman named Wally Pipp and a superb young starting pitcher named Bob Shawkey. And still the team was terrible.

With the brilliance of all major league club owners, Ruppert and Huston decided the fault lay with the manager, so they fired Donovan and looked around for someone else. Huston wanted the someone else to be his friend Wilbert Robinson, the fat, jolly, profane manager of the Brooklyn Dodgers, but Ruppert had other ideas. He wanted the best man he could find and therefore consulted Ban Johnson, still the president and guiding light of the American League. Johnson recommended that Ruppert dip into the National League and sign Miller Huggins, the scrawny, little (five feet six inches, 140 pounds) manager of the St. Louis Cardinals. Huggins had managed the Cardinals for five years and had finished last, third, sixth, last and third. Not a very consistent record, but Johnson assured Ruppert that Huggins was the man to get.

By this time Huston was off in France with the army, and Ruppert, acting on his own, hired Huggins to take over in 1918. Huston was furious when he heard the news in France, and a breach opened between him and Ruppert that never really healed. After the war, when he was again involved in the operation of the ball club, Huston never warmed to Huggins and often criticized him loudly and publicly. But Ruppert, convinced he had made the right choice, stood behind the little manager all the way.

In Huggins' first year the team moved up only slightly in the standings, from sixth to fifth, but in 1919 the club finished third (behind Chicago's infamous Black Sox and a strong Cleveland Indian team). Huggins had plucked second baseman Del Pratt from the Cardinals and put together the solid, hard-hitting, euphoniously named infield of Pipp, Pratt, Peckinpaugh and Baker. The outfield was not as strong but had a couple of fair hitters in Duffy Lewis, who with pitcher Ernie Shore had been the first Red Sox players to come to the Yankees, and the colorful Ping Bodie. These 1919 Yankees led the league in home runs, with forty-five—remember that Ruth hit twenty-nine all by himself for the Red Sox that year. In the New York sports pages, the Yankees were occasionally referred to as Murderers' Row, a name that would be revived and applied with more justification to the Ruthian lineup.

Better than the hitting was the pitching staff Huggins put together around Bob Shawkey, a staff which in midseason of 1919 was greatly helped by the addition of another player from Boston, righthanded pitcher Carl Mays.

Mays, a longtime teammate of Ruth's (together they were Providence's best pitchers in that late-season pennant drive in 1914 and the best pitchers in Boston's late-season pennant drive in 1918), had soured on the Red Sox and in July had jumped the club and gone home. He should have been suspended by the Red Sox management, but the opportunistic Harry Frazee got in touch with the Yankees and soon sold the recalcitrant pitcher to Ruppert and Huston for $40,000, a staggering, Steinbrenner-like sum in that day. This deal outraged Ban Johnson and led to a furious legal battle, which the Yankees won decisively. Johnson suspended Mays, but the Yankees went into court and got an injunction against the suspension.

Mays won nine games for his new team from August 9 to the end of the season, but the power struggle between the league president and the Yankees continued after the season when the Yankees and two other anti-Johnson clubs threatened to secede from the American League and join a new, expanded National League. Johnson was hamstrung. Antagonism toward his dictatorial control of the league he conceived, bore and nurtured to greatness spilled over and led directly to the appointment a year later (just after the Black Sox scandal) of Judge Kennesaw M. Landis as the Commissioner of Baseball, with almost absolute authority over both leagues and both league presidents.

At any rate, by the end of 1919 the Yankees were a recognized power in baseball, an upcoming team on the field and a force to be reckoned with in the front office.

During the late fall and early winter of 1919, Frazee, who had already sent three players (Lewis, Shore and Mays) to the Yankees for considerable sums of money, mentioned to his good friend and drinking companion Colonel Huston that it was just possible he would sell Babe Ruth if he could get the right price for him. Huston consulted Ruppert, with whom he still had a good working relationship despite their differences over the hiring of Huggins. Ruppert was interested. In fact, a year and a half earlier, after watching Ruth hit a towering home run in the Polo Grounds against the Yankees, he had offered to buy the Babe, but Frazee had laughed at the idea.

Now, financially strapped, Frazee worked out a complex financial deal. The Yankees would get Ruth. Frazee would get $25,000 in cash and three $25,000 promissory notes at 6 percent. The first note was due on November 1, 1920, the second on November 1, 1921, the third on November 1, 1922, which meant that by the time the notes were redeemed the Yankees had paid close to $110,000 for the Babe's contract. Ruppert also arranged for a $300,000 loan that Frazee needed, which was secured by a mortgage on Fenway Park. Imagine the Yankees holding the mortgage on Fenway Park; imagine if they had *foreclosed* the mortgage.

Ruppert, Huston and Frazee reached agreement in December 1919, but the sale was not announced until January 5, 1920, in order to give Miller Huggins time to go to California and talk to Ruth, who was on a barnstorming tour. After considerable haggling, Huggins and Ruth settled the salary terms: the Yankees gave the Babe a $1,000 cash bonus and a two-year contract at $20,000 a year, which doubled his 1919 salary and was four or five times larger than most big-league salaries at that time.

Now the Babe was in tow. The Yankee dynasty was ready to begin.

It was a new era. Prohibition went into effect eleven days after the announcement of Ruth's sale. Skirts were higher, hair was shorter. Postwar euphoria continued. There was a partying atmosphere, and baseball was part of the party. Baseball was *the* sport, about the only truly big sport in the country except for boxing and college football, and the crowds poured into the ballparks. The Giants had set the single-season attendance record of 910,000 in 1908 (no other team had ever attracted as many as 700,000), but in 1920 the Yankees, outshining McGraw's Giants in their own ballpark, drew 1,289,000, up more than 40 percent from the old mark.

Ruth, obviously, was a major factor. He was very much in evidence in New York, roaring through the streets in his racy cars, hopping from one gala party to another, hitting home runs in extravagant numbers. He started the season in a slump, missed several games with a pulled muscle and did not hit his first homer until May 1, a couple of weeks after the season had begun. But then he began to pole them out: a dozen in May, a dozen in June, thirteen in July, leaving his year-old record of twenty-nine far behind. He finished with fifty-four, an awesome total even today but almost incomprehensible in 1920.

No other player that season hit more than nineteen; no other *team* hit as many as the Babe did. The bereft Red Sox had only twenty-two —all season long.

The Yankees, paced by Ruth and a fine pitching staff (Mays won twenty-six games; Shawkey, twenty), were in the pennant race all the way and finished a close third, only three games behind the pennant-winning Indians. That was the year the Indians lost their fine shortstop, Ray Chapman, when he was beaned in the Polo Grounds by a pitch thrown by Mays. Taken to a hospital, Chapman died early the next morning. There was an angry reaction around the league against Mays, who was a cold, hard competitor, not at all averse to brushing a batter back. But those close to the scene agreed that Chapman, a plate-crowder, seemed to freeze on the pitch instead of ducking away. Mays

Carl Mays

Bob Shawkey

Waite Hoyt

Ed Barrow

returned a week later, pitched a shutout and went on to complete his season.

Several new faces other than Ruth's worked their way into the Yankee picture that year. Aaron Ward, a hard-hitting Southerner, took over third base in the absence of Home Run Baker, who sat out the year in voluntary retirement because of his wife's serious illness. Bob Meusel, a big righthanded-hitting Californian, played several games at third base but eventually moved to the outfield, where he was a fixture for ten seasons.

Ruppert and Huston, casting about later in the year for a "secretary" (now known as a general manager), hired Ed Barrow away from the Red Sox. One of Barrow's first moves for the Yankees was to engineer another deal with the Red Sox—well salted with money, of course— for a young righthander named Waite Hoyt, who was later elected to the Hall of Fame, and catcher Wally Schang, who had played on three pennant winners with the Philadelphia Athletics and the Red Sox, and who was one of baseball's best catchers.

The Red Sox had become a Yankee farm club.

The following season, 1921, was a joy for New York. The Giants, after finishing second three years in a row, swept to the National League pennant, and the Yankees, with the Babe having an even better season than in 1920—he hit 59 homers, drove in 170 runs, scored 177 and batted .378—won their first American League pennant. They had fought the defending champion Indians game for game throughout the summer and into the fall. In late September, with the Yankees ahead by two percentage points, the Indians came in for a four-game series. The Yanks won the first game; the Indians, the second. In the third, played on a Sunday before a huge crowd, the Yankees behind Mays opened a 15–0 lead and went on to win, 21–7. In the final game Ruth hit two home runs and a double as the Yankees won, 8–7, to knock the Indians out of the race.

New York had the World Series all to itself—the first "Subway Series," although all the games were played in the Polo Grounds, the home field for both clubs. It was a marvelous confrontation. In one corner the Giants, for more than thirty years the darlings of New York, pennant winners for the ninth time, led by John McGraw, the most famous manager in the game. In the other corner the *parvenu* Yankees, for two decades a seedy collection of also-rans, now force-fed into a pennant by Ruppert's money and the rape of the Red Sox.

In the opener Mays shut out the Giants, 3–0, then Hoyt threw another 3–0 shutout. Mays had pitched a five-hitter, four by Frank Frisch, the Giants' young third baseman. Hoyt pitched a two-hitter, and Frisch had one of those. In other words, except for Frisch, the powerful Giants were able to get only two hits in two games. When the Yanks opened a fast 4–0 lead in the third game, the Series seemed to be developing into a rout. But the Giants finally came alive, pounded out twenty hits and won the game, 13–5. This was the last best-five-out-of-nine Series, and dreams of an easy Yankee victory quickly disappeared. For one thing, Ruth was hurt. He scraped his elbow sliding into third in the second game (he startled the crowd by stealing second and then third after reaching first on a walk), and infection set in. He damaged the elbow again in the third game, and the Yankees announced he would probably miss the rest of the Series.

But, his arm bandaged and obviously bothering him, the Babe was in the lineup for the next game and hit a home run, the first of his fifteen World Series homers. Even so, the Giants won, squaring the Series at two games apiece. Ruth played again the next day, his arm still bandaged, a tube draining the wound, and was the hero, beating out a surprise bunt in the fourth inning with the score tied 1–1 and coming all the way around to score on Meusel's subsequent double. Hoyt pitched strongly, and the Yanks won, 3–1, to take back the Series lead.

That was the Babe's last gasp. He did not even put on a uniform for the next two games, both of which the Giants won, and did nothing more than pinch-hit futilely in the eighth and final game, in which the Giants beat Hoyt, 1–0, to take the Series. Hoyt, incidentally, allowed only two unearned runs in twenty-seven innings.

Ruth's arm injury had further repercussions. During the Series a New York sportswriter named Joe Vila wrote sarcastically about Ruth's injury, recalling numerous occasions during 1920 and 1921 when the Babe, apparently grievously ill or injured, was back playing almost immediately, none the worse for wear. Vila strongly implied that Ruth was dogging it, particularly since he played so well in the two games in which he appeared with the bandage on his elbow. Ruth, furious at Vila's comments, went over to him before the start of the sixth game and in full view of the crowd yelled angrily at him, gesturing at his wounded arm.

If nothing else, that served to focus attention on Vila's accusations, and even though the Babe's arm was indeed badly infected, a specter of doubt was raised that later backfired. Ruth was now about to go one-on-one with Judge Landis, that crusty, imperious and almost brand-new Commissioner of Baseball.

After the 1919 and 1920 seasons Ruth had earned tremendous fees in postseason exhibition tours, and he had lined up a similar trip for the fall of 1921. Meusel, Mays and Schang were among the players going with him. But Landis reminded Ruth and the others of a baseball rule then in effect that specifically barred members of World Series teams from playing in postseason exhibition games. This was a rule the owners had established years before when they were afraid such exhibitions might drain interest away from the World Series itself—if, for example, the two teams that had met in the Series traveled around the country afterwards playing each other day after day. Landis implied that he did not necessarily feel the rule as applied to individual players was fair or right, but it was part of baseball law and he was damned well going to enforce it.

The Commissioner's reasons were obvious. Baseball had come to near anarchy only two seasons earlier in the great dispute between the Yankees, together with the other rebelling teams, and Ban Johnson. The scandal of the Black Sox, which had burst open late in 1920, was still a sore and sensitive subject. There were other rumors of fixes or attempted fixes or generally unsavory situations. Landis was determined to establish his authority over everyone in baseball in order to deal forcefully with such matters as they arose. He felt strongly that he could not waive a rule for anybody at this precarious time in the game's history—particularly not for the boisterous, carefree, authority-flouting Babe Ruth. Landis was going to control baseball, not Ruth.

Landis ordered Ruth not to go on the barnstorming tour. Ruth, his mind on all that money he expected to earn, insisted he would go. Mays and Schang, worrying about what might happen, withdrew. Meusel, a stubborn, taciturn man, agreed to go along with whatever Ruth decided.

With Ruth and Landis on a collision course, the trip was a lively subject of discussion as the Series ended. People asked how the Babe could go off on an exhibition tour if he was not well enough to play in the last three games of the Series. "I heal quick," Ruth explained.

That was true—he had remarkable recuperative powers—but it did not sit well. And then Ruth defied Landis and went on the tour, which turned out to be an artistic and financial flop, one of his few unsuccessful postseason ventures ever. In time Landis ruled that Ruth and Meusel be fined the amount of their World Series shares and suspended for the first six weeks of the 1922 season. Ruth howled, but baseball supported the Commissioner. The Yankees, who had gone into court to overturn the Ban Johnson decision, accepted this ruling without an argument.

Even though Ruth and Meusel had driven in more than 300 runs in 1921 (Babe led the league with 170, Meusel was third with 135), the Yankees did not seem to miss them much in the early weeks of the 1922 season. The team was in first place or close to it most of the time. Barrow had made another deal with the Red Sox, obtaining Sam Jones and Joe Bush, two of the best pitchers in the league, and Everett Scott, a deft little shortstop who had been on three Red Sox pennant winners in Boston and who had played every game for them since the middle of the 1916 season. With the Yankees he would extend that consecutive-game streak to 1,307, then the longest in baseball history, ending it early in 1925, a month before Lou Gehrig began his own streak of 2,130 games as the Yankees' first baseman.

The lineup was becoming more and more solid. The pitching—with Hoyt, Mays, Shawkey and now Jones and Bush—was overpowering. Schang was a strong, hard-hitting catcher. Pipp at first base had driven in 97 runs in 1921 and would average better than 100 over the next three seasons. Aaron Ward had switched from third base to second when Baker returned to the team in 1921, and was quick and sure there. Scott was the league's best fielding shortstop. At third base Baker was nearing the end of the line, and the Yankees were looking for someone to take over for him. But they had obtained Whitey Witt from the Athletics to fill the hole in center field. Witt, a short, slender, blond Pole from Massachusetts, was a superior fielder and a sharp hitter who got on base often and scored runs. He played only three full seasons with the Yankees but, with Ruth and Meusel, helped give the club the first of its memorable outfield combinations.

When the suspension of Ruth and Meusel ended in May, it was expected that the Yankees would win the pennant handily. It didn't happen. Meusel hit well enough, but Ruth was simply awful. The grip he had on the affections of the crowd rapidly disappeared. The previous winter, when the ill-fated barnstorming trip was over, he had gone on a successful vaudeville tour from which he had earned more than $50,000. And early in the spring he had signed a new contract with the Yankees for $52,000 a year, an increase of $32,000 over his old contract and far and away the most money a baseball player had ever received up to that time—equivalent to at least $500,000 a year now and proba-bly more, if thought of in relation to other players' salaries. Established veterans like Schang, Pipp and Witt were making $10,000, $6,500, $4,000. Home Run Baker, a longtime star and one of the highest-paid players ever, was making $16,000.

Men supporting families on salaries of $40 a week who had come to the ballpark for the fun of seeing Ruth hit a homer soured quickly on the slumping slugger. Toward the end of May, when his batting average had fallen to an almost unbelievable .093, the boos and taunts got to the hot-tempered star. He had an argument with an umpire and was thrown out of the game. The crowd got on him as he walked in toward the dugout, and he suddenly charged into the stands after one particu-larly aggravating tormentor. For this he was fined $200 (a *big* fine) and suspended for several days, less than two weeks after his six-week suspension had ended. And a month later, hitting by now, he got into another furious argument with an umpire. Again he was tossed out. The next day, just before game time, word came that Ruth had been suspended again, this time for three days. Exploding with anger, Ruth went for the umpire, was restrained and had an extra two days' suspension tacked on to the earlier sentence.

The Babe calmed down then, made his peace with the umpire and behaved for a while. But late in the season he let off a choice stream of obscenities at a plate umpire who had called him out on strikes. He was suspended yet another time—the fifth that season. Roger Maris would break Ruth's single-season record for home runs, and Henry Aaron would surpass his lifetime record, but it is hard to imagine anyone ever breaking the Babe's record for suspensions.

Meanwhile the Yankees found themselves in a ferocious fight for the pennant with the St. Louis Browns, whose star first baseman, George Sisler, batted .420 that season. At one stage he batted safely in forty-one straight games. The Yankees were so busy squabbling among themselves, perhaps even more so than the current Yankees have, they hardly had time to pay attention to the race. Al De Vormer, a reserve catcher, had a fight one day with Carl Mays and another the next day with reserve catcher Bootnose Hofman. Meusel and Schang got in a fight on the bench during a game with the Browns, and later the same afternoon Pipp and Ruth exchanged blows. And poor little Miller Huggins even had trouble with his players. The manager got into a loud argument on the street with Mays in spring training. Mays was in disfavor after that, pitched less and less, and after the 1923 season was sold to the Cincinnati Reds, with whom he won twenty games the next year. Huggins also tangled with Waite Hoyt on the bench.

Despite this unruly behavior, the Yankees continued to play good ball. Barrow raided the Red Sox again, getting Joe Dugan, who some thought was the best third baseman in the league, to fill the gap left by the fading Baker and give the club a strong lineup from top to bottom. In September, leading the Browns by half a game, the Yankees went into St. Louis for a showdown and won two out of three games in one of the most memorable regular-season series the club ever played. The Yankees won the first game, 2–1, but in the ninth inning, as Whitey Witt raced back for a fly ball, a thrown pop bottle hit him on the forehead and knocked him unconscious. Bandaged, he played again the next day and even ran into the overflow crowd in the outfield to make a brave catch.

But the Browns won the second game behind Hub Pruett, a rookie lefthander remembered now for the uncanny hold he had over Ruth that season. He had struck Ruth out ten times in the first thirteen times he faced him (the Babe walked twice and tapped back to the mound in his other three appearances). Three times Pruett had come in from the bullpen to strike him out, once with the bases loaded. In that loss to the Browns in September, the Babe finally broke the spell, hitting a homer and a single off Pruett, and the following year the total domination was pretty well gone—although Pruett continued to strike him out now and then.

Pruett's victory over the Yankees that day brought the Browns back to within half a game of the lead. In the final game the Browns led in the ninth, 2–1, knowing that a victory would lift them into first place. But the Yankees rallied, scored twice and won, 3–2. As far as the Yankees were concerned, that was it—they had won the pennant—and they were correct. They held on to their slim margin to win by one game. Then they again lost the World Series to the Giants, who swept them, four games to none, with one game tied. Ruth had a bad Series, batting only .118, with one single, one double and no home runs.

In the eighth inning of the last game Huggins had a public quarrel with pitcher Joe Bush when he ordered Bush to walk a Giant batter purposely. Bush glared back in anger, walked the batter, gave up what proved to be the game-winning hit and yelled bitterly at Huggins from the mound. After the game Huston, venting his displeasure with Huggins, declared loudly that this little manager had worked his last Yankee game. Ruppert, never a man to get excited, refused to be swayed by Huston's argument and insisted that Huggins remain. Interestingly, he was supported by Ed Barrow, who had come to the Yankees primarily because of Huston's friendship with Harry Frazee, the Red Sox owner. Huggins was well aware of Huston's distaste for him, knew that Huston and Barrow were friends and, when Barrow arrived, felt that his days as manager were numbered. But for all his arrogance and insistence on running things his way, Barrow had a deep respect for Huggins' managerial skills. Early in his tenure he went to the manager and assured him of his support. He even persuaded Ruppert and particularly Huston, who loved to mingle with the players, to stay out of the Yankee clubhouse, declaring that it was the manager's territory. And so Barrow, despite his affection for Huston, sided with Ruppert in backing Huggins as manager.

That meant the end of Huston as co-owner. He asked Ruppert to buy him out, and the Colonel agreed to, although the two decided their uneasy partnership should continue for several months until Yankee Stadium, which was then being built, opened for the 1923 season. About a month later Huston sold his half of the club to Ruppert for $1.5 million, six times what he had paid for his share eight years earlier.

The 1923 season was as serene and fulfilling for the Yankees as 1922 had been tumultuous and frustrating. Opening at home in their splendid new stadium before the biggest crowd then to see a major league game (reportedly 74,217, actually between 60,000 and 65,000), the

Site of the Stadium before construction began   The New York Yankees

Opening Day at Yankee Stadium, April 18, 1923   UPI

Yankees marched easily to their third straight pennant. Ruth batted
.393, second to Harry Heilman's .403, led the league with forty-one
homers and batted in 130 runs. The pitching staff, augmented by the
stylish lefthander Herb Pennock, another Hall of Famer siphoned away
from the Red Sox by Ruppert's money, was much the best in the league.
In the World Series, facing the Giants for the third straight year, the
Yankees, trailing two games to one (the Giants wins were on home runs
by outfielder Casey Stengel), came back with three straight victories for
their first Series championship.

Of the twenty-four Yankee players eligible for that Series, eleven had
come from the Red Sox, including the catcher (Schang), the shortstop
(Scott), the third baseman (Dugan), the rightfielder (Ruth) and the
starting pitchers in five of the six games (Hoyt, Pennock, Jones, Bush
and Pennock again).

There were also six rookies on the Yankee roster for that World
Series, only one of whom, pitcher George Pipgras, developed into an
outstanding performer. Rookie centerfielder Earle Combs had broken
an ankle after playing only twenty-four games and was not on the
roster; another rookie, first baseman Lou Gehrig, joined the team too
late in the season to be eligible. Huggins obviously was aware that his
powerful team was getting on. The squad was lucky in 1923, with
almost no injuries to the regulars, but Huggins knew replacements
would soon be needed in several positions.

In 1924 the team slipped to second place, two games behind the
Washington Senators, who were winning their first pennant behind the
23-and-7 pitching of thirty-six-year-old Walter Johnson and the inspired leadership of their "boy manager," twenty-seven-year-old Bucky
Harris. The Yankees did not play badly that year—Ruth hit a league-
leading .378 with 46 homers, the pitching was sound, the same solid
lineup performed as usual. The team simply did not play well enough.

The underlying weakness became glaringly evident in 1925 when
Ruth collapsed in spring training, was hospitalized and was out of the
lineup until June. With his first marriage falling apart, the Babe had
been drinking and carousing and generally raising hell, and the immediate cause of his collapse was an intestinal abcess, or ulcer. The gossip
that he was hospitalized with a venereal disease had no truth to it. He
may at times in his festive life have contracted social diseases—it would
be mildly surprising if he hadn't, considering his promiscuity—but in
the hospital he was operated on for an ulcer. He had a long vivid scar
on his belly just below the ribcage when he returned to the team.

Three years earlier, when both Ruth and Meusel were suspended for
almost the same length of time that Ruth was ill in 1925, the Yankees
did not falter. Now, however, they were a disaster. The infield was a
mess. Pipp at first base was in a dreadful slump. Ward, for years so

dependable, was no longer making the plays at second. Scott, exhausted and thin as a piece of string after all those years of playing every day, was finally benched. Witt, not yet thirty, was suddenly washed up. Schang caught only a third of the games and was gone before the 1926 season came around.

Even though Meusel led the league with 33 home runs and 138 runs batted in, even though a fill-in outfielder named Benny Paschal filled in surprisingly well for Ruth (.360 average, 12 home runs, in the equivalent of half a season) and even though young Combs stepped smartly into Witt's place in the outfield, the Yankees sorely missed Ruth and his extravagant bat.

Yet when the Babe returned to the lineup on June 1—much too soon after his operation—it didn't help. For one thing, he was not in playing shape. He was woeful at bat, hitting barely .250 and managing to clout only a few home runs. For another, the usually bouncy, ebullient Babe had become sullen and insolent. He openly defied Huggins, contemptuously referring to the pint-sized manager as Little Boy or as the Flea. He was having well-publicized personal difficulties—his first wife, Helen, whom he had married in 1914, was about to leave him, and he was deeply involved with Mrs. Clare Hodgson, who would later become his second wife. On the road with the team, he was out on the town every night, drinking, chasing women, staying away from the team hotel.

With the Yankees wallowing near last place in August, Ruth disobeyed Huggins' orders twice during a game in Chicago, once bunting when the manager wanted him to hit and then swinging away when the manager wanted him to bunt.

Huggins and Ruth had a showdown a few days later in St. Louis, and Ruth lost. After being assured of support by Ruppert and Barrow, the manager confronted Ruth in the locker room when his rightfielder arrived late to dress for a game—after again having been away from the hotel all night. Huggins told him he was indefinitely suspended and was being fined $5,000. Ruth stomped out and, in a long, interrupted trip that was followed almost hour by hour in the nation's newspapers, made his way from St. Louis to Chicago to New York, at first defying Huggins and declaring that he would never again play for New York as long as Huggins was managing the team, and then little by little calming down.

By the time he reached New York and went to see Colonel Ruppert, the Babe was almost humble. Ruppert told him the matter was entirely in Huggins' hands. Even though Ruth by now was eager to apologize, the little manager let him stew for a week, refusing to talk to him or let him play or even put on a uniform. The cold-shoulder treatment worked. When they finally sat down to talk, and Huggins agreed to accept Ruth's apology, the big slugger was contrite. When he returned to the lineup after his suspension, he was his old self again and hit the ball hard and often. In the few weeks remaining in the season the team played well. Although the Yankees finished seventh in that 1925 season, the future seemed promising.

Behind the furor created by Ruth (his collapse in spring training, his well-publicized return to the lineup in June, his bad behavior and suspension in August, his second return in September), Huggins and Barrow had been working to rebuild the team. With the Babe back, Meusel as dependable as ever and Combs, who batted .342, the outfield was set. Huggins experimented with a shortstop named Pee Wee Wanninger, who was as small as Scott and not nearly as good, but late in the season installed a six-foot, 180-pound rookie named Mark Koenig in that position—Colonel Ruppert liked big players. Barrow picked up a dependable righthander, Urban Shocker, from the Browns and purchased Tony Lazzeri, a hard-hitting shortstop, from Salt Lake City in the Pacific Coast League, for 1926 delivery. Huggins moved Lazzeri to second base, where he proved to be one of the best for the next decade.

But the most important of all the new players was Lou Gehrig, the big first baseman. He was only twenty-one, still eighteen days short of his twenty-second birthday, when he pinch-hit for Wanninger on June 1, 1925, the day Ruth returned to the lineup after his operation. The next day he started at first base in place of Pipp and remained in the lineup, never missing a game, for the next fourteen years.

Despite his youth, Lou Gehrig was by no means an unknown. Five years earlier, in 1920, when he was playing for the High School of Commerce in New York, he was recognized as the best high school baseball player in the city and possibly in the nation. Commerce won the New York public high school championship and went to Chicago that spring to play Lane High, the Chicago champions, in Wrigley Field. With the score 8–6 in Commerce's favor in the ninth inning, Gehrig won the game by hitting a grandslam homer.

After finishing at Commerce a year later, Gehrig accepted an athletic scholarship to Columbia, where his German-immigrant parents earned their living by working in a fraternity house at which he had often waited on tables. But during the summer, before his freshman year, he was approached by John McGraw, who persuaded him to sign a contract *sub rosa* and go off to Hartford in the Eastern League to play minor league baseball under an assumed name. No one would know, McGraw assured him, and in the fall he could go to Columbia and play football and baseball there.

The eighteen-year-old "Lou Lewis" had played only a dozen games for Hartford when Columbia officials got word of the situation and

Lou Gehrig as a Yankee rookie in 1923

hurriedly went to rescue him. His contract with the Giants was abrogated, possibly because he was under age, and his amateur status was somehow restored, although he was barred from playing football or baseball as a freshman.

As a sophomore in 1922 he played football—he was a hard-driving fullback, about six feet tall and weighing more than 200 pounds. And in the spring of 1923 he had his one and only year of college baseball. He was both a pitcher and a slugger, as the Babe had been, but the major league scouts were after him only for his hitting. Paul Krichell, a well-known Yankee scout, offered him a contract under which he would receive a $1,500 cash bonus for signing and $3,000 for the remainder of the season. A dutiful only son who was always close to his parents, particularly his big, domineering mother, Gehrig talked things over at home and debated whether to sign at once or finish his remaining two years of college and then sign. Money was the deciding factor. His parents were not destitute, but $1,500 in hand and $3,000 for four months' work seemed like a fortune. He signed.

Again he was sent to Hartford, the Yankees having arranged a "working agreement" with the Hartford club, where he proved to be little short of sensational. His batting average was only .304, but in fifty-nine games he hit twenty-four home runs and forty of his sixty-nine hits were for extra bases. Barrow brought him up to the Yankees at the end of the 1923 season to give Huggins a closer look at him. In thirteen games (this was the year the Yankees won the pennant by sixteen games) he batted .423 and hit his first big-league home run. In the last week of the season, when regular first baseman Wally Pipp injured himself and appeared unable to play in the World Series, the Yankees asked Judge Landis for permission to let Gehrig play first base even though he had joined the club too late to be technically eligible for Series competition. Landis agreed to approve the request if McGraw, whose Giants were to play the Yankees, had no objection. McGraw, still disgruntled at having lost his prize two years earlier, flatly refused. Pipp had to play, strapped up.

In 1924 the young first baseman—he turned twenty-one on June 19 —played in Hartford again. Over a full season he batted .369, hit forty doubles, thirteen triples and thirty-seven home runs. Again recalled by the Yankees near the end of the season, he batted .500 with six hits in twelve at-bats and drove in six runs.

He certainly seemed ready, but first base was still Pipp's, and for the first six weeks of the 1925 season Huggins used Gehrig only to pinch-hit (he didn't do much) and play a few games in the outfield. Then Pipp got a headache that day in early June and was unable to play. Huggins put Gehrig into the lineup. The rest is history.

Gehrig batted .295 that season, not as good an average as it sounds.

Bob Meusel

Earle Combs

Herb Pennock

Tony Lazzeri

Joe Dugan

Mark Koenig

The league average was .292, tying the league record set in 1921, which meant that Gehrig had a so-so season as far as batting averages went, but he showed promising power, with twenty home runs, fifth best in the league. He was massively built, with powerful legs and an extremely broad back. Ruth's home-run swing was long, smooth, free, even wild; Gehrig's was compact and controlled. Neither fast on his feet nor quick with his hands, he had to work hard around first base to become an acceptable fielder. And he did work hard. Gehrig was the Super Straight Arrow, a virtuous, well-behaved, well-mannered young man who was good to his parents, respectful to his superiors, obedient to authority. Except in the matter of pulverizing a baseball, he was about as unlike Babe Ruth as a man could be.

As the 1926 season began, the rebuilding Yankees had (1) a couple of nonentities handling the catching duties in place of the departed Schang, (2) the still unproven Gehrig starting his first full season at first base, (3) a total rookie, Lazzeri, at second base, (4) a near rookie, Koenig, at shortstop, (5) Combs, also with only one big-league season behind him, in center field. Dugan at third base and Meusel and Ruth in the outfield were solid—although there were quite a few observers who felt that Ruth at thirty-two was very possibly over the hill despite his apparent reform. And the pitching was strong.

When they began to play spring exhibition games, the team worked smoothly. After they started a long exhibition tour north with the Dodgers with a couple of victories, Colonel Ruppert beamed and predicted he wouldn't be surprised if the team rose from seventh place into the first division. Ruth, more optimistic, said, "If we keep beating the Dodgers, we're going to win the pennant." The Yankees did keep beating the Dodgers—a dozen times, in fact—and won sixteen consecutive exhibition games before the regular season began. Ruth was correct; the Yankees sustained that winning pattern throughout the season and won the pennant by three games. Ruth hit 47 home runs and drove in 155 runs to lead the league in both categories; his .372 average was second. Gehrig, still maturing, had only 16 homers, but he drove in 107 runs. Lazzeri, in a marvelous debut, had 18 homers and 114 runs batted in.

Ruth, Ruppert and the entire ball club expected to win the World Series easily from the St. Louis Cardinals, who had won their first National League pennant with the lowest winning percentage in baseball history at that time: .578 (89 victories, 65 defeats). But the Cardinals, with Grover Cleveland Alexander only four months shy of his fortieth birthday, upset the Yankees, four games to three. Alex twice evened the Series with complete-game victories in the second and sixth games. And in the seventh inning of the seventh game, with the bases filled and the Cardinals leading, 3–2, he came out of the bullpen to strike out the dangerous Lazzeri, then stopped the Yankees in the eighth and ninth innings. Ruth hit three home runs in the fourth game to set a record only he was able to equal until Reggie Jackson hit three in the last game of the 1977 Series, but otherwise the Babe's performance was no more than ordinary. He even caused the last out in the ninth inning of the last game when he was caught in an ill-advised attempt to steal second. Nobody's perfect.

But in 1927 the Yankees were virtually perfect—as perfect as a baseball team can be.

They won 110 games and lost only 44, for a .714 percentage. They took the pennant by nineteen games. Their team batting average was .307, best in the league. Their pitchers' combined earned-run average was 3.20, by far the best in the league that year. Ruth batted .356; Meusel, .337; Combs, .356. Gehrig batted .373; Lazzeri, .309; Koenig, .285. Gehrig batted in 175 runs; Ruth, 164; Meusel, 103; Lazzeri, 102. Of the beautifully balanced seven-man pitching staff that accounted for all but five of the team's victories and defeats, six won more than twice as many games as they lost. Wilcy Moore, a thirty-year-old rookie whom Barrow found hidden in the minors, won nineteen games, starting occasionally but pitching more often in relief. Hoyt won twenty-three games; Pennock, nineteen; Shocker, eighteen. Hoyt, Shocker, Moore and Pennock had the four best won-lost averages in the league. Hoyt and Shocker had the two best earned-run averages, 2.63 and 2.84; Hoyt tied for the most wins.

The pitching was, in a word, superb. But the hitting made the team famous. Gehrig and Ruth were first and second in the league in runs batted in. Ruth and Gehrig were first and second in slugging averages. Gehrig and Ruth were first and second in total bases, with 447 and 417, respectively. Gehrig led the league in doubles. Combs led in triples. Ruth led in bases on balls. Meusel was second in stolen bases. Combs had the most hits; Gehrig was second.

Oh, yes. Ruth hit sixty home runs, and Gehrig hit forty-seven—no one other than Ruth had ever hit that many. The third highest home-run total in the league was Lazzeri's eighteen.

The home-run race between Ruth and Gehrig in 1927 was unlike anything baseball had ever experienced. For the first time the Babe had a challenger going nose to nose with him, trying to unseat the Home Run King. In 1918, when he had tied for the home-run championship, the Babe had hit all his eleven homers by midseason and was caught later on by Tillie Walker of the Athletics. When he lost the title in 1922 and 1925, he had missed most of the first two months of the season each time and was never really in the hunt. In the other years, when he won the crown outright, he was far out in front all season long.

But now Gehrig was matching him homer for homer. The Babe started slowly, with only one in his first ten games, but late in April he found the range and started to pop the ball over the fence with devastating regularity. Before the end of May he had hit homers in seven of the eight ballparks around the league (the eighth, spacious Comiskey Park in Chicago, had to wait until July). By June 16, after fifty-five games, he had twenty-two home runs—keeping a pace that would have given him sixty-two for the year. But he went into a long slow period and from the middle of June until the middle of August, a stretch of fifty-eight games, added only fourteen more. Gehrig, meantime, was hitting them steadily and on August 15 was ahead of the Babe, thirty-eight homers to thirty-six.

Then Lou slowed down—he would hit only nine more the rest of the season—just as the Babe began his astonishing drive toward the magic sixty. There were only forty-two games left; in these games Ruth hit twenty-four homers, a furious pace that would have produced nearly ninety over a full season. He started his surge with four in ten games to reach forty and then began belting them in explosive bursts. He hit four in five games to jump to forty-four as the season moved into September. On September 6 he hit three in a doubleheader and the next day added two more to lift his total to forty-nine. Lou was now hopelessly far behind. With the Ruth-Gehrig battle no longer operative, and the pennant race a runaway, the fans seemed interested only in whether or not the Babe was going to reach and surpass his old record of fifty-nine.

He failed to hit one, failed again the next day, failed a third day, then rallied for three in his next three games to move to fifty-two. Another frustrating dry period followed—only one homer in six games—and hope for the record was fading. He had fifty-three, but there were only nine games left. He needed six to tie, seven to reach sixty. Impossible.

But again he hit homers in three successive games to move to fifty-six. He was stopped the next two games. Now there were only four games left, and he was still four homers away from sixty. On September 27 he hit a grandslam home run off Lefty Grove, the great Philadelphia pitcher, to move to fifty-seven. What he did in the next game should be etched in bronze and put on the outfield wall in Yankee Stadium. The Babe hit his fifty-eighth home run, hit a triple off the rightfield fence, hit his fifty-ninth homer and hit a long fly that the rightfielder caught at the fence. The next day, September 30, he got number sixty, a long fly down the rightfield line that stayed just fair. And there was still one game left in the season (Babe, the record in his pocket, went oh for three).

It was some team. *Some* team. And this time in the World Series it

The Babe connects for his 60th homer, September 30, 1927

Wide World Photos

The 1927 Yankees *(front row)* Julie Wera, Mike Gazella, Pat Collins, batboy Eddie Bennett, Benny Bengough, Ray Morehart, Myles Thomas, Cedric Durst; *(middle row)* Urban Shocker, Joe Dugan, Earle Combs, coach Charlie O'Leary, manager Miller Huggins, coach Art Fletcher, Mark Koenig,

Approaching the plate that day,
he is greeted by Gehrig

Wide World Photos

Dutch Reuther, Johnny Grabowski, George Pipgras; *(back row)* Lou Gehrig, Herb Pennock, Tony Lazzeri, Wilcy Moore, Babe Ruth, Don Miller, Bob Meusel, Bob Shawkey, Waite Hoyt, Joe Giard, Ben Paschal, Walter Beall, trainer Doc Woods

The New York Yankees

showed, the Yankees wiping out the Pirates in four games. Ruth and Gehrig drove in eleven runs between them.

The Yankees won again in 1928, their second set of three consecutive pennants in the decade, but they had trouble. Ruth and Gehrig were once more overwhelming. Meusel, Lazzeri, Koenig and Combs continued to hit hard. But cracks were beginning to show.

Lazzeri hurt his shoulder and missed forty games. Koenig's fielding was beginning to slip. Leo Durocher, a twenty-three-year-old rookie, filled in brilliantly at both shortstop and second base, but he couldn't hit a lick. Dugan, suffering from a bad knee, had missed forty games in 1927; he missed sixty in 1928, and there was no replacement in sight. Meusel had had nine highly productive seasons (averaging well over .300 and with more than 100 runs batted in), but he was hurt. Huggins sensed that he was near the end and proved to be correct. Meusel appeared in only 100 games for the Yanks in 1929, had one more big-league season with Cincinnati, and then was gone. Combs, injury-prone, sprained his wrist and missed the 1928 Series; so did the aging Pennock, who hurt his arm and was only a spot pitcher after that. Wilcy Moore's magic subsided, and he became just another arm in the bullpen. Finally, something had to to be done about the catching. Three second-stringers—Benny Bengough, Pat Collins and Johnny Grabowski—had been responsible for most of the catching for four years, none of them appearing behind the plate in more than 100 games in a season, none of them establishing himself as *the* catcher.

Despite all this, the 1928 Yankees looked terrific early in the season, roaring through the league in the early months and opening a thirteen-and-a-half-game lead by July 1. Then the improving Philadelphia Athletics, with Lefty Grove, Mickey Cochrane, Jimmy Foxx, Al Simmons, George Earnshaw, Jimmy Dykes and a host of other fine players, began to cut into the lead. By the second Saturday in September the A's had caught the Yankees and moved past them into first place. But in a climactic battle at the Stadium the Yankees swept a three-game series from the A's to recapture the lead and, as it turned out, the pennant.

Their late momentum carried into the World Series, in which Ruth and Gehrig all by themselves destroyed the Cardinals in four straight games. Now the Yankees had swept the Series in two successive years, something no team had ever done before and which only the Yankees would ever do again. No two players on one team ever put on a show to match Babe and Lou in that 1928 Series. Ruth hit .625, highest of all Series batting averages, and Gehrig hit .545. They had five of the Yankees' seven hits in the first game, with Ruth scoring two of the team's four runs and Gehrig batting in two (Meusel drove in the other two with the only World Series home run of his career). Gehrig hit a three-run homer off Grover Alexander in the first inning of the second game to lead a rout of the now forty-one-year-old pitcher. He hit two more home runs in the third game, and another in the fourth. Ruth, who had no home runs in the first three games, hit three in the fourth to equal the record he had set two years earlier. The two sluggers batted in fourteen runs between them, scored thirteen and had eleven extra-base hits (including seven home runs) in their sixteen hits.

There were two marvelous, unforgettable moments in the fourth game. The desperate Cardinals were leading, 2–1, when Ruth came to bat in the seventh with the bases empty. Bill Sherdel, the Cardinals' star lefthander, got two strikes on the Babe and then tried to quick-pitch him. This once legal maneuver—throwing the ball over the plate before the batter expected it—had been declared illegal for the Series, and the plate umpire ruled it "no pitch." The Cardinals protested bitterly, their bench emptying, the players surrounding the umpire and shouting at him. The no longer hot-tempered Ruth watched the argument with a big grin, taking no part in it. When Sherdel finally returned to the mound, the Babe made an insulting remark, and Sherdel reacted with a few barbed comments of his own.

"Put one in here again," Ruth said, "and I'll knock it out of the park for you."

Sherdel missed the plate with two pitches to even the count at two balls and two strikes, and then did indeed come in with one. Ruth knocked it out of the park to tie the score. Gehrig followed with another home run to put the Yankees ahead, and the Cardinals never did catch up.

They tried, though, rallying in the bottom of the ninth. But their last batter lofted a foul fly down the leftfield line, where temporary box seats encroached on the field. Ruth, playing left field, raced over, reached into the boxes, caught the fly to end the game and the Series and, still running, waved the gloved ball high and tauntingly at the Sportsman's Park crowd as he headed in toward the dugout.

With that catch the first great Yankee era ended, although no one (except possibly Miller Huggins and perhaps Ed Barrow) was aware of it. The team entered a curious kind of doldrums and in the next seven seasons was able to win the pennant only once. Not until the roster had an almost complete change of personnel would the Yankees again dominate baseball.

Death even touched those Yankee teams. Shocker, who had pitched so well in 1926 and 1927, had a serious heart condition, became gravely ill early in the 1928 season and died in September. In January 1929 Ruth's first wife, Helen, died in a fire in Boston (three months later, Babe married Clare Hodgson). Huggins, edgy and restless during the

1929 season, developed erysipelas (blood poisoning), entered a hospital on September 20 and died five days later.

The A's won the pennant by eighteen games in 1929 and won it again easily in 1930 and 1931. The once magnificent Yankee pitching staff had disintegrated. Pennock was old, Shocker was dead, Hoyt was traded away after the 1929 season. Except for George Pipgras, who pitched well, the staff seemed composed of strange and ephemeral names. Even though Shawkey, the pitching mainstay of earlier years, was the new manager (Ruth wanted the job and made no bones about it, but he got along well enough with Shawkey), the pitching did not improve, although Barrow took a step for the future—and echoed the past—by acquiring a strong righthander named Charles (Red) Ruffing from the Red Sox.

After the 1930 season the Yankees abruptly fired Shawkey and replaced him with Joe McCarthy, who himself had been dismissed by the Chicago Cubs, with whom he had won the 1929 National League pennant. The appointment of McCarthy, a shrewd, efficient manager who kept a tight hold on his team, angered Ruth, who felt that this time *he* deserved the job. On the other hand, Gehrig, who was comfortable with discipline, got along well with McCarthy; so did Lazzeri and Combs and a young catcher named Bill Dickey, who had taken over in 1929 and soon established himself.

There were several new players on the team now: Ruffing, slowly developing into one of baseball's best righthanders; Lefty Gomez, a thin, humorous rookie with a blazing fastball; Ben Chapman, a hot-tempered Southerner who could hit hard and steal bases. Chapman had come up as a third baseman, but in 1931 the Yankees obtained veteran shortstop Joe Sewell from the Indians. McCarthy had installed Sewell at third and put the fleet-footed Chapman in the outfield. Chapman was a good hitter who could bat in runs and score them, an excellent fielder and a superb baserunner (he led the league in stolen bases for three straight years), but somehow he never really fit into the Yankee pattern.

Koenig was traded in 1930 as the search for a new shortstop continued. Durocher was found wanting and was sent to the Cincinnati Reds. Lyn Lary took over in 1930 and 1931, and while adequate he is remembered mostly for one bonehead play he pulled in 1931. He was on first base when Gehrig hit a high fly ball to right field that fell into the seats for a home run. Lary for some reason thought the ball had been caught and as he passed third base trotted off the field and into the Yankee dugout. Gehrig, who modestly looked at the ground during his home-run trot, did not notice Lary's departure and was called out for "passing another runner on the basepath" and credited with a triple rather than a homer.

The mistake proved costly. Gehrig had finished second to Ruth in home runs the four previous seasons, but in 1931 he and the Babe shared the title with forty-six each. If it had not been for Lary's goof, Gehrig would have had forty-seven and the championship to himself.

Gehrig just could not escape from Ruth's shadow. His hitting through these years was as good as Ruth's—the Babe hit more homers, Lou batted in more runs—but Ruth was the headliner. His salary battles with Colonel Ruppert at contract-signing time were big news, and the formal signing of his contract was covered like a Presidential press conference. No one really noticed when Lou signed.

The one pennant the Yankees won through these years came in 1932, when McCarthy found a shortstop (twenty-one-year-old Frank Crosetti, who played for the next seventeen seasons) and a brilliant rookie pitcher (the volatile Johnny Allen, who between fits of temper won seventeen games and lost only four). Gomez blossomed into a twenty-four-game winner, and Ruffing, Pipgras and a revived thirty-eight-year-old Pennock rounded out a formidable array of starters. Ruth lost the home-run title to Jimmy Foxx of the A's (who hit 58), but he still hit 41 and drove in 137 runs, even though he was beginning to sit out the second games of doubleheaders. Gehrig, in the prime of his career, drove in 151 runs and hit four homers in one game, something the Babe had never done; in fact, it was the first time in the twentieth century that any major leaguer had done it. Lazzeri batted in 113 runs; Chapman, 107. The team rolled to an easy pennant and finished the season by sweeping the Chicago Cubs in the World Series, the *third* straight time the Yanks had swept the Series in four games.

Ruth and Gehrig again dominated the Series, the Babe by his personality and flair for the dramatic, Lou by the astonishing power of his bat. This was the Series in which the Babe "called his shot," and people still argue over whether he actually pointed to a precise spot in the bleachers and then hit the ball there. He didn't. But what he did do—as he had done before, as he had done in the 1928 Series, for example—was defy the opposing team, indicate that he was going to do *something,* and then do it.

Ruth had been riding the Cubs unmercifully throughout the Series, calling them basically a bunch of cheapskates for the miserly way they had divided their World Series shares. They voted nothing to Rogers Hornsby, who had been dismissed as manager in midseason, and only a half share to Mark Koenig, the old Yankee who had joined the Cubs in midseason and proved a key factor in their pennant success. Ruth's scathing comments were richly embellished, of course, and the Cubs, stung by his vulgar wit, rode him hard in return, calling him fat and old and a variety of other pungent epithets.

In the third game, the first played in Chicago, Ruth messed up a play

in the outfield that helped the Cubs tie the score, and when he next came to bat the entire Cub bench was at the top of the dugout steps hooting and hollering at him. Ruth grinned and jeered back at them. When he took a called strike, the Cubs' jockeying grew louder, but Ruth held up one finger as if to say, "That's only one." The count went to two balls and two strikes, and the hooting became more intense on every pitch. Ruth, relishing the moment, called out something to the Chicago bench. According to Gabby Hartnett, the Cubs' catcher, Ruth's words were, "It only takes one to hit it"—and the Chicago pitcher, Charley Root, yelled something to the effect of "Get in there and hit."

Ruth pointed at Root, and Gehrig, waiting on deck, heard him say, "I'm going to knock the next pitch down your goddamned throat." It was more a challenging remark than an angry one.

Root pitched, and Ruth hit a tremendous home run to center field, supposedly the longest ever hit in Wrigley Field to that time. It put the Yankees ahead to stay (it was the gamer, as they say today), and it stunned the Cubs and Chicago. Ruth chortled as he rounded the bases, kidding each infielder as he passed, shouting again at the Cub dugout when he rounded third. It was a marvelous moment for him. As he said afterwards, "That's the first time I ever got the players and the fans going at the same time. I never had so much fun in all my life." He later told the renowned Chicago sportswriter John Carmichael, "I didn't exactly point to any spot. All I wanted to do was give the thing a ride out of the park. I used to pop off a lot about hitting homers."

Ruth's spectacular home run effectively obscured Gehrig's performance. The Babe provided the fun and the thrills, but Lou dominated this four-game sweep. In the first game he had two hits, including a home run, scored three runs and drove in two. In the second he had three hits, scored two runs, drove in one. In the third—the "called-shot" game— he hit two home runs, one right after the Babe's famous blast. In the fourth he had a double and a single, scored two runs and drove in three. He led the Yankees in everything—hits, runs, home runs, runs batted in, batting average. He hit .529 (Babe hit .333), the second consecutive Series in which he batted over .500.

The Yankees were back in the doldrums the next season, finishing second behind the Washington Senators in 1933 as they would finish second behind the Detroit Tigers in 1934 and 1935. Ruth had thirty-four homers and batted .301, but he was winding down, playing less and less. The pitching fell off sharply (Ruffing was 9-14, for example), and the club was generally uneasy. Ruth's dislike of McCarthy was very much in evidence, and it was clear that the thirty-nine-year-old Bambino was now more of a detriment to the team than he was a help.

Gehrig, on the other hand, was the club's bulwark, although Lazzeri, whose great skills often are forgotten today, drove in more than 100

The face that made
the Yankees famous
The New York Yankees

The Babe and Lou
enjoy a day off together
The New York Yankees

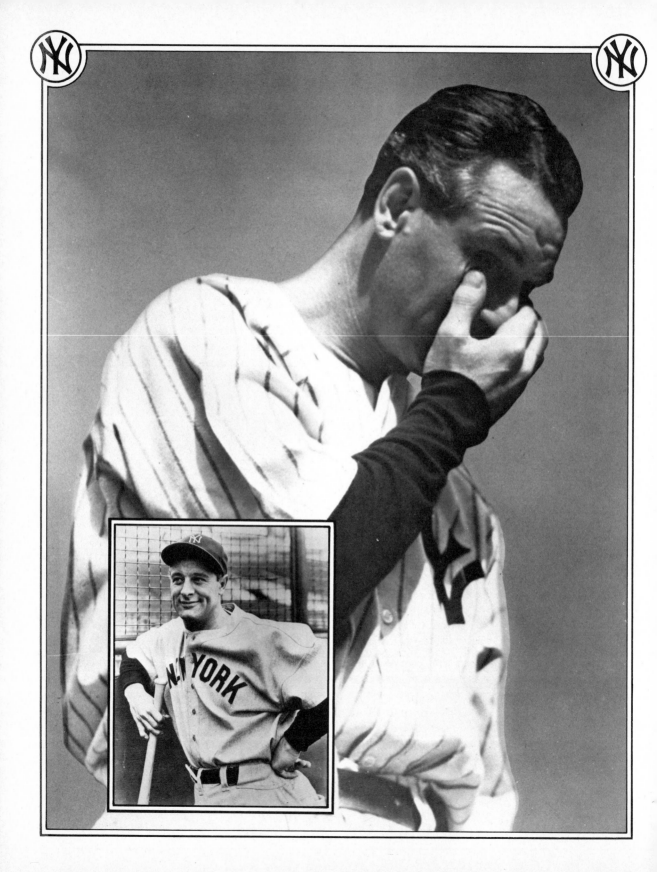

runs for the sixth time in the eight years since he had become the second baseman. He was also the leader of the infield, a smart, poised, capable ballplayer, the one the pitchers looked to for comfort and advice.

Gehrig, still playing every day (he passed Everett Scott's mark in 1933 and continued through five more seasons) had his greatest year in 1934. In a sense, he was fully mature now. He had been a mama's boy, but he gently defied his mother late in 1933 and at the age of thirty married a charming young woman named Eleanor Twitchell, whom he had met in Chicago. With the Babe in his last season as a Yankee, playing only about half the time, batting under .300, hitting only twenty-two home runs, the kid who used to be called Buster by the Babe was now obviously the star of the team. Gehrig hit .369 to lead the league, won the home-run title outright for the first time with forty-nine, and drove in 165 runs to win that title too for the Triple Crown. He had come into his own. Henry Louis Gehrig, not George Herman Ruth, was now baseball's best player.

Ruth departed the Yankees the following winter, after demanding once again that McCarthy be deposed and he himself be made manager. The Yankees courteously—and undoubtedly with relief—gave Babe his unconditional release so that he could sign a complex contract with the Boston Braves. The Babe was to be vice president, part-time coach and full-time ballplayer with the Braves, according to the contract, and the Babe fondly assumed it meant a managerial role in the future. In truth, the Braves, a wretched team, wanted him as a gate attraction only. His final flourish occurred on May 25, 1935, when he hit three homers in one game at Forbes Field in Pittsburgh, but less than two months into the season he retired, finished as a player after twenty-two seasons. Of his 714 homers, a total that would be his monument for nearly four decades until Henry Aaron surpassed it with 755, the Babe had hit 659 for the Yankees.

Ruth served as a coach for the Brooklyn Dodgers for a few months in 1938, but otherwise, in the years before his death in 1948, he never again had any official connection with the game that was his life.

Gehrig's performance declined slightly in 1935 as the Yankees suffered through another frustrating second-place season, but he came back strongly in 1936, when McCarthy's patient search for the kind of player he wanted finally paid off. Ed Barrow had purchased Joe Di-Maggio from the Pacific Coast League, and DiMaggio was the kind of efficient, undemonstrative player McCarthy loved. In their own ways the moody DiMaggio and the amiable Gehrig were very much alike. Dickey, now standing alone as the best catcher in the league, was another in the same mold, even though he had once broken Carl Reynolds' jaw with a single punch after the Senators' outfielder had bar-

"The luckiest man
on the face of the earth"
The New York Yankees

Lou Gehrig—the
"Iron Horse" first baseman
The New York Yankees

reled into him at home plate. Red Rolfe, a taciturn New Englander, had come up as a shortstop, but McCarthy kept the quiet Crosetti at that position and put the quiet Rolfe at third base, where he was one of the best in the game year after year as McCarthy's teams won pennant after pennant. George Selkirk stepped into Ruth's outsize shoes in right field and played well, batting hard and often for four straight seasons before breaking his collarbone in a fall and never fully regaining his early promise.

It was McCarthy's team now, with Gehrig and Lazzeri the only players left from the super Yankees of the 1920's. Both had little time to go in the majors. Gehrig was superb in 1936, although after only one season out of Ruth's shadow he now had to contend with the young DiMaggio's extraordinary presence. And there was another shadow— in the 1937 Series, "suffering from lumbago," Lou again batted under .300 and drove in only three runs, hardly a typical Series performance for him.

Gehrig's brief time on top between the descending Babe and the rising Joe was over. Only thirty-four as the 1938 season began, he was still bothered by the "lumbago." His average fell to .295. While he hit twenty-nine homers and batted in 114 runs (the thirteenth straight year that he had more than 100 runs batted in), he was no longer among the league leaders in either category. He had been first or second in runs batted in for nine of the previous eleven seasons, and first, second or third in home runs in ten of those seasons. Now he was an also-ran. It didn't seem right. He was too young to be getting old.

And, of course, it wasn't right. He wasn't getting old. He was deathly ill. In spring training of 1939 it was apparent that he no longer had proper muscle coordination. He worked hard trying to regain it and opened the season at first base, but he managed only four singles in twenty-eight at-bats in the first eight games. When two teammates praised him extravagantly after he made a routine play on a ground ball, he knew it was time to quit. And on May 2, 1939, in Detroit, he told McCarthy to take him out of the lineup—after 2,130 consecutive games.

Soon after that, Gehrig went off to the Mayo Clinic in Rochester, Minnesota, for a thorough physical examination. There the dreadful truth was discovered. Gehrig at thirty-five was suffering from amyotrophic lateral sclerosis, a form of progressive paralysis that was incurable and fatal. He lived for two more years but never played another inning, although he remained in uniform as a "coach" through the rest of that 1939 season. On July 4 a Lou Gehrig Day was held at Yankee Stadium. Two moments are vividly remembered from that afternoon. One was Gehrig's speech, heard often in retrospective films and recordings, in which this dying man thought not of his dismal future but of his glowing past.

"All in all," he said, "I can say on this day that I consider myself the luckiest man on the face of the earth."

The other was the presence of the beefy, still healthy Babe Ruth, who had had a serious falling out with Gehrig some years earlier after saying something critical about Gehrig's mother. Usually a flip, breezy, unsentimental type, the Babe impulsively put his arms around Lou and hugged him. The sight of these two, so close for so long in majestic accomplishment, now close again, provided an unforgettable ending to an unforgettable era of Yankee history.

The Babe hugs Lou Gehrig on July 4, 1939—the end of an era

The New York Yankees

The Joe DiMaggio Years
by Dave Anderson

PLEASE PRONOUNCE HIS name the way he does. It's not DiMadge-ee-o, it's DiMah-zhee-o, as if he were an Italian nobleman. And he justified that pronunciation. Joseph Paul DiMaggio, Jr., played baseball with an almost royal elegance that nobody else has ever quite matched.

In the batter's box he settled his spikes into the dirt in a wide-legged stance, pumped his bat once and, staring at the pitcher, held it still with a silent dignity. His swing was quick but smooth, with a sweeping follow-through: no other hitter has ever had a follow-through like it. And in center field he seemed to catch everything, running with easy, flowing strides.

During his thirteen seasons from 1936 through 1951, from the midst of the Depression through the post–World War II boom, he batted .325 with 361 homers (despite Yankee Stadium's vast left-centerfield) and 1,573 runs batted in. But the true measure of his importance to the Yankees is their success as a team—ten pennants and nine World Series championships in those thirteen seasons.

In a time before the frequent use of the word "superstar" cheapened the entire galaxy, the word "star" was enough. Joe DiMaggio was the Yankees' star, baseball's star.

He had several nicknames—the Yankee Clipper, the Jolter, Joe D—but some people called him simply the great DiMaggio and that said it all. High above Fenway Park a small plane once towed a banner with that phrase on it. And in Ernest Hemingway's classic *The Old Man and the Sea* he is identified that way.

"I would like to take the great DiMaggio fishing," the old man said. "They say his father was a fisherman."

Babe Ruth always had trouble remembering names. When he couldn't put a face and a name together, he just said "kid," as if that covered everybody. In a way, it did. Shortly after the kid centerfielder joined the Yankees, however, the Babe visited the clubhouse. He addressed player after player as "kid," but when he got to the new centerfielder he said, "Hiya, Joe."

The clubhouse was DiMaggio's throne room. When he arrived there, he would wink at Pete Sheehy, the clubhouse custodian then as now, and request half a cup of coffee.

"Never a full cup, always half a cup," Sheehy says. "Twenty half a cups a day. But when he walked in the clubhouse, the lights flickered. Joe DiMaggio was a star."

His presence demanded decorum. "I can't ever remember Joe being in a clubhouse argument," Tommy Henrich has said. "He had too much class for that." Joe DiMaggio popularized the word "class" in baseball. Handsome, with gleaming black hair then, he maintained his elegance in his dress, favoring dark blue suits, white shirts with a figured tie, glossy black shoes. In cool weather he wore a camel's hair coat or had it draped over one arm. He escorted beautiful women. He married two—Dorothy Arnold, who bore him his only child, Joe Jr., and actress Marilyn Monroe, then the nation's sex symbol. Both marriages ended in divorce.

Pete Sheehy

But his class endured. Ever since Marilyn Monroe's death, fresh flowers have been placed on her grave in Los Angeles twice a week. Joe DiMaggio gets the bill.

His teammates remember his generosity. He once invited Hank Bauer, then a rookie, to dinner. When the check came, Joe grabbed it. Bauer protested, but Joe said, "When you eat with the dago, the dago pays." Using the word "dago" to describe himself might be considered insulting to some people of Italian descent, but on the Yankees in those years he turned it into a term of endearment. He had too much pride for it to be anything else. His pride was always evident. In a mixup once he was fined $100 for missing a photo session. When he hit a home run that night, Larry MacPhail, then the Yankees' president, handed him a $100 bill, ostensibly as a bonus.

"Send it," Joe said easily, "to the Damon Runyon Cancer Fund."

Another time, in the sweltering heat of St. Louis before a double-header with the last-place Browns, he was talking about how he looked forward to playing that day.

"In this heat?" a bystander said. "How can you enjoy playing a doubleheader in this heat?"

"Well," he said, with a glance at the grandstand, "maybe somebody never saw me before."

Joe DiMaggio often wore pin-striped suits, just as he wore a pin-striped uniform. It was almost as if the Yankees were part of him, as if he would have appeared to be someone else in another team's uniform. Back in those years when Joe DiMaggio was at his best, some baseball writers were wondering how "the great DiMaggio" would have appealed to the people of Brooklyn if he had played for the Dodgers.

"Joe never could've played in Brooklyn," one said. "He's too perfect."

When the Babe went to the Boston Braves in 1935, the Yankees already had purchased DiMaggio from the minor league San Francisco Seals for 1936 delivery. DiMaggio was then only twenty years old. Ed Barrow didn't want to rush him; the general manager also thought the Yankees might be good enough to win the 1935 pennant without him. Joe McCarthy had a solid team: Gehrig, Lazzeri, Crosetti and Rolfe in the infield; Selkirk, Combs and Chapman in the outfield; Dickey catching; Gomez, Ruffing and Allen as starting pitchers and Johnny Murphy in the bullpen.

Through June and into July the Yankees were in first place, but then the Detroit Tigers took command.

Gehrig was having an off-year, batting only .329 with thirty homers. Combs, his average slipping to .282, was in his last season; he was benched as Chapman moved to center field, with Myril Hoag or Jesse Hill in left. Ruffing had a 16-11 record, but he had won 19 the year before. Gomez was down to 12-15 from his marvelous 26-5 the year before. McCarthy was frustrated. In his five seasons the Yankees had won only the 1932 pennant and finished second the other four years. But the manager's frustration would end with the arrival in 1936 of the kid outfielder from San Francisco.

Fisherman's Wharf hasn't changed. Small boats cling to the old wooden docks by the bay. Sometimes the boats are silent and still, sometimes they bob and creak in the breeze that blows through the Golden Gate Bridge from the ocean where the salmon and crab are. Back when Joe DiMaggio was small, his father's boat had his mother's name, Rosalie D, painted across the stern. His father, Giuseppe, a small, mustachioed man, had grown up in Isola delle Femmine, an islet off Palermo where generations of DiMaggios had fished the Sicilian waters. Not long after his parents' wedding at the turn of the century, Rosalie's father, who had immigrated to Collinsville, a tiny town halfway between San Francisco and Sacramento, wrote them about how good the fishing was off the California coast.

"Giuseppe," he suggested, "can make a better living here."

Giuseppe decided to try California for a year. If the fishing was better, he would stay. When he left, Rosalie was pregnant with their first child, Nellie, and the next year his wife and daughter joined him in Martinez on San Pablo Bay above the Oakland-Berkeley area. Giuseppe and Rosalie had eight more children: Mamie, Tom, Marie, Michael, Frances, Vincent and, born on November 25, 1914, in their little Martinez home, their fourth son, Joseph Paul Jr.; by the time their last child, Dominic, was born, the DiMaggios had moved across the bay to a four-room apartment on Taylor Street not far from where the Rosalie D was docked. Giuseppe expected his sons to be fishermen, but Joe resisted. He often got seasick. He preferred to play baseball on a dirt lot where dairy horses were kept.

"The man who owned the dairy let us play," he once recalled, "but first we had to round up the horses and tie them up. The bases were chunks of concrete, two feet high. Home plate was a big piece of wood. You needed a pillow to slide."

But his father didn't approve of baseball. *"Lagnuso,"* his father snapped in his Sicilian dialect. *"Meschino."*

Lazy. Good for nothing. That's what the old fisherman thought of his fourth son, even though Joe contributed to the family finances by selling newspapers on street corners. On good days Joe cleared $1, including tips. His brothers were different. Tom and Mike worked the fishing boat, although Tom also played baseball. "Maybe the best in the family," Joe has said. "He could hit a ball a mile, but as the oldest son he had to have a steady job." Vince worked in a fruit store. Vince also was gifted—he could sing. His parents even considered sending him to Italy for operatic training. They never did, but still Vince was gifted; perhaps that's why they understood when Vince wanted to play baseball. He hit .347 for Tucson of the Arizona-Texas League in 1932 before he was called up by the San Francisco Seals to finish the Pacific Coast League season.

Vince had just turned twenty; Joe, at seventeen, a dropout from Galileo High School, hit .633 that year as a shortstop for Sunset Produce, a good semipro team. Earlier he had played for the Rossi Olive Oil sandlot team.

"I didn't work for them, that was just the firm that bought our uniforms," he has said, "but I had a few jobs. I crated oranges for one day. I picked crabmeat in a cannery for a day. I got $3 for picking shrimp. When the Rossi team, the Jolly Knights, won the championship, we got little gold baseballs to put on our watch chains. We didn't have any watches, but that little gold baseball was the first thing I ever got out of baseball."

He never got much out of high school. He wanted to take a phys-ed course, but it was filled. He had to take ROTC instead. He didn't like to drill, so he played hooky.

"They finally caught me. They told me to make up my credits and I did, but they wouldn't take me back for some reason. I remember waiting to see the principal, waiting and waiting, but the principal never showed. That really made a ballplayer out of me. I remember I won a pair of featherweight spikes for being the best player in the sandlot league. They cost $22.50—what a touch that was. I've wondered what would've happened if the principal took me back in school that day."

Shortly after Vince reported to the Seals, the other San Francisco team in the PCL, the Missions, offered Joe a contract for $150 a month.

His father, realizing that Joe would never be a student, agreed. Tom and Mike encouraged their younger brother, but first Joe wanted to talk to Vince, who was over at Seals Stadium that day. With no money for a ticket, Joe was peeking through a hole in the fence when a Seals scout, Spike Hennessey, spotted him.

"C'mon in with me," Hennessey said. "I'll get Vince for you, but first I want you to meet Charlie Graham."

Inside, the scout introduced Joe to the Seals' owner not only as Vince DiMaggio's brother but also as a "good-looking prospect, this kid can hit." Graham sized up the slim teenager with the long legs and long muscular arms.

"You're big for your age," Graham said. "How'd you like to work out with the Seals?"

One workout was enough. The Seals asked Joe to join them for the final week of the season. He agreed, even though he had no contract and no salary. That would be unthinkable today, but then, a quarter of a century before the major leagues moved to Los Angeles and San Francisco, minor league baseball was important. And in San Francisco the Seals were more important than the Missions. Another factor, of course, was that Vince would be a teammate. And his first time up, Joe tripled.

"Sign with us for next year," Graham said, "and we'll give you $225 a month."

That was twice what the average rookie made in the PCL then, but Joe DiMaggio more than earned it. He also discovered his proper position. Early in the 1933 season the Seals' manager, Ike Caveney, once an infielder with the Reds, used Joe as a pinch-hitter. The eighteen-year-old rookie walked. At the end of the inning he was trotting back to the dugout when Caveney called to him.

"Get your glove, kid," the manager said. "Finish up in right field."

Joe had never played the outfield. But, except for one game at first base late in his Yankee career, he would never play anywhere else from then on. Although he had his troubles there that year, making seventeen errors, he led the league with thirty-two assists. He also led the league with 169 runs batted in while hitting .340 with twenty-eight homers. Even more memorable, he hit safely in sixty-one consecutive games, breaking the PCL record of forty-nine set by Jack Ness in 1914 —a feat that would ease the burden of his famous fifty-six-game hitting streak with the Yankees in 1941—all this at age nineteen.

"I was just a kid then, I never felt any pressure in that streak," he has said. "I was having too much fun."

One night during the 1934 season the fun stopped. After a doubleheader at Seals Stadium, Joe had dinner at the home of one of his married sisters. He was tired from the long day and took a cab home.

Sitting awkwardly in the small back seat, he didn't realize that his left foot had fallen asleep. As he got out of the cab, he put all his weight on his left foot.

"I went down like I'd been shot," he later said. "There was no twisting, just four sharp cracks at the knee. I couldn't straighten out my leg. The pain was terrific, like a whole set of aching teeth in my knee."

He hobbled to a nearby movie theater from which the manager, a friend of his, drove him to a hospital. The diagnosis was sprained tendons. He was told to go home and apply an epsom-salt solution and hot towels. But the next morning his leg collapsed again. He went to the ballpark and mentioned the injury to Ike Caveney.

"I can play, though," Joe said.

As a precaution, Caveney wisely chose to rest his nineteen-year-old slugger. Late in the game, however, the manager used him as a pinch-hitter. DiMaggio smashed a homer but *walked* around the bases.

"Is your knee that bad?" Caveney asked.

"No use running on it," DiMaggio said.

Two days later Joe pinch-hit again. He doubled but hobbled weakly into second base. Ordered to see the Seals' orthopedist, he learned that he had suffered torn cartilage. His left leg, from ankle to thigh, was put in an aluminum splint which he wore for three weeks. Then, shortly after he rejoined the Seals, he slipped in the dugout and his leg collapsed again. He was through for the season. Several major league teams had talked to Charley Graham about purchasing the young outfielder. Selling his best players is how the Seals' owner turned a profit. The offers for DiMaggio had escalated to $75,000—a tremendous sum in those days. But the knee ailment scared away most teams. Only the Yankees were still interested. Two of their scouts, Joe Devine and Bill Essick, had raved about him in their reports to Ed Barrow.

"Don't back off because of the kid's knee," Essick said. "He'll be all right. And you can get him cheap."

Barrow phoned Graham, who demanded $40,000. The Yankees' general manager offered half that, and eventually they compromised at $25,000 and five players (outfielder Ted Norbert, first baseman Les Powers, third baseman Ed Farrell, pitchers Jim Densmore and Floyd Newkirk), with DiMaggio to stay with the Seals during the 1935 season as Yankee property. But one stipulation remained. DiMaggio had to have his knee examined by a physician of the Yankees' choice. Graham agreed. DiMaggio went to Los Angeles, where he was checked by Dr. Richard Spencer, a noted orthopedist. Dr. Spencer advised the Yankees that, at his age, DiMaggio should make a full recovery. Barrow phoned Graham.

"We got a deal," the general manager said.

An 18-year-old Joe DiMaggio scores during his 61-game hitting streak for the San Francisco Seals

The Yankees also had a bargain. As fast and as sure-footed as ever, the twenty-year-old centerfielder tore the PCL apart in 1935, batting .398 with 34 homers and 154 runs batted in. Joe DiMaggio was ready.

In those years the Yankees trained in St. Petersburg, Florida, a long train ride from San Francisco, where two other Yankees of Italian descent lived—Tony Lazzeri, the veteran second baseman, and Frank Crosetti, the young shortstop. For the trip that year Lazzeri had purchased a shiny '36 Ford sedan. He invited Crosetti to join him, then phoned Joe DiMaggio.

"Go to Florida with Frank and me in style," Lazzeri said. "In my new car."

The rookie was flattered. He had become acquainted with Lazzeri and Crosetti, but he didn't know them well; he also didn't know that his brother Vince had asked the two Yankees to watch over him. The first day of the trip DiMaggio, shy and quiet, sat in the back seat while Lazzeri drove. Crosetti then slid behind the wheel, and after another few hours Lazzeri turned to the rookie.

"Your turn to drive," he suggested.

"I'm sorry," Joe said. "I don't know how."

Lazzeri stared at Crosetti, who stared back. "Let's throw the bum out," Lazzeri said. "Let's leave him here in the middle of nowhere."

Curled comfortably in the back seat, DiMaggio grinned. "Let's go," he said. "I got a date with the Yankees."

And the Yankees were waiting—the Yankees who had not won the American League pennant since 1932, the Yankees who needed another big bat. The day he arrived at Huggins Field the other players sized him up as soon as he walked into the clubhouse. Lazzeri took him around and introduced him to the other players. Lou Gehrig shook hands and greeted him warmly, saying, "Nice to have you with us, Joe." The others were pleasantly polite, except for Red Ruffing, who stared at him with a half smile and a half sneer.

"So you're the great DiMaggio," the tough righthander said.

Lazzeri glared at Ruffing, but DiMaggio glanced at him without a change of expression and apparently without resentment. He knew he was a rookie. He knew that what he had done in the PCL meant nothing to his new teammates. All that mattered to them was what he did from now on. The introductions over, Lazzeri ushered DiMaggio into Joe McCarthy's office, then left them together. When the rookie emerged, the newspapermen covering the Yankees surrounded him.

"What," one asked, "did the manager say to you?"

"Not much," Joe said.

"Did he tell you which outfield position you would play?"

"No."

"Did you express any preference?"

"Wherever he puts me is all right."

"Left field is the sun field at Yankee Stadium," one said. "Have you ever played the sun field?"

"No," the rookie answered.

"Ruth never would play it."

"I'll play it if Mr. McCarthy wants me to."

"More likely he'll put you in center field."

"That's all right with me."

But he didn't play center field immediately. When the season opened, he wasn't playing at all. Shortly after the exhibition games began, he twisted his left foot. Diathermy was prescribed. The second day of treatment he had his sore foot under the heat lamp when he suddenly felt a burning sensation. He yanked the foot away, but too late. Somehow the diathermy machine had generated more heat than planned. His foot was badly burned. After missing the first sixteen games of the season, he finally made his Yankee debut on May 3 at the Stadium when he played left field and batted third (behind Crosetti and Rolfe, with Gehrig as cleanup) against Jack Knott, the St. Louis Browns' big righthander. His first time up he lined a single to left. He got another single and a triple as the Yankees won, 14–5.

At the time Ben Chapman was the Yankees' centerfielder. Six weeks later the quarrelsome Chapman was traded to the Washington Senators for Jake Powell, a quiet leftfielder. DiMaggio was installed in center field.

"I wanted him to be comfortable before I put him in center," Joe McCarthy said years later. "He needed the room in center to roam, especially in Yankee Stadium, the toughest center field in baseball. There's so much ground out there. Only the great ones can play it. And he did everything so easily. You never saw him make a great catch. You never saw him dive for a ball. He didn't have to. He was already there to catch it. That's what you're supposed to do—catch the ball, not make exciting catches."

Once in the lineup, DiMaggio played in each of the Yankees' remaining 138 games. He batted .328 with 206 hits, including 29 homers. He knocked in 125 runs and scored 132.

The Yankees finished first by nineteen and a half games, clinching the pennant on September 9, the earliest in American League history. In his first World Series the rookie centerfielder batted .346 with three doubles, as the Yankees defeated the Giants in six games, including 18–4 and 13–5 routs. Not only had the rookie made it, he had made the difference between the Yankees being a contender and a champion. And for one, Red Ruffing no longer was skeptical of "the great Di-Maggio"—the thirty-two-year-old righthander won twenty games for the first time in his thirteen big-league seasons. Monte Pearson, a slim righthander acquired from the Indians, won nineteen and Lefty Gomez was 13-7.

Lou Gehrig had a tremendous season, winning the Most Valuable Player award with a .352 average, 49 homers and 152 runs batted in. Bill Dickey hit .362 with 22 homers and 107 runs batted in. Red Rolfe batted .319 and led the league with 116 runs. But in Yankee history 1936 was the first of the Joe DiMaggio years.

When the 1937 season began, Joe was no longer the only DiMaggio in the big leagues. Older brother Vince was with the Braves; in his other travels around the National League with the Reds, Pirates, Phillies and Giants, his career average would be .249 with 125 home runs. His best season would be 1941 with the Pirates, when he hit 21 homers and drove in 100 runs.

But in 1937, with a wink at some bystanders as Joe sat at a nearby locker in the Yankee clubhouse, Lefty Gomez said, "Nice guy, this DiMaggio, his brother Vince gets him a trial with the Seals—and he beats his brother out of a job."

"I didn't do that," Joe said, looking up.

"Sure you did," Gomez said. "You were together on the Seals in the spring of 1933, weren't you?"

"Yes," Joe said.

"Vince was a regular in the outfield, wasn't he?"

"Yes."

"And after a while you were a regular?"

"Yes."

"And whose place did you take?"

"Well, but . . ."

"But what?" Gomez said, grinning.

"I don't know."

"You don't know! What happened to Vince?"

"Hollywood bought him."

"Hear that—'Hollywood bought him,'" Gomez said of the Hollywood team then in the PCL. "You mean the Seals sold him to Hollywood to make room for you. See, this DiMaggio is nothing but an ungrateful bum who beat his brother out of a job."

Joe smiled, enjoying the fun that Gomez was poking at him.

None of the other Yankees talked to Joe that way. Still somewhat shy, still somewhat remote from his teammates, he preferred his privacy. His shyness, he believes now, developed when his parents used to tease him about his mistakes in speaking Italian as a youngster; rather than risk the teasing, he kept quiet. Still, in his shyness, he enjoyed Lefty Gomez; they had dinner together on road trips, they went

Red Ruffing   Joe McCarthy   Lefty Gomez

The '37 Yankees: DiMaggio, Crosetti, Lazzeri, Dickey, Gehrig, Powell, Selkirk

The New York Yankees

out on the town together. They were baseball's odd couple—the intro-verted slugger, the extroverted pitcher.

"Opposites attract," Joe once explained.

Except for demeanor, however, they weren't that opposite. Their roots were similar—one of Italian ancestry, the other of Spanish. Gomez also was from California, and he had pitched for the Seals before the Yankees purchased him. He had been their ace lefthander since 1931, when he had a 21-9 record with a 2.63 earned-run average. The next year he had a 24-7 record, and in 1935 he was 26-5 with a league-leading 2.33 earned-run average. Now, in 1937, he led the league with 21 victories (against 11 losses), a 2.33 earned-run average and 194 strikeouts. He always led the league in laughs.

"I've got a new invention," he said one day. "It's a revolving bowl for tired goldfish."

There were many laughs for the Yankees that year as they breezed to another pennant, by thirteen games. The second-place Tigers were never a threat after their manager and catcher, Mickey Cochrane, was beaned May 25 by Bump Hadley at the Stadium, two days after the Yankees had moved into first place. Instead of being afflicted with the so-called sophomore jinx, DiMaggio got better, as the great players usually do. He batted .346, hit 46 homers and drove in 167 runs. Gehrig had another big year—.351, 37 homers, 154 runs batted in. Dickey hit .332 with 29 homers and 133 runs batted in. Ruffing had a 20-7 record; Johnny Murphy was 13-4 with 10 saves, earning his "Fireman" nick-name.

And that year a new face appeared, the hawk-nosed, smiling, boyish face of Tommy Henrich.

In 1937 they obtained Tommy Henrich in an auction, which was almost unheard-of at the time. Henrich had signed with the Indians in 1934, but when he found himself sidetracked in the minors, he wrote to Commissioner Landis claiming that the Indians' general manager, Cy Slapnicka, was deliberately preventing him from advancing to the Cleveland roster. After an investigation, the Commissioner found the Indians guilty and declared Henrich a free agent.

Pursued by eight teams, Henrich joined the Yankees for a $25,000 bonus. When the 1937 season opened, the twenty-four-year-old out-fielder was in Newark. Then McCarthy became annoyed with outfielder Roy Johnson and told Barrow to get rid of him.

"Who'll replace him?" Barrow asked.

"The kid in Newark," McCarthy said.

Hitting .320 in sixty-seven games, the kid was in Yankee Stadium to stay, mostly as the rightfielder alongside DiMaggio and later as the first baseman. Another rookie that year was Spurgeon (Spud) Chandler, a chunky righthanded pitcher who twice would be a twenty-game winner and would emerge as the Yankees' all-time leader with a .717 percentage. As the new faces appeared, the old ones departed. Tony Lazzeri's bat was slower. He hit only .244 and drove in only seventy runs. His legs around second base also were slower. Still, when the Yankees disposed of the Giants in the World Series in five games, Lazzeri batted .400; his six hits included a homer and a triple. At the end of the Series, Philip K. Wrigley, the Cubs' owner, phoned Barrow.

"I'd like to have Lazzeri," he said. "Tony has just what my team needs—that Yankee spirit."

Barrow had no objections. After consulting Lazzeri, who also had no objections, the Yankees gave him his unconditional release. Then the Cubs signed him. But the Yankees weren't concerned about replacing him at second base. They had another "kid in Newark" named Joe Gordon, typical of their flourishing farm system.

Joe DiMaggio's salary as a rookie was $8,000; his salary in 1937 was $15,000. Each year he also collected a winning World Series share of about $6,400. Now, in the winter of 1938, he wanted a $40,000 salary. When he mentioned that to Ed Barrow, however, the general manager glared.

"Young man," he said, "do you realize that Lou Gehrig only makes $43,000 a year after thirteen years?"

"In that case, Mr. Barrow," DiMaggio said respectfully, "Mr. Gehrig is a very underpaid ballplayer."

The best that Barrow offered, with Colonel Ruppert's blessing, was $25,000. And when the Yankees gathered for spring training, the centerfielder remained in San Francisco, where DiMaggio's restaurant had opened on Fisherman's Wharf the previous year.

"The restaurant is going good," DiMaggio told newsmen. "For what the Yankees are offering, I can't afford to leave."

That was a bluff, of course. The restaurant's popularity depended on Joe DiMaggio's popularity as a baseball player, not on his presence. But he was obstinate. He remained in San Francisco throughout spring training, which annoyed his teammates. Almost to a man, they considered $25,000 a generous salary for a third-year player, even one of DiMaggio's talent. They also wanted him in St. Petersburg, preparing himself for the season. When the Yankees arrived in New York for their opener, the impasse still existed. Around that time Joe Gould, a New York boxing manager who knew DiMaggio, phoned him.

"You have a chance this year to break a lot of records and then get the money you want," Gould said. "But you can't break any records in San Francisco."

The next day DiMaggio phoned Barrow and accepted the $25,000 offer. He also had to accept the hoots of fans who, during the Depression, resented his "greedy" demands. But in the face of his stoic manner the jeers soon turned to cheers. He didn't break any records that year, but as the Yankees breezed to their third consecutive pennant, he earned his money. Missing only seven games, he led the Yankees with a .324 average, 32 homers and 140 runs batted in. Gordon had taken over at second base, batting only .255 but smashing twenty-five homers and, with Crosetti, forming an acrobatic double-play combination.

Ruffing was 21-7; Gomez, 18-12; Pearson, 16-7, including a 13–0 no-hitter against the Indians in which he faced only twenty-seven men. Two baserunners who had walked were erased by double plays.

While the Yankees, who finished nine and a half games ahead of the Red Sox, clinched the pennant, the Pirates were building a World Series press box on their Forbes Field roof. But then the Pirates lost three straight to the Cubs in late September; the second game was decided by a ninth-inning homer by Gabby Hartnett at Wrigley Field as twilight dissolved into darkness. And so the Yankees went to Chicago, where Tony Lazzeri was waiting. During the Cubs' workout the day before the Series opened, one of the New York sportswriters approached the swarthy ex-Yankee who now was the Cubs' utility infielder.

"Well," the reporter said, "do you give up?"

"Give up what?" the ex-Yankee wanted to know.

"Give up on the Series with the Yankees."

"Give up?" he snapped, glowering. "What for? We're as good as they are."

"Who's 'they'?"

"The Yankees," he said. "I'm not on their side any more. We'll beat their brains out."

"You really think so?"

"I really think so."

Not many of his teammates did. Of all the other Cubs, only Dizzy Dean put up much resistance. Still uninhibited and colorful, the big righthander, whom the Cubs had obtained from the Cardinals for $185,000, no longer had his fastball, but he had a 7-1 record. In the second game his soft stuff had the Yankees fooled, 3–2, going into the eighth. But then Selkirk singled and Crosetti homered. In the ninth Henrich singled and DiMaggio homered. That was all for Diz—and all for the Cubs, as the Yankees swept the Series in four games.

Jake Ruppert was dying. At the hospital Babe Ruth visited the Yankee owner who had always called him "Ruth," and the old millionaire looked up at him, smiled and whispered, "Babe, Babe." He died on January 13, 1939, with the Yankees passing into the control of the Ruppert estate. And in June the heart went out of the Yankees when Lou Gehrig was discovered to be fatally ill. His iron-man streak had ended on May 2, with Ellsworth (Babe) Dahlgren inserted at first base. Joe DiMaggio had never been close with Gehrig, but they had always been friendly. In the old Yankee clubhouse on the third-base side of the Stadium their lockers were side by side near a window. To pass the time before a game they often looked out the window, trying to gauge the size of that day's crowd by the number of customers out on the sidewalk.

DiMaggio also had always been grateful for the time Gehrig stuck up for him early in his rookie year. Against the Tigers in Detroit one day, the rookie centerfielder let a questionable high pitch go by. Behind him, George Moriarity, a crusty old umpire, bellowed, "Strike one!" The rookie didn't complain. But when the second pitch was at eye level and Moriarity roared, "Strike two!" the rookie glanced back.

"Turn around," Moriarity snapped.

From the on-deck circle, Gehrig disputed the old umpire, yelling "Leave the kid alone, George. If you call 'em right, he won't have to turn around."

Now, his strength and reflexes gone, Gehrig would never swing a bat or play first base again, but he continued to sit in the dugout and travel with the team that won another pennant so easily without him. Babe Dahlgren, playing 144 games at first base, knocked in 89 runs with a .235 average and 15 homers, but the new name was Charley Keller, the rookie outfielder who hit .334 with 11 homers. His bushy eyebrows and his bulging biceps earned him the nickname King Kong.

"He's the first player brought back by Frank Buck," cracked Gomez, referring to the popular big-game hunter.

DiMaggio meanwhile hit for the highest average of his career, .381, with 30 homers and 126 runs batted in, earning his first MVP award. Gordon had 28 homers and 111 runs batted in; Dickey, 24 and 105; Selkirk, 21 and 101. Rolfe again led the league with 139 runs. Ruffing was 21-7 with a 2.93 earned-run average, while six other pitchers thrived. Atley Donald, a rookie righthander who opened with 12 consecutive victories, finished at 13-3. Pearson was 12-5; Gomez, 12-6; Hadley, 12-6; Steve Sundra, 11-1; Oral Hildebrand, 10-4. Out of the bullpen, Murphy was 3-6 but had 19 saves as one of the first famous relief pitchers.

Finishing 17 games ahead of the Red Sox, the Yankees had a 106-45 record for a .702 percentage, joining the 1927 team (110-44, .714) as the only American League teams at that time to have bettered the .700 mark.

But in the World Series the Yankees figured to have trouble with the Cincinnati Reds' two aces, 27-game winner Bucky Walters (the National League's most valuable player) and 25-game winner Paul Derringer.

Charley Keller   Joe Gordon   Tommy Henrich

DiMaggio after setting the American League record of hitting in 42 consecutive games

The New York Yankees

In the Stadium opener Ruffing outpitched Derringer with a four-hitter, winning, 2–1, in the ninth when Keller tripled, DiMaggio walked and Dickey singled. In the second game Pearson fired a two-hit shutout, 4–0, as Dahlgren homered off Walters. With only five hits, the Yankees won the third game, 7–3, but four of those hits were homers—two by Keller, one each by DiMaggio and Dickey. Desperate now to avert a sweep, the Reds' manager, Bill McKechnie, used Walters in relief of Derringer to protect a 4–2 lead going into the ninth of the fourth game, but then the Yankees rallied to tie. In the tenth Crosetti walked and Rolfe sacrificed, then Keller was safe on shortstop Billy Myers' error. DiMaggio singled for one run, and when the ball got away from right-fielder Ival Goodman, Keller also scored, slamming into catcher Ernie Lombardi and jarring the ball loose.

As the ball sat there only a few feet from the dazed Reds catcher, DiMaggio kept running and also scored on what had only been a single.

In baseball history that scene would be remembered as "Lombardi's Snooze," courtesy of Charley Keller, the rookie who also stunned the Reds with six runs batted in and a .438 average on seven hits that included three homers, a triple and a double. When the Yankees triumphed the next day, 7–4, they became the first team to win four successive World Series, the last two in eight consecutive games. The cry "Break up the Yankees" was heard in the land, but that night in Cincinnati a Reds rooter shook his head.

"The hell with breaking up the Yankees," he said. "I'll be satisfied if they break up Keller."

By then the Yankees were on their way back to New York, celebrating on the train. Some of the players began to parade through the Pullman cars. But when Joe McCarthy heard the commotion, he leaned out of his stateroom.

"Cut that out," he barked. "What are you—amateurs? I thought I was managing a professional club. You're worse than college kids."

In 1940 the Yankees had nothing to celebrate. In last place for two weeks in May, they were no better than .500 in early August as the Tigers and the Indians battled for the lead. Then the Yankees streaked, winning sixteen out of nineteen, and moved into first place after the opener of a September 11 doubleheader in Cleveland, but they lost the second game and drifted back. With an 88-66 record, they finished third, two games behind the Tigers, who lost the World Series to the Reds, and one game behind the Indians.

DiMaggio won his second (and last) batting title with a .352 average, along with 31 homers and 133 runs batted in. Gordon had another big year (30 homers, 103 runs batted in). Keller hit .286 with 31 homers and 93 runs batted in, and Henrich hit .307, but several Yankees skidded—notably Dickey, to .247, 9 homers and 54 runs batted in.

Ruffing had a 15-12 record, but Gomez developed arm trouble, appearing in only 9 games for a 3-3 record. Marius Russo, a slim left-hander in his second season, was 14-8, but the Yankees' best pitcher over the last two months was Ernie (Tiny) Bonham, a well-padded righthander who was 9-3 with a league-leading 1.91 earned-run average after his promotion from the Kansas City farm in the American Association.

The third-place finish annoyed McCarthy, who decided to make changes for the 1941 season. Dahlgren was sold to the Boston Braves because, as the manager explained, "His arms are too short. He makes easy plays look hard."

McCarthy wanted to try Gordon at first base in order to open up second for Gerry Priddy, a rookie who had come up from Kansas City along with a tiny shortstop named Phil Rizzuto, the heir apparent to Crosetti's job. When Priddy wrenched an ankle just before the season opener, however, Gordon returned to second and Johnny Sturm, also up from Kansas City, emerged as the first baseman.

But the 1941 season, more than any other in his career, belonged to Joe DiMaggio.

Occasionally, a baseball player has a year that is his alone, a year with which he is identified forever. Babe Ruth had 1927 when he hit sixty home runs. Roger Maris had 1961 when he hit 61 home runs. Ron Guidry had 1978 when he won twenty-seven games and lost only three, including two victories in the World Series and the American League championship series. Joe DiMaggio had 1941 when he hit safely in fifty-six consecutive games.

In nearly four decades since then nobody has threatened DiMaggio's record; only Pete Rose has even approached it. Rose was stopped after forty-four games in 1978, a streak that hypnotized the nation but ended twelve games short of equaling DiMaggio's record. As much as anything else, Rose's accomplishment was merely a reminder of what DiMaggio had done in the summer of 1941, when baseball was merely a game in a world of harsh reality. Japanese admirals were plotting their Pearl Harbor attack. President Franklin Delano Roosevelt spoke of a "national emergency" and warned of Hitler's plan to "extend his Nazi domination to the Western Hemisphere." In the coastal cities people listened to a new sound: the ghostly wail of air-raid sirens signaling test blackouts. But there was time to sing a silly tune that went "Hut sut rawlson on the rillerah," and there was time, for several weeks that summer, to check whether Joe DiMaggio got his hit that day.

In mid-May, however, the two-time batting champion was struggling at .306; the Yankees also were struggling. By the morning of May 15 the Yankees had lost four straight and seven of their last nine. They were in fourth place, five and a half games behind the league-leading Indians.

That afternoon at the Stadium the Yankees lost again, 13–1, but in the first inning DiMaggio singled off Edgar Smith, the White Sox stocky lefthander. The streak had begun, but the team slump was the story. YANK ATTACK WEAKEST IN YEARS, declared a New York *Journal-American* headline. Not even DiMaggio was commanding the respect a hitter of his stature deserved. Against the Tigers the next week at the Stadium he extended his streak to seven games with two early hits, but with the score 4–4 in the ninth the Yankees had the winning run on third base with nobody out and DiMaggio up. Rather than order an intentional walk, Del Baker, the Tigers' manager, told righthander Al Benton to pitch to him. DiMaggio grounded out. The Yankees won in the tenth inning, but the Tigers, the defending American League champions, had insulted the Yankees' big hitter.

At the Stadium three days later the Red Sox also insulted him. In the seventh the Yankees were losing, 6–5, but DiMaggio was up with runners on third and second. Although again an intentional walk appeared to be the logical move, the Red Sox manager, Joe Cronin, told lefthander Earl Johnson, "You can get him out, don't walk him."

On the first pitch DiMaggio singled for the winning run. This hit stretched his streak to ten games, but virtually nobody was aware of it yet. Not even DiMaggio, who was more concerned with a swollen neck. "This neck is driving me crazy," he told Lefty Gomez, "but don't say anything about it." DiMaggio kept getting his hits, but in the Memorial Day doubleheader in Boston he made four errors. In the first game he dropped a fly ball. In the second he fumbled a grounder and twice threw wildly.

"If you're not going to say anything about that neck," Gomez told him later, "then I will."

The secret was out, but DiMaggio shrugged it off, saying, "I get it every year. It'll go away."

Then suddenly DiMaggio's neck didn't seem too important. The afternoon of June 2 the Yankees lost to Bob Feller, 7–5, in Cleveland and traveled over to Detroit afterwards. In the lobby of the Book-Cadillac the hotel manager was waiting for Joe McCarthy.

"Mr. McCarthy," he said, "there's an important message for you. Lou Gehrig died tonight."

The manager was shaken. So was Bill Dickey, once Gehrig's roommate. McCarthy and Dickey returned to New York for the funeral on June 4, but two days later McCarthy was in the Yankee dugout at Sportsman's Park before the opener of a weekend series with the Browns, and his team was on his mind again.

"The boys," McCarthy said, "are just waiting for Joe to show 'em how to do it."

That day DiMaggio got three hits. The next day, in a doubleheader, he slugged three homers and a double. The Yankees had an eight-game winning streak, and DiMaggio had a twenty-four-game hitting streak. And the newspapermen covering the Yankees had dug up the Yankee record for hitting safely in consecutive games—twenty-nine, shared by Roger Peckinpaugh and Earle Combs.

"That's when I became conscious of the streak, when the writers started talking about the records I could break," DiMaggio said later. "But at that stage I didn't think too much about it."

Early the following week, on June 17, he broke the Yankee record on a bad-hop single off the shoulder of Luke Appling, the White Sox shortstop—one of the few times luck helped. But by now DiMaggio was more than a baseball idol. He was a national celebrity. The next night he and a pal, ticket-broker George Solitaire, went to the first Joe Louis–Billy Conn heavyweight title fight at the Polo Grounds, and he needed a police escort to keep him from being mobbed.

"There were so many people asking for his autograph," Solitaire once said, "he had almost as many cops around him as the fighters did on their way into the ring."

By now other forgotten records had been unearthed. There hadn't been a significant hitting streak since 1922, when George Sisler of the Browns went forty-one games for the American League record. That same year Rogers Hornsby of the Cardinals went thirty-three games for the modern National League record (increased to thirty-seven games by Tommy Holmes of the Boston Braves in 1947 and then to forty-four by Pete Rose), but in 1897, aided by the old rule that foul balls were not strikes, Wee Willie Keeler hit in forty-four games for the Baltimore Orioles, then in the National League—the major league record that DiMaggio was most aware of now. But all the talk didn't seem to phase him, perhaps because of his sixty-one-game streak in San Francisco.

"I never saw a guy so calm," Lefty Gomez has said. "I would up with the upset stomachs."

With four hits, two each off Bobo Newsom and Archie McKain, on July 20 against the Tigers at the Stadium, DiMaggio matched Hornsby and lifted his average to .354. His teammates were rooting openly for him, but each opposing pitcher bore down more than usual against him, hoping to be the one to stop the streak. And the fielders were more alert. Human nature had intruded on the plot. In the thirty-sixth game an eighth-inning single preserved the streak against Bob Muncrief, a rookie righthander for the Browns.

"It wouldn't have been fair to walk him—to him or to me," Muncrief said. "Hell, he's the greatest player I ever saw."

Two days later, on June 26, after the Yankees had finally climbed into first place, they were leading the Browns, 3–1, at the Stadium going into the last half of the eighth. DiMaggio had been up three times without a hit against Eldon Auker, a submarine-ball righthander. Unless the Yankees got a runner on in the eighth, he would not get another chance. Johnny Sturm popped up, but when Rolfe walked, Henrich turned back from the on-deck circle.

"If I hit into a doubleplay, Joe won't get up," he reminded Joe McCarthy. "Is it all right if I bunt?"

McCarthy agreed. Henrich bunted, moving Rolfe to second. On the first pitch, DiMaggio doubled to left.

But not every pitcher was willing to let the hits fall where they may. Two days later the Yankees were playing the A's at the Stadium; the A's pitcher was righthander Johnny Babich, who had been in the Yankee farm system and now had a reputation as a Yankee-killer. He had beaten them five times in 1940 to wreck their pennant hopes. And now, on June 28, he predicted that he would halt Joe DiMaggio's streak.

"He was out to stop me," DiMaggio has often said. "Even if it meant walking me every time up."

And his first time up, DiMaggio walked. His second·time up, Babich threw three wide fastballs. DiMaggio glanced at Art Fletcher, the Yankees' third-base coach, to see if he would be permitted to swing at the 3-0 pitch. Fletcher, relaying a signal from McCarthy, flashed the "hit" sign.

"The next pitch was outside," DiMaggio once recalled, "but I lined it between Babich's legs. After I took my turn at first, I looked over at him. His face was white as a sheet. McCarthy was great to me. He let me hit the 3-0 pitch quite a few times, but that's the one I remember best."

The next day, against the Washington Senators in a Griffith Stadium doubleheader, DiMaggio tied Sisler's record at forty-one with a double off knuckleballer Dutch Leonard in the sixth inning of the opener. But between games a fan jumped on the field near the Yankee dugout, snatched DiMaggio's favorite bat and escaped into the stands. In the second game DiMaggio twice lined out and then flied out against Arnold Anderson, a journeyman righthander. But in the seventh inning he appropriated Henrich's bat and singled to left, extending his streak to forty-two games for the American League record. Henrich's bat actually was a DiMaggio model that the rightfielder had borrowed. In the dining car on the way back to New York that night DiMaggio ordered beer for all his teammates and explained why he missed his own bat.

"Most of my models are thirty-six inches long and weigh thirty-six

One of these bats was stolen during the 56-game hitting streak

ounces," he said, "but I had sandpapered the handle of this one to take off one-half to three-quarters of an ounce. It was just right. I wish that guy would return it. I need it more than he does."

The bat thief was never identified, but DiMaggio learned later that the youngster lived in Newark, New Jersey, across the Hudson River from New York City. The boy bragged about having stolen the bat, and when the word got around he was quickly confronted by some men whom DiMaggio described as "good friends of mine." The bat was returned to the Yankee clubhouse at the Stadium in time to help DiMaggio challenge Keeler's record in a July 1 doubleheader with the Red Sox.

In the fourth inning of the opener he hit a tricky bouncer to third baseman Jim Tabor, who, hurrying his throw, fired wildly past first base.

Hit or error? That was the question as DiMaggio looked up at the press box on the mezzanine level behind home plate where the official scorer, Dan Daniel of the New York *World-Telegram,* was about to make his decision. Moments later Daniel raised his right arm, the signal for a hit. DiMaggio sighed.

"That was one of the few times I got a break from the scorer on a questionable play," he has said. "Instead of giving me the benefit of the doubt—not that I was asking for it—they usually made sure it was a clean hit."

All around the American League the official scorers, each an experienced baseball writer, were under ethical pressure. They knew that awarding DiMaggio a tainted hit would cheapen the streak. But in the second game that day a scorer's decision was not needed. DiMaggio drilled a clean first-inning single off righthander Jack Wilson that tied Keeler's major league record at forty-four games. Then an element of timing, if not luck, surfaced when the game was rained out after five innings. The next afternoon forty-one-year-old Bob (Lefty) Grove, then nearing his three hundredth victory, begged off as the Red Sox starter because of the sweltering 94.8° heat. Not that DiMaggio got a break: righthander Heber (Dick) Newsome, a nineteen-game winner that season, started instead. His first time up, DiMaggio hit a liner to right field, where Stan Spence, after momentarily misjudging the ball, ran back to make a leaping catch. In the third he grounded out. But in the fifth, on a 2-1 count, he hit his eighteenth homer into the lower leftfield stands. In his long stride, he rounded the bases and tipped his cap to the ovation from 52,832 spectators as he approached the Yankee dugout, then behind third base.

"You not only broke Keeler's record," Gomez told him, "you even used his formula—you hit 'em where they ain't."

After the game, surrounded by newspapermen, DiMaggio sat at his locker, puffed a cigarette, sipped coffee and talked about the record. "I don't know how far I can go," he said, "but I'm not going to worry about it now. I'm glad I got the record; it got to be quite a strain the last ten days. I was swinging at some bad pitches so I wouldn't be walked, but now I can go back to swinging at good pitches." Reaching into his locker, he picked up a stack of fan mail. "The pressure has been as tough off the field as on it. I've got so much fan mail I've had to turn it over to the front office to answer it for me."

And the pressure off the field still existed. When he left the Stadium late that afternoon, he needed a police escort to get to Gomez's waiting car for the ride to his West Side apartment.

"That apartment," Gomez has recalled. "Remember how in those days every time a guy hit a home run, they gave him a case of Wheaties cereal? I once opened a door to an extra closet in Joe's apartment, and there were cases of Wheaties up to the ceiling."

The record his, many people assumed that DiMaggio would have an emotional letdown. Instead, he was swinging even more smoothly. With the streak at forty-eight games, he went to Detroit for the All-Star game, which would not count. But after two hitless at-bats and a walk, he doubled in the eighth inning off Claude Passeau, the Chicago Cubs' big righthander, and scored the American League's third run on a single by his brother Dominic, who had joined the Red Sox as their centerfielder the year before. The next inning Joe drove in the fourth run with a force-out just before Ted Williams crashed a three-run homer off Passeau for a 7–5 victory, one of the most memorable games in All-Star history.

When the regular schedule resumed, DiMaggio was a sideshow freak. For the opener of a three-game series in St. Louis on July 10, the Browns took three-column newspaper ads that announced: "The Sensational Joe DiMaggio Will Attempt to Hit Safely in His 49th Consecutive Game Tonight!"

And he succeeded, cracking a single off Johnny Niggeling, a knuckleball righthander. The next afternoon he had four hits, including a homer, for the fourth time in the streak. As the Yankees traveled on to Chicago and then to Cleveland, he easily extended it to fifty-six games. In the eleven games since establishing the record, he had batted .545 with twenty-four hits in forty-four official at-bats, including four doubles, a triple, two homers and eleven runs batted in. During the fifty-sixth game, on a Wednesday afternoon in old League Park in Cleveland, he had three hits, two off lefthander Al Milnar, the other off righthander Joe Krakauskas.

In those years the Indians split their schedule, using huge Municipal Stadium for their more attractive dates. And now, on July 17, the Indians had a Thursday night game—one of their seven night games that season—at Municipal Stadium with Joe DiMaggio's streak on the line.

Late that afternoon DiMaggio and Gomez got into a taxi for the short ride from the downtown Hotel Cleveland to the big fortress-like ballpark on the Lake Erie shore. Up front, the cabdriver glanced into his rear-view mirror and recognized DiMaggio.

"I got a feeling," the driver volunteered, "if you don't get a hit the first time up, they're going to stop you tonight."

DiMaggio didn't say anything, but Gomez was annoyed. "What the hell is this?" he said. "What are you trying to do, jinx him?"

Al Smith, a lefthander who would have a 12-13 record that year, was the Indians' pitcher. Many in the crowd of 67,468 were hoping that DiMaggio would get a hit that night so that Bob Feller, blazing to a 25-13 record with 260 strikeouts, would stop him the next afternoon. But now, as DiMaggio settled into the batter's box in the first inning, third baseman Ken Keltner moved back near the edge of the outfield grass.

"He was daring me to bunt on him," DiMaggio said later. "I didn't bunt during the entire streak."

On a 1-0 count DiMaggio smashed a sharp grounder down the third-base line. Keltner, agile and sure-handed, lunged to his right, made a backhand stab and, from foul ground, threw DiMaggio out. On the bench, Gomez grumbled, "That cabdriver, that lousy cabdriver." In the fourth DiMaggio walked. In the seventh he hit another hot shot at Keltner, who threw him out again. But in the eighth the Yankees knocked out Smith and took a 4–3 lead with DiMaggio coming up. Indians manager Roger Peckinpaugh brought in Jim Bagby, Jr., a young righthander who would have a 9-15 record that year with the fourth-place Indians.

With a count of two balls and one strike, DiMaggio drilled a hot grounder that took a bad hop, but shortstop Lou Boudreau grabbed the ball shoulder-high and started a double play.

"DiMaggio," wrote Herb Goren in the New York *Sun* the next day, "rounded first base, picked up his glove and trotted to center field. There was no kicking of dirt, no shaking of the head."

The next morning, in newspapers all over the country, there were head shots of Smith, Bagby and Keltner side by side, as if they were the three assassins of a king. During those fifty-six games, DiMaggio had batted .408 with ninety-one hits, including sixteen doubles, four triples and fifteen homers; he had scored fifty-six runs, driven in fifty-five. He had 160 total bases. He had struck out only seven times. And, most important to the Yankees, they had won forty-one and lost only thirteen (two games had gone to no-decision) for a remarkable .759 percentage. But the night the streak ended, when he filed into the

Yankee clubhouse in Municipal Stadium and reached into his locker for
a cigarette, he said softly to nobody in particular, "Well, that's over."

When the newspapermen came in, he told them, "I can't say that I'm
glad it's over. I wanted it to go on as long as it could."

The streak had ended, the streak that had millions of Americans
talking. Soon, however, they were humming and singing a new tune.
One night in the Log Cabin Farm, a nightclub north of New York City,
a twenty-nine-year-old disc jockey named Alan Courtney had scribbled
some lyrics on a tablecloth. He turned to bandleader Les Brown and
said, "See if you like this."

"Not bad," Brown said after reading the lyrics. "I'll get Ben Homer
to do the arrangement—hey, that's a helluva name for a guy arranging
a DiMaggio song."

They laughed, then Courtney said, "I'll work on it some more, but
if we can get it on the market quick, it might sell. Let's hope he keeps
hitting."

When the streak ended, Courtney was able to write it into the lyrics
of the song recorded by Les Brown and his band and sung by Betty
Bonney:

Hello Joe, whatdya know
We need a hit, so here I go.
Ball one (rah), ball two (rah), strike one (boo), strike two (boo) . . .
    whack, yeah, a case of Wheaties.

Who started baseball's famous streak
That's got us all aglow
He's just a man and not a freak
Jolting Joe DiMaggio.

Joe, Joe DiMaggio, we want you on our side.

He tied the mark at 44 July the first, you know
Since then, he hit a good 12 more,
Jolting Joe DiMaggio.

Joe, Joe DiMaggio, we want you on our side.

From coast to coast, that's all you hear
Of Joe the one-man show
He's glorified the horsehide sphere

Joe, Joe DiMaggio, we want you on our side

He'll live in baseball's Hall of Fame
He got there blow by blow
Our kids will tell their kids his name

Joe, Joe DiMaggio, we want you on our side—we dream of Joey with
  the light brown bat.

And now they speak in whispers low
Of how they stopped our Joe
One night in Cleveland—oh, oh, oh
Goodbye streak, DiMaggio

But against Bob Feller the next day DiMaggio started a new streak.
This one lasted sixteen games (of which the Yankees won fourteen) and
ended August 3 when Johnny Niggeling of the Browns stopped him at
the Stadium in the opener of a doubleheader—the only doubleheader
the Yankees lost all season. He had hit safely in seventy-two of his last
seventy-four games, and going back to May 2 it was the first game in
eighty-four that he had not been on base. By now the Yankees were
running away with the pennant. Their final margin over the second-
place Red Sox was again seventeen games. Ted Williams batted .406
that season, the last major leaguer to hit .400 or over, but Joe DiMaggio
was voted the Most Valuable Player award for the second time in three
years. DiMaggio polled 291 points; Williams, 254.

"Did DiMaggio spark the Yankees to their fifth pennant in six years
or was it the other way around?" Dan Daniel wrote. "The writer
believes Joe did the sparking. The Yankees really won their pennant
with their streak of 14 in a row from June 28 to July 13—right in the
middle of the DiMaggio skein."

DiMaggio batted .357 that year, third behind Williams and shortstop
Cecil Travis of the Senators, who hit .359, but he led the league with
125 runs batted in and 348 total bases. He had 43 doubles, 11 triples
and 30 homers. He struck out only 13 times and hit into only 6 double
plays. Keller hit .298 with 33 homers and 122 runs batted in; Henrich,
.277 with 31 homers and 85 runs batted in; Gordon, .276 with 24
homers and 87 runs batted in. The tiny rookie shortstop, Phil Rizzuto,
batted .307. Of the pitchers, Ruffing was 15-6; Gomez, 15-5; Russo,
14-8; Murphy, 8-3 with a 1.98 earned-run average and 15 saves. But all
those teammates had honored DiMaggio long before the MVP award
was announced. After a tiresome train ride from St. Louis to Washington on August 29, the Yankees checked into their rooms at the Hotel
Shoreham; they had the night off, but George Selkirk was phoning the
other players and the newspapermen. Meanwhile, in the room Gomez
shared with DiMaggio, the lefthander was taking a long shower.

"C'mon, Lefty, let's go," DiMaggio urged. "All the steaks will be
gone."

Gomez shrugged and suggested that his roommate relax. On the way
to the elevator he said, "I just remembered something, Joe. I've got to

go by Selkirk's room down the hall here."

"I'll get a table and order," DiMaggio said. "I'll meet you in the dining room."

"No, no, stay with me," Gomez said. "It'll only take me a minute. Stay with me."

"All right," DiMaggio grumbled, "but hurry up, damn it, all the steaks will be gone."

From behind the door of room 609D, Selkirk peeked down the corridor. "Here he comes," he whispered to those who had congregated in his room. "Quiet, here he comes." And entering the room Joe DiMaggio was startled to see nearly forty men with raised champagne glasses. There were cheers and songs, then Gomez presented DiMaggio with a gift-wrapped package. Inside was a sterling-silver cigar humidor. Atop the cover was a statuette of the Yankee centerfielder in his classic swing. On one side was "56" for the number of games in the streak; on the other was "91" for the number of hits in the streak.

"Presented to Joe DiMaggio," the inscription read, "by his fellow players on the New York Yankees to express their admiration for his consecutive-game hitting record, 1941." Below were the engraved autographs of all his teammates.

"This is swell," Joe mumbled, "but I don't deserve it." Then he opened the lid of the humidor and called out in jest, "Cigars, cigarettes." To further lighten the atmosphere, Joe Gordon turned to Gomez and said, "Lefty, I want to congratulate you. This is the first time in history you kept a secret." Then the relief pitcher, Johnny Murphy, offered a toast. "Joe," he said, "we just wanted you to know how proud we are to be playing on a ball club with you and that we think your hitting streak won the pennant for us."

The thoughtful present and party had sprung from a conversation a couple of weeks earlier involving Selkirk, Henrich, Dickey and Murphy. Dickey had suggested that the team should do "something special" to honor the centerfielder's streak. And now, at the noisy party in room 609D, that something special, the sterling silver humidor, gleamed in Joe DiMaggio's hands.

"We got it," Murphy said proudly, "at Tiffany's."

Joe DiMaggio remembers that party often. "It was just a little party in a hotel room," he says, "but it was the biggest party I'll ever go to."

The Yankees clinched their 1941 pennant on September 4, but when the World Series was about to begin they were upstaged by the Brooklyn Dodgers, who had won their first National League pennant since 1920—"dem Bums" from Brooklyn who were managed by Leo Durocher, who had Dolph Camilli at first base, Pete Reiser in center field, Pee Wee Reese at shortstop, Whitlow Wyatt on the mound, and who

The New York Yankees

Johnny Murphy

also had the nation rooting for them.

The opener at the Stadium attracted 68,540, then a Series record. Ruffing outpitched Curt Davis, 3–2, but the Dodgers won the second game behind Wyatt, 3–2—the Yankees' first Series loss after ten consecutive victories since 1937.

Then at Ebbets Field the Yankees got two breaks. In the seventh inning of the scoreless third game Marius Russo cracked a line drive off Fred Fitzsimmons' left leg. The ball richocheted high in the air to Reese for the third out, but Fitz was hobbling. He had to be helped into the dugout. At the start of the eighth Hugh Casey was the Dodger pitcher. Singles by Rolfe, Henrich, DiMaggio and Keller produced the runs for a 2–1 victory. In the ninth inning the next day Casey again was the Dodger pitcher, this time with a 4–3 lead, two out and nobody on as a prelude to one of the most famous rallies in World Series history.

Throwing what Casey later confessed was a spitball, the heavy right-hander appeared to have Henrich struck out on a lunging swing. But the ball skidded past Mickey Owen, the Dodger catcher, for an error as Henrich hurried to first base.

Afforded another life, the Yankees pounced. DiMaggio singled sharply to left. Keller, on an 0-2 pitch, doubled off the rightfield wall, scoring both Henrich and DiMaggio for a 5-4 lead. Dickey walked. Gordon doubled to left for a 7–4 lead. That was the final score as the Dodgers, stunned and shaken, went out meekly for Johnny Murphy in the bottom of the ninth. In the fifth game Tiny Bonham completed the Yankees' fifth World Series championship in six years with a four-hitter, 3–1, that is remembered best for the Brooklyn Eagle headline that was to become the Dodgers' motto—WAIT 'TIL NEXT YEAR—and for a rare display of angry words by DiMaggio with an opposing player.

In the fifth Henrich had hit a homer off Wyatt for a 3–1 lead. Up next, DiMaggio twice was knocked down by Wyatt before hitting a long fly ball that Reiser caught near the centerfield wall. As he trotted across the infield grass toward the Yankees' dugout behind third base, Di-Maggio yelled at Wyatt, who yelled back. They began to move toward each other, but teammates quickly separated them.

Nearly a decade later, Wyatt told Red Barber, then the voice of the Dodgers, that Mickey Owen had ordered the two knockdown pitches. "Mickey told me later," Wyatt explained, "that he heard Joe had said before the game that Mickey had it coming to him for dropping that strike the day before because Mickey had gone out of his way to slide into Rizzuto earlier in that game." And when Barber relayed Wyatt's story to DiMaggio, the Yankee Clipper nodded in understanding.

"I still say," DiMaggio said, "that was a lousy play, that slide into Rizzuto."

By the time the 1942 season began, the nation was at war following the Pearl Harbor attack. And when Joe DiMaggio understandably asked for a raise over the $37,500 he had earned with his fifty-six-game hitting streak, he was not only refused, he was also asked to take a $5,000 cut. He was even humiliated by Ed Barrow, the crusty general manager.

"Soldiers are making $21 a month," Barrow told the newspapermen, "but DiMaggio wants a big raise."

Barrow, meanwhile, had told DiMaggio not to speak to the newspapermen, but he had sent the Yankees' traveling secretary, Mark Roth, to the centerfielder's New York apartment with a contract calling for the same salary. DiMaggio eventually signed for $43,750, but that bitter contract dispute still rankles.

"What letters I got after Barrow mentioned the soldiers," he has said. "Baseball owners ruled with an iron hand then. Now, with the free-agent situation, the shoe is on the other foot. And deservedly so."

Perhaps disenchanted, DiMaggio responded with an off-year—.305, 21 homers, 114 runs batted in—but the Yankees coasted to another pennant, 10 games ahead of the Red Sox. Joe Gordon was voted the Most Valuable Player award with a .322 average, 18 homers and 103 runs batted in. Keller drove in 108 runs with a .292 average and 26 homers. Bonham had a 21-5 record, Spud Chandler was 16-4 and Ruffing, at age thirty-eight, was 14-7.

But maybe the Yankees won too easily. After taking the World Series

The 1941 World Series: Mickey Owen muffs Tommy Henrich's third strike   UPI

opener, they were ambushed by the Cardinals in the next four games. Johnny Beazley, a young righthander, beat them twice.

By 1943 the Yankees, along with most teams, were depleted by the military effort. DiMaggio was in the Army Air Force, Rizzuto in the Navy, Henrich in the Coast Guard. But the Yankees won again, outdistancing the Senators by fourteen games. Nick Etten, a burly first baseman obtained from the Phillies, knocked in 107 runs, and Billy Johnson, a chesty third baseman, knocked in 94 runs. Spud Chandler had a 20-4 record and a 1.64 earned-run average (the league's lowest since Walter Johnson's 1.49 in 1919). He also was voted the Most Valuable Player award—the first pitcher so honored since Lefty Grove of the A's in 1931, the first year the Baseball Writers Association of America governed the balloting.

After the Yankees sagged to third place in 1944, the Ruppert heirs sold the club for $2.8 million to an unlikely triumvirate: playboy millionaire Dan Topping, construction tycoon Del Webb and bombastic Larry MacPhail, once the Dodgers' and Reds' general manager.

MacPhail had introduced night baseball to the big leagues in Cincinnati a decade earlier; he would install lights at the Stadium for the 1946 season. But under the new owners in 1945 the Yankees dropped to fourth place, although some players flourished. Etten led the league with 111 runs batted in, while George (Snuffy) Stirnweiss, a chunky second baseman, won the batting title with a .309 average that symbolized the loose level of wartime competition.

World War II ended in August of 1945, and by the next season the real Yankees had returned. But they were more rusty than real. So rusty that Bob Feller fired a no-hitter against them, 1–0, on April 30 at the Stadium—the first no-hitter against the Yankees since Ray Caldwell of the Indians in 1919, the year before Babe Ruth arrived.

Irritable under the new owners, Joe McCarthy resigned on May 24; Bill Dickey was appointed the new manager, but he resigned on September 12 and Johnny Neun completed the disastrous season. Finishing third with an 87-67 record, 17 games behind the first-place Red Sox, the Yankees never threatened. Spud Chandler was the only Yankee to produce a big season—20-8 with a 2.10 earned-run average. Joe DiMaggio hit .290 with twenty-five homers and ninety-five runs batted in.

But that season Joe wasn't even the best DiMaggio—his little brother Dom was, batting .316 as the Red Sox centerfielder.

Keller, who had missed only the 1944 season, hit .275 with thirty homers, but of the others who returned from military service Rizzuto batted .257 and Henrich .251. Gordon hit only .210 with only eleven homers, only forty-seven runs batted in. Even so, the Indians, looking to 1947, wanted Gordon to be their second baseman alongside Lou

Yogi Berra Night in St. Louis, 1947   UPI   Joe Page, Bucky Harris and Joe DiMaggio celebrate
winning the '47 World Series   UPI

Boudreau, the manager and shortstop.

"You can have one of two pitchers," offered Bill Veeck, the Indians' owner. "Embree or Reynolds."

Charles (Red) Embree, a slender righthander, was only twenty-nine years old compared to thirty-one for Allie Reynolds, a thick-bodied righthander who was nicknamed Chief because of his Creek heritage. Embree also had compiled a slightly better record than Reynolds that season—8-12 and 3.47 with 87 strikeouts to 11-15 and 3.89 with 107 strikeouts. But during the World Series, which the Cardinals won from the Red Sox in seven games, Dan Topping asked Joe DiMaggio which pitcher the Yankees should take.

"Reynolds," he replied.

That was the trade—Gordon for Reynolds, who emerged as the Yankees' big winner in 1947 with a 19-8 record. But there were other reasons why the Yankees, in a return to normalcy, won the pennant. Bucky Harris, brought in by MacPhail as the new manager, restored order and harmony to the clubhouse with his quiet experience. DiMaggio, hitting .315 with twenty homers and ninety-seven runs batted in, earned his third Most Valuable Player award. George McQuinn, acquired from the Browns, turned out to be the Yankees' best first baseman since Lou Gehrig, with a .304 average and eighty runs batted in. Keller, bothered more and more by a spinal disc ailment, slipped to .283, but Henrich hit .287 and Johnson .285 with ninety-five runs batted in. Johnny Lindell, once a righthanded pitcher but now an outfielder, hit .275 with eleven homers and sixty-seven runs batted in. The new name was Lawrence (Yogi) Berra, who hit .280 with eleven homers in only eighty-three games, mostly as a catcher but a few times in the outfield. His tutor as a catcher was Bill Dickey, now a coach.

"Dickey," said Yogi in one of his first memorable phrases, "is learning me his experience."

Perhaps the difference in the Yankees' 97-57 record, twelve games ahead of the Tigers, was the emergence of Joe Page as their bullpen savior. After pitching poorly in a May 10 game at Fenway Park, however, the handsome dark-haired lefthander appeared to be on his way back to the minors. That night Page justified his roustabout reputation, returning long after midnight and waking up DiMaggio in the hotel room they shared.

"What the hell are you doing?" DiMaggio scolded. "The way you live, you're letting the team down and you're letting yourself down."

The next morning DiMaggio requested a single room on future road trips, paying the difference himself between the single and double rates, although he never snitched on his pal being out long after the club curfew. And on May 26, before 74,747 at a Stadium night game, still the Yankees' single-game attendance record, Joe Page hopped over the low bullpen fence in right field and strode in to face Ted Williams with the Red Sox leading, 3–1, two on and nobody out in the third inning. Williams squirted a grounder off McQuinn's glove for an error, filling the bases. Rudy York, the husky first baseman, was up next. The count went to three balls and no strikes. Another ball, Bucky Harris acknowledged later, and Joe Page would have been on his way to the Newark farm. But he got one strike, then another, then York struck out. Bobby Doerr, the clutch-hitting second baseman, was up now. Again three balls and no strikes. Again one strike, two strikes, and Doerr struck out. The next batter, shortstop Eddie Pellagrini, lifted a routine fly ball to Henrich in right field, and the Yankees were out of the inning. They went on to win that night, 9–3.

Joe Page's world had turned. That season he had a 14-8 record with a 2.49 earned-run average and 17 saves. In the World Series against the Dodgers he was credited with the victory in the decisive seventh game, with a one-hitter over the last five innings after having saved two other triumphs. But that Series is best remembered for two other moments.

In the fourth game Floyd (Bill) Bevens, who had a 7-13 record during the season, nearly pitched the first no-hitter in Series history. He had been wild, issuing ten walks; two of them, along with a sacrifice and an infield out, had produced a Dodger run in the fifth. So the stocky righthander had only a 2–1 lead with one out in the ninth when Carl Furillo walked. Spider Jorgensen fouled out, but Al Gionfriddo was inserted as a pinch-runner and stole second. Bucky Harris then ordered pinch-hitter Pete Reiser to be intentionally walked. Harris would be second-guessed for putting the potential winning run on base. Eddie Miksis soon represented that run when he took a lead off first base, having replaced Reiser, who was limping on an ailing ankle.

Moments later, on Bevens' second pitch, Cookie Lavagetto, pinch-hitting for Eddie Stanky, whacked a double off the rightfield wall at Ebbets Field as Gionfriddo and Miksis scored for a 3–2 victory on one hit.

In the sixth game, with the Dodgers leading 8–5, the Yankees had two men on in the sixth when DiMaggio smashed a long high fly ball toward the Stadium's leftfield bullpen. He thought he had a homer that would have tied the score, but little Al Gionfriddo, inserted that inning for defense, scurried back to the low bullpen fence, stabbed at the ball with his glove and made a one-handed catch. For one of the rare times in his career, DiMaggio displayed some emotion. Nearly at second base when Gionfriddo made the catch, he kicked the bag in disgust.

During the locker room celebration after the Series ended, Larry MacPhail announced his decision to sell his one-third interest to Topping and Webb for $2 million.

Not a bad return for MacPhail on his investment, which was merely his baseball know-how. But he had earned it. In a statement later he mentioned that in his three years as president the Yankees had made $2 million each year before taxes; that the Yankees had made more money in those three years than any other big-league team ever had in ten years; and that the Yankees had drawn more spectators in those three years (notably 2,265,512 in 1946 and 2,178,937 in 1947) than any other team ever had in six years.

With baseball still in a postwar boom, the carryover of MacPhail's know-how enabled the Yankees to set their club attendance record in 1948 with 2,373,901, including 49,641 on June 13 when Babe Ruth made his last Stadium appearance.

The new general manager was George Weiss, who had been in charge of the Yankee farm system. Portly and shy, Weiss was a career baseball man. He had operated semipro and minor league teams before entering the Yankee organization. Now he was running the team that had won the World Series, but during his first year the Yankees finished two and a half games behind the Indians (who won the pennant in a one-game playoff with the Red Sox). For the Yankees, third place was no place. DiMaggio, despite a painful heel ailment, led the league with 155 runs batted in while hitting .320 and walloping 39 homers. Henrich hit .308

A weeping Larry MacPhail announces his retirement, as Del Webb and Dan Topping look on   UPI

Casey Stengel arrives in 1948 to join his old friend, general manager George Weiss

Babe Ruth's "3" is retired in his farewell Yankee Stadium appearance   The New York Yankees

with 25 homers and 100 runs batted in; Berra hit .305 with 14 homers and 98 runs batted in. But the pitching staff was shaky. Vic Raschi, a big righthander, was 19-8. Eddie Lopat, a soft-stuff lefthander obtained from the White Sox, was 17-11 and Reynolds was 16-7, but Page skidded to a 7-8 record and a 4.25 earned-run average. Frank (Spec) Shea, a 14-game winner the year before, dipped to 9-10.

Weiss, who had inherited Bucky Harris from the MacPhail regime, blamed the manager's loose rein. Weiss even hired private detectives to follow Page and Shea, among others, on their nocturnal adventures.

When the Yankees didn't win the pennant, Weiss changed managers. He selected one of his longtime pals, a manager he knew he could work with but one who had never been much of a success anywhere else. His name was Charles Dillon (Casey) Stengel, and he would be the most famous manager in Yankee history, but when his appointment was announced at a news conference at the posh "21" club on October 12, 1948, he was looked upon as more of a comedian.

In *The New York Times* the next day John Drebinger described him as a "onetime hard-hitting outfielder, manager of both major and minor league clubs, sage, wit, raconteur . . . glib with the wisecrack."

Nobody considered Casey Stengel a brilliant manager. In nine seasons, directing the Brooklyn Dodgers and Boston Braves, his teams had finished as high as fifth only twice. In his twelve seasons in the minors, with Worcester, Toledo, Milwaukee, Kansas City and Oakland, his teams had won only two pennants—twenty years apart. His one season in Kansas City, then a Yankee farm, in 1945 had been important. That's when George Weiss got to know him best. But when he was introduced as the Yankees' manager he justified his billing.

"I want first of all," he opened, "to thank Mr. Bob Topping for this opportunity."

Dan Topping, of course, was the Yankees' co-owner, not his brother Bob, but the mixup was somewhat understandable. Bob Topping had been in the headlines recently for his marital problems with Arlene Judge, the film actress who once had been Dan's wife. Not that Dan Topping was annoyed at Casey's goof. He laughed along with everybody else. Laughter was to become the most common reaction to Casey Stengel over the next thirteen years—laughter at his syntax, at his inspired one-liners, and *his* laughter on the way to the bank with World Series shares.

DiMaggio had been asked to attend that news conference, the Yankees knowing that his presence would imply approval of Casey Stengel as the new manager.

DiMaggio appeared, smiling and gracious. Asked if he hoped to manage the Yankees himself someday, he said, "Not me. I'm just a ballplayer with one ambition and that's to give all I've got to help my

The 1949 season began
with DiMaggio in topcoat,
ended victoriously with a
fatherly arm around Joe Jr.

ball club win." Afterwards the new manager and his centerfielder walked around the corner to Toots Shor's restaurant on West 51st Street and had lunch together.

"You're the old standby, Joe," the new manager said. "I'm going to be asking for your help."

"Anything you need from me," the centerfielder replied, "I'll be very happy to give it."

As the 1949 season approached, the Yankees were not concerned with the heel ailment that had bothered DiMaggio the previous year. He had undergone surgery in November at Johns Hopkins in Baltimore, and when he was discharged he had obeyed his doctor's orders and stayed on crutches for six weeks. He seemed fine. What did concern the Yankees was DiMaggio's contract. His salary in 1948 had been $70,000; he also had earned another $10,000 because of an attendance bonus. Now it was time to negotiate his 1949 contract, and DiMaggio talked to his confidant, Toots Shor, over lunch in Toots' restaurant on a Saturday afternoon.

"They're offering me $85,000 plus the attendance bonus," DiMaggio said. "What do you think?"

"Go for the $100,000—no bonus," Shor said. "No ballplayer ever made that much. You deserve to be the first. The year you had, they got to give it to you."

"But with the attendance bonus," DiMaggio said, "I could go over $100,000 if the crowds are good."

"Don't take a chance," Shor said. "Suppose the team has a bad year. Be the first to make $100,000."

Just then, Topping, Webb and Weiss walked in for lunch. DiMaggio joined them at the bar later. During the conversation he asked Topping about his contract.

"Come over to my apartment tomorrow night," Topping said. "We'll talk about it there."

The next night at his Park Avenue apartment Topping agreed to the $100,000 salary but warned DiMaggio that Webb, as his partner, also had to agree. Webb, meanwhile, was in Toots Shor's, discussing DiMaggio's contract with the proprietor.

"I'm not going higher than $90,000—plus the bonus deal," Webb said. "If he makes more than $100,000 with the bonus, fine, but not flat."

"Del," said Shor, "ain't it worth another ten G's to you to get your picture in all the papers with baseball's first $100,000 player?"

Webb grinned. Soon both Topping and DiMaggio arrived. Topping and Webb chatted privately for a few minutes, then each shook hands with DiMaggio on the deal—$100,000 flat.

But in February, with spring training only two weeks away, Joe DiMaggio's heel began bothering him again. When the Yankees assembled in St. Petersburg, he was in agony. Pads in his footwear did not alleviate the pain that he has described as "like having a nail in your heel." He spent more time in the trainer's room than in the batting cage. Playing two innings here, three innings there, he was unable to hit consistently or even run hard. As the Yankees swung through Texas on their barnstorming tour north, he was batting .216 with only seven hits.

"I never hit a ball that even looked like a home run," he later said. "In the field I felt awkward because the leg muscles couldn't work into shape the way I was favoring them."

Finally, on April 11 in Dallas, with the season opener only a week away, DiMaggio limped back to the dugout after two innings and told Stengel the pain was unbearable. The next day he left for an examination in Baltimore by Dr. George Bennett, the famous orthopedist who had performed the November bone-spur surgery. Dr. Bennett recommended x-ray treatments and salt injections for "immature calcium deposits in tissues adjacent to the heel bone." After several treatments DiMaggio returned to New York, where the Yankees were about to open the season. DiMaggio's questionable condition had many baseball writers picking the Yankees for third place. Not that Stengel complained.

"Third ain't so bad," the new manager said. "I never finished third before. Third's pretty high up."

But for nearly two months DiMaggio stayed mostly in his suite at the Mayflower Hotel; when he got out of bed each morning, pain shot through his heel. Wincing, he would touch the heel with his fingers.

"It really was hot," he has said. "I could feel the fever in it."

Then one morning in early June he put the heel down on the floor and got up. No pain. No heat. No fever. Time had healed it. When the Yankees returned from a Western trip to open a home stand, he surprised Stengel and his teammates by strolling into the Stadium clubhouse. He put on his uniform and took batting practice, blistering his hands. Since he was not on the active roster, he was ineligible to wear a uniform during the game. Dressed in his dark suit and tie, he stood in the tunnel leading to the Yankee dugout and peeked at the game. The next day he took batting practice again, then handled a few grounders in the infield. The third day he also shagged fly balls in center field. The heel was holding up; a little sore but cool. And his spirits were soaring, especially when Lou Boudreau, the Indians' manager, told him that it could be arranged for him to play in the All-Star Game if his heel was sound.

"Thanks," the still idle DiMaggio said. "Maybe by that time I'll be able to pinch-hit if you need me."

Buoyed by that conversation, DiMaggio waited until the Stadium had emptied after the game. He trotted out to center field and had Gus Niarhos, one of the Yankees' reserve catchers, loft fungoes to him for half an hour. He later ran two laps around the field. The next morning his heel remained cool. About a week later, in an exhibition game with the Giants at the Stadium, he went up to swing against Kirby Higbe, a twenty-two-game winner for the Dodgers in 1941 but now hanging on as a thirty-four-year-old knuckleball pitcher.

"Remember," wrote Frank Graham in the New York *Journal-American,* "how he swung at the first pitch . . . and popped it into the air? He had to hit that first one. He couldn't wait. You see, he had waited so long."

But now the waiting was over. Now the Yankees had a three-game series in Boston, and after the team departed on the morning train DiMaggio took an afternoon plane. Shortly after 5 o'clock he was in the Yankees' clubhouse at Fenway Park, and at 6 he walked into Casey Stengel's office.

"I'm ready," he told the manager, "if you want me."

The manager wrote DiMaggio's name into the cleanup spot on the Yankees' batting-order card. Maurice (Mickey) McDermott, a skinny lefthander with a hissing fastball, was the Red Sox starter. After fouling off several pitches his first time up, DiMaggio slapped a single into left field. In the third inning, after a single by Phil Rizzuto, he smacked a home run into the screen atop the high green leftfield wall. As he crossed home plate, he shook hands with Rizzuto, who was jumping up and down, yelling, "Nice hitting, Jolter," and in the dugout his teammates swarmed around him. The next day he got a telegram from Del Webb, who had been told by DiMaggio not to expect him in the lineup until mid-July, that read, "You're crossing me up. How am I going to explain this to my friends?" DiMaggio let out a loud laugh.

"Joe," said one of his teammates, "that's the first time I've seen you laugh all year."

That night he hit two more home runs. After the second, Stengel hopped out of the dugout and greeted him with a deep bow. The next afternoon, with a small plane towing a fluttering THE GREAT DIMAGGIO sign above Fenway Park, he hit another homer. During the three-game series, he had four homers, knocked in nine runs and scored five: the first-place Yankees now had a five-and-a-half-game lead, eight and a half over the Red Sox.

More important, Joe DiMaggio had emerged as a national hero as never before. During the fifty-six-game streak he was admired, but primarily as an attraction. But for what happened in Boston, he was admired as a human being in a spectacular return from adversity. Two

Joe DiMaggio Day in 1949: Dom, Mom, brother Tom, Joe and Joe Jr.

weeks later, as the All-Star centerfielder, he drove in three runs with a double and a single as the American League won, 11–7, at Ebbets Field.

On September 18, with the Yankees holding a two-and-a-half-game lead over the Red Sox, viral pneumonia knocked DiMaggio out of the lineup again. He lost eighteen pounds in ten days. Slowly, the Red Sox pulled ahead.

Entering the last two games of the season on Saturday and Sunday at the Stadium, the Red Sox had a one-game lead. But by then DiMaggio, though still weak, had recovered enough to play following Joe DiMaggio Day ceremonies before the Saturday game. Wearing a Yankee jacket in the cloudy chill and standing with two of his brothers, Tom and Dom, his mother and little Joe Jr., he acknowledged the cheers and the gifts—an automobile for himself and another for his mother, a yacht and a TV set, among others. He also acknowledged Joe McCarthy, now the Red Sox manager.

"If we can't win the pennant," he said, "it's nice to know my old manager will win it."

That Saturday the Yankees won, 5–4, on Joe Page's relief pitching and Johnny Lindell's tie-breaking homer in the eighth. Moments after that homer the Yankees' traveling secretary, Frank Scott, on instructions from DiMaggio, had ushered Joe's mother down under the Stadium to avoid the crush of spectators. She was waiting on a chair outside the clubhouse later when Scott walked over.

"Joe's going to be a long time," Scott said. "Let me take you upstairs where you'll be more comfortable."

"No, no," replied the gray-haired Mrs. DiMaggio, smiling softly. "Take me over to Dominic—he lose today."

The next day Dominic lost again, 5–3, as Vic Raschi pitched the Yankees to the pennant. Joe DiMaggio batted .346 that season, but with only 272 at-bats he was ineligible for the batting title that George Kell, the Tigers' third baseman, won with a .343 average. In only seventy-six games, DiMaggio hit fourteen homers and knocked in sixty-seven runs. Berra had ninety-one runs batted in and twenty homers, Henrich had eighty-five and twenty-four. But perhaps the most important factor was the resurgence of Joe Page to 13-8 with a 2.60 earned-run average. Vic Raschi was 21-10, Reynolds was 17-6, a sometimes wild lefthander named Tommy Byrne was 15-7 and Lopat was 15-10.

In the World Series opener against the Dodgers a homer by Henrich leading off the ninth against Don Newcombe provided Reynolds with a 1-0 two-hitter. Henrich was "Old Reliable," the nickname awarded to him by Russ Hodges, then a second banana to Mel Allen in the Yankee radio booth.

Preacher Roe, the Dodgers' crafty lefthander who confessed after his retirement that the outlawed spitball had been his money pitch, won the second game, 1–0, with a six-hitter, but then the Yankees rolled to another Series victory in five games. The turning point occurred in the third game when Johnny Mize, a muscular first baseman obtained from the Giants in an August waiver deal, delivered a two-run pinch single against Ralph Branca during a three-run ninth-inning rally that produced a 4–3 triumph.

All of which meant that, in Casey Stengel's first season as manager, the Yankees had won the World Series.

The clown was now a genius at age sixty; so was George Weiss for choosing him. Stengel would always cherish that first season. When he was elected to the Hall of Fame, his wife Edna wept and said, "I can't get over it. This is even greater than winning the World Series in 1949." Perhaps the first is always the best, but 1950 wasn't bad. Joe Page went sour again, popularizing the theory that a relief pitcher couldn't put two good seasons back to back (a theory since refuted by Sparky Lyle, among others). But at the time all Casey Stengel cared about was that he needed another relief pitcher. George Weiss obtained one from the Browns, a chubby righthander named Tom Ferrick, who had a 9-7 record as the Yankees, with a 98-56 record, finished three games ahead of the Tigers.

DiMaggio, healthy again, hit .301 with 32 homers and 122 runs batted in. Berra, now the everyday catcher, hit .322 with 28 homers and 124 runs batted in. Rizzuto hit .324, shared the league lead with 125 runs and was voted the Most Valuable Player award. Hank Bauer, a

UPI

Phil Rizzuto, the 1950 MVP, hops with glee as Hank Bauer smiles

Whitey Ford has his hair mussed by Reynolds, Ferrick, Raschi and Lopat

UPI

combative outfielder, hit .320.

Raschi again was the big winner, with a 21-8 record. Lopat was 18-8; Reynolds, 16-12; Byrne, 15-9. But there was a new pitcher, a twenty-one-year-old lefthander who had been brought up from the Kansas City farm at midseason and who posted a 9-1 record. His name was Edward Ford, nicknamed Whitey by Lefty Gomez, one of his minor league managers. And after Raschi, Reynolds and Ferrick, in relief of Lopat, had won the first three games of the World Series against the Phillies, young Whitey Ford was credited with the triumph that completed a sweep.

That year another rookie arrived—a scrappy second baseman named Billy Martin, who had played for Stengel in Oakland.

Martin made more noise than hits. He batted only .250 with only one double, only one homer, only three runs batted in. Still, when Stengel once listed him eighth in the batting order, he glared at the manager.

"What is this, a joke?" he snapped.

Stengel didn't mind. He enjoyed Martin's aggressive attitude. So did DiMaggio, who adopted him, perhaps because Martin was of Italian descent and from Berkeley, California, across the bay from where Joe lived. But by now DiMaggio didn't always enjoy Stengel, who had insulted him occasionally. Once the manager put Johnny Mize in the cleanup spot, with DiMaggio batting fifth. That hurt. So did the idea of Stengel giving him a rest in a game in Washington; as a mild protest Joe sat in the bullpen that day instead of in the dugout. DiMaggio also played first base in Washington one day after Dan Topping had asked him if he would.

All the signs were there. Joe DiMaggio was getting old. And in 1951 one Yankee era ended as another began.

The Yankees won their third consecutive pennant, a 98-65 record lifting them 5 games ahead of the second-place Indians, but Joe Di-Maggio was no longer the Jolter—he slumped to .263 with only 12 homers and 71 runs batted in. Berra was the Yankees' most dangerous hitter now, with 27 homers and 88 runs batted in. And the new era began with the arrival of a kid outfielder named Mickey Mantle, who batted .267 with 13 homers and 65 runs batted in. Another new name, third baseman Gil McDougald, was the league's rookie of the year with .306, 14 homers and 63 runs batted in. Even with Whitey Ford in the army, the pitching held up. Lopat was 21-9 with a 2.91 earned-run average. Raschi was 21-10. Reynolds was 17-8, including no-hitters against the Indians at Cleveland on July 12 and the Red Sox at the Stadium on September 28 when Berra muffed Ted Williams' pop foul for what would have been the final out; on the next pitch Williams lifted another pop foul that Yogi held on to.

"When I die," Del Webb later told Berra, "I hope they give me a second chance the way they did you."

In the World Series a grandslam by McDougald in the fifth game was the big blow as the Yankees won in six games from the Giants, the "Miracle of Coogan's Bluff" team. They had won the National League pennant when Bobby Thomson hit a three-run homer at the Polo Grounds off Ralph Branca of the Dodgers for a 5–4 victory in the ninth inning of the decisive third playoff game.

DiMaggio, after eleven hitless trips, walloped a homer in the fourth game off Sal Maglie, the Giants' ace righthander, and in the sixth game he doubled to right off Larry Jansen, the Giants' other twenty-game winner that year—they would be his last homer and his last hit, respectively. Not long after the Series ended, DiMaggio arranged a meeting with Topping and Webb in Topping's apartment. He told the co-owners that he had decided to retire. His body was aching. His skills had deteriorated.

"I'm finished," he said. "I can't play any more."

"Take some time to think about it," Topping said.

"Don't worry about the money," Webb said. "You can have the same $100,000 next year. We'll get the contract drawn up and send it to you."

"It's not the money, it's me," DiMaggio said. "I don't want to play baseball like this."

Several weeks later *Life* magazine printed a scouting report on the Yankees that included a sad perspective of DiMaggio's skills. The report had been compiled mostly by Andy High, a Dodger scout who had followed the Yankees for the final month of the season. When the Dodgers didn't win the pennant, their front office presented the scouting report to the Giants in a show of National League unity. After the Giants won the Series opener, Leo Durocher raved about the scouting report, saying, "It's great. I never saw a report like it." The report couldn't win the Series for the Giants, but its disclosure embarrassed DiMaggio more than any other player:

Fielding—he can't stop quickly and throw hard. You can take the extra base on him if he is in motion away from the line of throw. He won't throw on questionable plays and I would challenge him even though he threw a man or so out.

Speed—he can't run and he won't bunt.

Hitting vs. righthanded pitcher—his reflexes are very slow and he can't pull a good fastball at all. The fastball is better thrown high but that is not too important as long as it is fast. Throw him nothing but good fastballs and fast curveballs. Don't slow up on him.

Hitting vs. lefthanded pitcher—will pull lefthand pitcher a little more than righthand pitcher. Pitch him the same. Don't slow up on him. He will go for a bad pitch once in a while with two strikes.

DiMaggio's friends knew that his pride surely would not let him play now that the erosion of his skills had been promulgated. And early in December, shortly after his thirty-seventh birthday, he phoned Topping, saying that he wanted to come to New York to announce his retirement. But he agreed to Topping's request for another meeting in his apartment the following Monday evening. That's when Topping played his last card: Stengel's plan to use him on a part-time basis, with DiMaggio determining when he would play.

"I appreciate that," Joe said, "but I'm not a part-time player."

His retirement was final except for the announcement. In those years the Yankee offices were in the Squibb Tower at 745 Fifth Avenue, on the northeast corner of 57th Street, and on Wednesday morning, December 12, the newsmen were handed a statement announcing Joe DiMaggio's retirement. Joe was there, of course, with Topping, Webb and Stengel alongside him.

When the questions began, one newspaperman naturally asked, "Joe, why are you quitting?"

"I no longer have it," he replied.

No matter what was said later, his retirement boiled down to that simple explanation. Now that his retirement was official, Joe DiMaggio smiled occasionally, even laughed. Watching him, Dan Daniel, the Yankee historian of that era, remembered the sadness that surrounded the 1935 announcement that Babe Ruth had been traded to the Boston Braves and the sadness that surrounded the 1939 announcement of Lou Gehrig's illness.

"Joe," the old baseball writer said, "you are a very lucky man."

Over in another corner of the Yankee offices other baseball writers had Casey Stengel surrounded.

"Who's your centerfielder now?" one wondered.

"The kid," the manager said. "Mickey Mantle."   ·

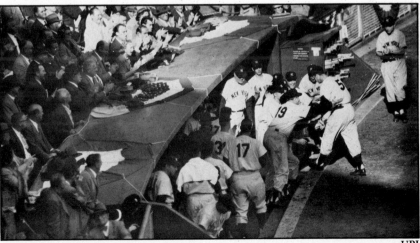

The Yankee dugout welcomes DiMaggio after the 1951 Series homer, his last

UPI

The New York Yankees

Mickey Mantle and Casey Stengel
by Harold Rosenthal

BABE RUTH HIT home runs lefthanded. Joe DiMaggio hit home runs righthanded. Mickey Charles Mantle hit them either way. And he left the customers wondering, after eighteen seasons with the Yankees: Was he more effective righthanded or lefthanded?

Of his 536 homers, he hit 373 lefthanded, 163 righthanded. That made him more effective lefthanded, correct? Not necessarily. You see more righthanded pitching, whether you're in the majors, the minors or in the Little League, simply because a greater proportion of people are righthanded.

Analyzing his home-run ability further, the record eighteen he belted in ten World Series also proved out at about the same left-right ratio —eleven lefthanded, seven righthanded. In the 1956 Series against the Dodgers he hit three, all lefthanded. In the 1960 Series with the Pirates, two of his three were righthanded. He hit his first Series homer in 1952 off Billy Loes, of the Dodgers, who won't ever be in the Hall of Fame, and his last in 1964 off the Cardinals' Bob Gibson, who will. All this really proves is that Mickey Mantle was an awesome figure with a bat in his hand.

He was equally awesome at the box office. Often tortured by leg ailments, he was the number one draw in baseball for a solid decade, at a time when, if you turned around too quickly, you risked bumping into a star. His picture on a magazine cover guaranteed a strong sale. They wrote songs about him; silly songs, but there were no songs written about President Eisenhower, or John Foster Dulles, or the boss of the Atomic Energy Commission, or Jonas Salk or Milton Berle. Mickey's appearance in a three-game series in a place like Kansas City, Cleveland, Detroit or Chicago, where the home teams often were struggling at the gate, guaranteed a crowd. He was twenty-four-karat at the box office.

Where some players have two or three lines of records preceding their standard major league year-year-year statistics, Mantle has almost two dozen—a lifetime of thrills and accomplishment crammed into type almost too small to read without a magnifying glass.

He was the American League's Most Valuable Player three times, in 1956, 1957 and 1962. He put together the triple crown (batting average, homers and runs batted in) in 1956. He led the American League in walks five times and in slugging percentage four times. He also led the league in strikeouts three straight years—and held the major league strikeout record (his 1,710 broke Babe Ruth's mark and stood for ten years until eclipsed by Willie Stargell in 1978). He made the *Sporting News'* All-Star Major League team three years and its American League All-Star team six.

Mantle came into baseball when TV, a sleeping giant, was just beginning to stir fitfully. He left at a juncture where the game could no longer operate without TV revenue. He rode sleepers the first couple of years with the Yankees, who were never eager to put their teams into the air, and by the end of his career, jets. He was a gangling kid out of high school when the Yankees got him in 1951; when he left after the 1968 season, shortly before his thirty-seventh birthday, he was a solid 200-pounder. His listed height, six feet, stretched him a couple of inches, although sometimes he looked even shorter than five-ten because of a slight round-shoulderedness. His country background made him easy prey for big-city fast talkers with something a little slippery to sell. Even during his prime some of his investments turned out less than successful. And unlike Stan Musial, Ted Williams or any one of several contemporaries, when he left baseball it wasn't to join some million-dollar operation.

Mickey was the oldest child in his family. As a youth he never believed he was as talented as people told him. He had younger twin brothers who, to him, were much better than he. "Just wait until Roy and Ray come up," he once promised. "They'll make me look like nothing."

The Yankees would have given a formal tryout to the Mantle family cat. The twins got as far as Class A, then faded into history. Mickey could never understand why they didn't make it. It's the old story of someone touched with a special talent wondering why others have trouble doing what comes naturally to him. They have the same number of arms, legs, ears, and eyes, haven't they?

As the 1949 season moved along into June, an important little drama was evolving in the extreme northeastern corner of Oklahoma—which was still thought of by older baseball people as "Indian territory." It wasn't going to make the papers, even as a filler item in the country editions of the Tulsa *Tribune,* but a Yankee scout, Tom Greenwade, was signing a local high school shortstop who appeared to be a good prospect as a hitter. The prospect was Elvin (Mutt) Mantle's oldest boy, Mickey.

It was graduation time in Commerce, Oklahoma. As in most places, the last couple of weeks for high school seniors were devoted to trying to look busy. Mickey wasn't even trying. He was out playing baseball, most of the time with the Baxter Springs Whiz Kids. He would have been just as happy for them to mail his diploma. Eventually, someone did pick it up for him.

Area scouts had taken a look at Mantle, but Greenwade, a slow-talking Lincolnesque character out of Willard, Missouri, seemed to be the only one with any genuine interest in signing him. The old scout had seen the boy the previous year and inquired mildly whether he might be interested in playing for the Yankees.

"Interested?" father and son had replied simultaneously.

"Well," said Greenwade, "you're still in school, so I can't talk to you. I'll see you again this time next year."

As it developed, Greenwade often saw Mickey and Mutt, a zinc and lead miner up around Picher, Oklahoma, who still played semipro ball and was baseball-crazy. He had named his first son in honor of the Tigers' Hall of Fame catcher, Mickey Cochrane, unaware that Cochrane's real name was Gordon Stanley Cochrane. Mickey's middle name, Charles, came from someone in the family, but the "Mickey" came right out of the sports page.

Greenwade sent several players to the Yankees, including Hank Bauer, Ralph Terry, Jerry Lumpe, Tom Sturdivant and Bobby Murcer. No one is on record as ever having requested the minute details on the actual signing of any of these. But Greenwade has been asked to go over the Mantle signing a dozen times.

"I signed Mickey to a Class D contract with Independence, Kansas, while sitting inside my '47 Olds during a driving rain in Baxter Springs right after a Ban Johnson League game had been rained out. I told Mickey's father that I thought the boy would be able to play Class D, and when he asked how much it would pay I told him '$140 a month.' Mickey's father said the boy could make that much playing Sunday games with him at Spavinaw [Mickey's birthplace] and working around the mines during the week. I got a pencil and a large manila envelope, and we figured out just how much Mickey could make doing a lot of things and then how much he'd make playing in Class D. It figured up to a difference of $1,150, so that's what I paid him as a bonus.

"That bonus had to come as a check from the Independence club, naturally, and until the club folded, as did so many lower minor league clubs, I remember they had that check framed up there on the wall in the office."

Mickey played his first season in organized ball less than 100 miles from home. He was eighteen and green as a pea. But he had an understanding manager in Harry Craft, once a World Series outfielder with the Reds. Craft was smart enough not to emphasize too heavily the forty-seven errors his shortstop made, either around the clubhouse or

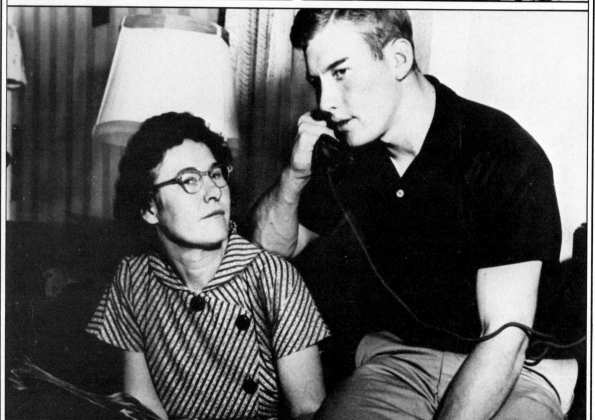

Back home in Oklahoma, little Mickey was bounced on his father Mutt's knee, grew up fishing with twin brothers Roy and Ray and sister Susie; and later was kept busy answering the phone, with his mother's help, as a Yankee celebrity

UPI

The New York Yankees

Mickey at fourteen on the
sandlots *(above)* and
at eighteen with Joplin,
where he batted .383

in his reports to the farm-system headquarters in New York.

The next year both Mantle and Craft moved up a notch to C ball in Joplin, Missouri. Mickey was still a short jump from home, and he was still a shortstop. He continued to throw the ball away, but he pulverized it at the plate with a .383 average. "I'd have hit .400," he once recalled, "except I didn't get a hit in the last two weeks."

Meanwhile, back in New York, Casey Stengel had won two pennants and two World Series in his first two seasons as manager. But he knew that basic repairs would have to be made if success was to continue. DiMaggio was coming to the end of his career. The manager already had looked at Whitey Ford, who now, in 1951, was on his way to the army for two years. He was a cocky lefthander, and Stengel liked cocky lefthanders. He had been a cocky lefthanded outfielder himself around New York with the Dodgers and Giants long before Whitey Ford was born.

Ford had come up through the Yankee farm system, starting a couple of years ahead of Mantle. He got a $7,000 bonus from Paul Krichell, the scout who had come up with Lou Gehrig off the Columbia campus. Ford, off the Astoria streets in Queens, had moved from Yankee farms like Butler, Pennsylvania, to Norfolk, Virginia, to Binghamton, New York, to Kansas City, always a step ahead of Mickey in the pecking order, each completely unaware of the other's existence.

When the Yankees called Ford up from Kansas City in 1950, he won nine in a row. They would never have won that pennant without Whitey, whose only loss occurred in relief late in the season.

As a reward, Ford started the fourth game of the World Series against the Phillies. The Yankees already had won the first three, and Ford had them ahead, 5–0, going into the ninth. But the Phillies got two runs off him, and the Old Man derricked him for Allie Reynolds, who got the final strikeout. Whitey got credit for the victory, the first of his World Series record of ten—an accomplishment duly noted on his Hall of Fame plaque in Cooperstown.

On the Yankee bench for that 1950 Series was Billy Martin, an infielder who had started the season with Kansas City. He had played for Stengel in Oakland in 1948, and a strong bond had developed. One of Stengel's first moves was to suggest the Yankees buy the kid. They did.

Ford and Martin were just casual acquaintances in the fall of 1950. Martin was more of a satellite circling the fabled Joe DiMaggio and the retinue that paid him court at his Hotel Elysée apartment in midtown. Ford also had a large retinue. But his was across the 59th Street Bridge in Astoria, made up mostly of admiring relatives. Mantle? His name never came up. Hotshot hitters down in Class C were a dime a dozen.

The Dodgers and Cardinals, with far more extensive farm systems, could probably produce a dozen at a moment's notice.

Little did this trio of Mantle, Ford and Martin know that their paths would cross shortly; that they would form a cabal that would be both a joy and a pain to the management; that two would gain the sacrosanct precincts of the Hall of Fame simultaneously, and that the other would manage the Yankees two decades later in two World Series and would on several occasions make larger headlines than the President of the United States.

Del Webb was a tall, stoop-shouldered multimillionaire who had come out of the hammer-and-saw ranks of pre–World War II construction workers to build an empire centered in the Southwest. He moved into the Yankee picture when the Ruppert heirs had to sell the club in a hurry. One of the three women mentioned in the Ruppert will was demanding her share, forcing a sale at a time when no one was breaking down any doors to buy a ball club. Webb, Dan Topping and Larry MacPhail, the baseball man who put the package together, got the biggest sports bargain of the century—the Yankees, their real estate, their farm system and its real estate, everything, all for $2.8 million.

Topping, a tin-millions heir, didn't know too much about baseball. He had gotten into sports via the late and unlamented pro football team known as the Brooklyn Dodgers.

Of the three Webb was (1) the most inarticulate, (2) the wealthiest and most powerful, and (3) the biggest fan. He had been a lefthanded semipro pitcher on the West Coast and had hoped in vain that a big-league team would give him a chance. Then he ran into a situation that changed his life. Pitching against a prison team, he drank from a bucket of contaminated water. He was stricken with a case of typhoid that hospitalized him for a year. During that time he swore off heavy drinking, decided that he had to make his way in something other than baseball. He moved to Phoenix, then practically pioneer country, got in on some government construction work for the army and after World War II emerged as a strong factor in the Las Vegas boom. He was squirmy in the presence of reporters but loved publicity. All those Sun Cities he built had Del Webb's name up front.

When the Yankees won the World Series in both 1949 and 1950, Webb started to pop his buttons a bit. Not bad for an old semipro pitcher now holding 50 percent of the club that had won the World Series three out of four years. Let's see, who could Del Webb impress?

Well, his Phoenix neighbors. They had never seen the Yankees, who were training in St. Petersburg, Florida, so there was no chance of bringing them out to the sage-and-cactus country. Phoenix, since becoming a spring training site, had been the exclusive domain of the New York Giants. Webb arranged that for one year—and one year only, 1951—the Giants and Yankees would trade training sites. It turned out to be an omen. Seven months later the Yankees and Giants met in the World Series for the first time since 1937.

Phoenix also set the stage for Mickey Mantle's debut in Yankee uniform. He had been moved up to the Kansas City roster and told to report to Phoenix for pretraining camp, which Casey Stengel called his "instructual" school. In Mantle the manager saw a shortstop who would have needed both of General George Patton's pearl-handled guns to take the job away from Phil Rizzuto, the previous year's Most Valuable Player in the American League.

"Kiddo," said the Old Man, "I think we'll try you in the outfield. Whaddya think of it?"

The "kiddo" was mute as he kept his eyes strictly on the ground. He still couldn't believe he was talking to the manager of the champion New York Yankees.

Not that Stengel was captivated only with the sandy-haired Oklahoma kid with the good arm, fast bat and more than average speed. There were several other prospects in camp. The Yankees had spent money on some. Jim Brideweser, a shortstop from Southern Cal, had received a $40,000 bonus.

Moving up from the Beaumont farm in the Texas League were Gil McDougald and Clint Courtney, who had played there for Rogers Hornsby. McDougald had hit .300 and had been the all-star second baseman. Courtney was a hydrant-shaped Louisianan who caught wearing thick glasses, not as commonplace then as today. Hornsby believed that both were ready to play in the majors, and he was right. McDougald was the American League rookie of the year; Courtney was traded to the St. Louis Browns, where he hit .286 in 1952, his first full season. In this atmosphere Mantle managed to demonstrate enough to continue training with the Yankees, instead of being sent to Florida to join the Kansas City Blues.

In sports it's a short, giddy ride from having to talk your way past the man at the gate to having people knocking down the same gate trying to get a look at you. Mantle took that ride in 1951. By the time the club left its Adams Hotel base in Phoenix for a ten-day trip up and down the West Coast, shaking the box-office gold out of the exhibition crowds in the minor league parks, he had become an attraction. They came to see him belt the long ones, and he didn't disappoint them. Against the University of Southern California he whacked three homers; perhaps he was aware of all those fat bonuses spread around that campus by the Yankees and other clubs.

The New York Yankees

At his first camp Mickey sometimes was too bashful to look at his manager

When Joe DiMaggio advised the Yankees that 1951 was going to be his last season, they were faced with a problem that did not seem to have an immediate solution. For almost thirty years there had always been a superstar in the lineup commanding attention, grabbing the headlines, filling the big ballpark in the Bronx. First it was the Sultan of Swat, then it was the Yankee Clipper. Suddenly, the only replacement possibility in the Yankee system was Mickey Mantle—raw, untutored, country-shy, but obviously able to knock the cover off the ball. And able to do it from *both* sides of the plate. His father, who thought of everything when it came to baseball, had started him on a program of switch-hitting at age five. Now it was a choice of either bringing up the kid or going outside the organization and spending big money for someone else's gate attraction. But the Yankees didn't do things that way then.

George Weiss, now in charge of the Webb-Topping baseball money, told key people to begin spreading the word, dropping it casually in the press boxes, around postgame bars, on trains as the writers bounced from one city to another. Managers, coaches, scouts, farm personnel all played the same then.

"This kid's gonna be the greatest," Paul Krichell once said. "You just wait 'n see."

"What kid?" a listener asked the Yankee scout.

"The Mantle kid. Greatest natural hitter I ever saw."

"Paul, what are you talking about? The kid didn't play higher than C ball last year."

"You wait and see. He'll make everyone forget DiMaggio, once he gets going."

"Krich," his listener said, "I think you're a helluva guy, but I think you're out of your mind to go along with Weiss's scheme. What are you trying to do, sell the kid for a couple of hundred grand?"

Paul Krichell, one of the great baseball talent hunters, was mute. He really didn't believe it, either.

And for the first couple of months it did appear as if George Weiss had gotten his well-groomed tail caught in a crack.

Mantle was in the opening-day lineup (along with Gil McDougald). As the season progressed, he got an occasional hit in his on-the-job training program in right field alongside DiMaggio, but by midsummer he had played himself back to Kansas City—although "back" was the wrong word, since he had never actually played there before. But now he was there, five notches higher in the Class AAA American Association than he had been the previous year.

But in only forty games with the Blues the kid hit .361 with eleven homers and fifty runs batted in.

Perhaps it was because Kansas City was closer to the rugged terrain

Mickey Mantle and Willie Mays were both rookies in the 1951 World Series

UPI

of his native Oklahoma where his father was ailing. Perhaps it was because his old manager, Harry Craft, was now the Blues' manager. Perhaps it was time. Perhaps there was less pressure in Kansas City about his 4-F draft status (for the osteomyletis in his leg) than there had been in the New York area, where there were still a dozen newspapers.

The kid returned to the Yankees on August 20, never to spend another moment in the minors.

Mantle's rookie year must have been nerve-racking for a country kid. Back home his mother had sewn every one of his baseball uniforms; in Yankee Stadium flunkies laid out a fresh one for you every day. Agents stuck checks into your hand and let you keep the pen after signing. Newsmen came back day after day with variations on the same questions, all boiling down to how come you hit the ball so much better than anyone else?

Mickey and his teenage wife, Merlyn, his school sweetheart in Commerce, Oklahoma, were overwhelmed by the towering buildings and the pace in the biggest city in the nation. People talked fast and said things a little differently from the way Mickey's ear had been trained to pick things up. He also was aware of the Yankees' campaign to build him up as Joe DiMaggio's successor.

His father's illness added to his troubles. It had been diagnosed as Hodgkin's disease, a form of cancer. The prognosis was poor. Mutt Mantle could no longer sleep in a bed; he had to sit up and try to get some rest in a chair. The kid's eyes were red a good deal of the time, and it wasn't just from the frustration of watching his batting average drop to a modest .267.

He also hit thirteen homers as a rookie. His first, for the record, was off Randall Pennington Gumpert, a former Yankee righthander and physical-fitness nut, in Chicago. It traveled 450 feet to deep center, and it gave the Yankee drum beaters a bit of a lift. And he hit one off the ancient Satchel Paige, the black righthander who was finishing up with Bill Veeck's moribund St. Louis Browns.

The day after Bobby Thomson's homer won the National League pennant for the Giants, the kid was playing in the first World Series game he had ever seen. Not only that, but he was the lead-off hitter. He did comparatively little, drawing two walks as Dave Koslo, a left-hander of modest abilities, beat the Yankees, 5–1, with a five-hitter.

The Yankees won the second game, but Mantle wasn't around to help celebrate. He started the game with a bunt single and ended in a room at Lenox Hill Hospital, with his father in the adjoining bed.

In the fifth inning Willie Mays—also in his rookie season—led off with a fly to right center. DiMaggio and the kid converged. At the last moment it appeared that Mantle, making a strenuous effort to avoid a collision, had ducked away and fallen. Actually, he had tripped on a sprinkler top and collapsed with a damaged knee—the first of a series of injuries that would plague him for his entire career. He was carried off the field and rushed by cab to Lenox Hill Hospital, used by the Yankees for four decades.

"Badly sprained right knee" was the report announced in the press box. "Mickey's father is in the hospital, too. He bumped his head getting into the cab taking Mickey downtown. The doctors thought he'd better stay for a day or two. They're in the same room."

It was, of course, not a bump on the head but the manifestation of cancer in the late stages, and more than "a day or two" would pass before the doctors permitted Mutt Mantle to leave the hospital. He returned to Oklahoma, where he died the following spring.

His father's death had a profound effect on Mantle throughout his career. He frequently mentioned that he would never get past forty because his father hadn't. Sometimes this attitude was reflected in his training habits, which could be less than casual. Mutt Mantle was denied watching most of his son's major league career, but at least he saw Mickey switch-hit in a World Series, righthanded in the first game, lefthanded in the second.

After that 1951 debut Mickey Mantle went on to dominate one of baseball's most famous dynasties. His Hall of Fame plaque (he was inducted in 1974) proclaims in bronze lettering his 536 homers, 4 league home-run titles, 2,415 hits, 3 Most Valuable Player awards, and his 20 All-Star teams. Also set down are some of his 10 World Series records: 18 home runs, 42 runs, 40 runs batted in, 123 total bases and 43 walks. His lifetime batting average is skipped, along with his 1,710 strikeouts, still a league record. Mickey was not a .300 hitter, finishing at .298 after subpar years in 1967 and 1968, his last two seasons.

The plaque also fails to note that he was the only Triple Crown winner during the 1950's. In 1956 he led the American League with 52 homers, 130 runs batted in, and a .363 average. For all this he was paid in the vicinity of $50,000, plus the slight fringe benefit of being able, along with Whitey Ford, to sign at the Yankee hotels on the road for anything reasonable. The owners considered this an equitable trade-off for their being reasonable in contract negotiations. Occasionally, another player would get wind of the arrangement and try his penmanship, only to be swatted down summarily. Like Billy Martin.

Mantle's Hall of Fame plaque should also have paid some sort of notice to his switch-hitting. As a lefthanded hitter, Mantle pulverized low pitches, golfing them prodigious distances. Righthanded, his best swing was a level one, generated a couple of inches below the shoulders. This swing produced line drives that outfielders simply couldn't get to in time.

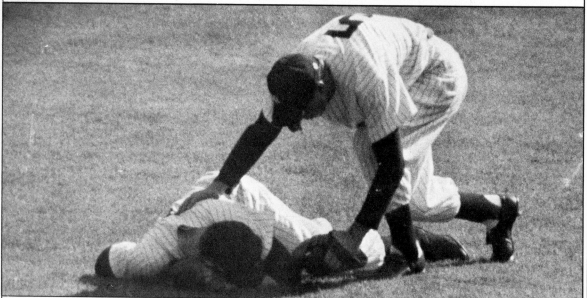

Helpless on the ground, Mickey Mantle has tripped over a Yankee Stadium drain in the 1951 World Series while Joe DiMaggio waits for Willie Mays's flyball; moments later, DiMaggio leans over the fallen rookie

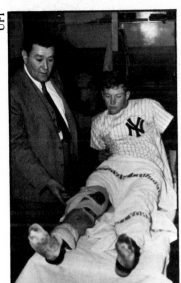

UPI

Mantle's damaged right knee is examined by Dr. Sidney Gaynor

His most famous righthanded homer occurred in Washington in 1953 at Griffith Stadium, a long-departed park set in the midst of private homes. Mantle tagged a pitch offered by Chuck Stobbs, a Senator lefthander, that cleared the fence in front of the centerfield stands, kept climbing, cleared the front wall of the stands, climbed even higher and caromed off the edge of a signboard atop the stands. The Yankees' press agent, Arthur (Red) Patterson, using Boy Scout heel-and-toe mathematics, quickly figured it was a 565-foot shot. That number was duly noted on the sign as long as it stood.

Pedro Ramos, another Senator pitcher and later a Yankee, was the victim of Mantle's best lefthanded shot. It traveled to the top of the façade of the Yankee Stadium roof in right field. No one has ever hit a fair ball out of Yankee Stadium, old or new. But that one came the closest.

The Yankees lay claim to two dozen Hall of Famers, more than any other club. The Mantle era generated a total of five inductees—Casey Stengel, George Weiss, Yogi Berra, Whitey Ford and Mantle himself. Berra and Mantle joined DiMaggio as three-time winners of the MVP award. Ford's plaque mentions that his .690 winning percentage is the best among twentieth-century pitchers. Weiss is honored as a builder of championship teams. Stengel was the manager whose teams won ten pennants (in twelve years) and seven World Series, including a record five in a row. Also listed on Stengel's plaque are his stops as a player, which read like a nonconducted tour of the Northeast sector of the United States—Brooklyn, Pittsburgh, Philadelphia, New York and Boston. He was also the first manager of the New York Mets.

Casey Stengel wanted Mickey Mantle the first day he saw him at that Phoenix school that preceded the 1951 training camp.

"That kid hits them pretty far. The stratmosphere around here helps," he said. "But you still gotta be pretty good to hit them that way."

"Stratmosphere" was Casey's reference to Arizona's hot, dry air that supposedly helped the ball travel.

Stengel won his third World Series that year. It's safe to say he could have won it without Mantle; it's also safe to say he couldn't have won the next two, 1952 and 1953, without him. The Old Man couldn't have won in 1953 without Billy Martin, either. Martin batted a meager .217 against the Dodgers in 1952 but saved the 4–2 victory in the seventh game with a memorable catch of Jackie Robinson's bases-loaded pop fly in the seventh inning. Then he went wild in 1953 with a six-game Series record average of .500. Mantle's efforts were directly opposite.

He had a great 1952 Series with a homer in each of the last two games for a .345 average, but he sagged to a .208 the following year. He struck out four straight times when Carl Erskine broke the Series record by fanning fourteen Yankees.

Not too many recall the details of any of Billy Martin's dozen Series hits in 1953, or for that matter the five he got in the 1952 Series, but that catch in 1952 is forever fixed in many memories.

The Yankees were leading, 4–2, in the seventh, having gone ahead in the top of that inning. Allie Reynolds, who had carried a heavy load in the Series, was tiring, and Stengel brought in Vic Raschi to start the inning. Carl Furillo led off with a walk. With one out, Billy Cox singled and Pee Wee Reese walked to fill the bases. Stengel summoned Bob Kuzava, a lefthander, to pitch to Duke Snider, who went after a high pitch and popped up to Gil McDougald.

Jackie Robinson, after working the count to three balls and two strikes, swung at a high curve and popped it up near the Ebbets Field mound. With the full count, the three base runners had been running on the pitch. And suddenly it was apparent that Joe Collins, the Yankee first baseman, had lost sight of the ball and neither McDougald, the third baseman, nor Kuzava was making any effort to go after it. But streaking in from between first and second came Billy Martin, his cap flying off. He was running full speed, glove hand extended. At the last second, just as the ball seemed to be sinking to the turf, he lunged an extra inch. He got the ball, flipped it over his shoulder and trotted toward the Yankee dugout. Two Dodger runs had already crossed the plate. What would have been a tie game remained a Series-winning 4–2 triumph.

About this time the baseball community, including the sportswriters, began to realize that the "clown" trappings that had clothed Casey Stengel in Brooklyn and Boston had been cast aside forever. No longer did he have to make jokes to cover up his players' deficiencies. Now he was in a position to pick and choose. He could be funny when he wanted to be or serious when he thought that was proper.

He also didn't have to use retreads, bunglers or novices who learned on the job. When he needed a player, he would drop by George Weiss's office. Four or five hours later he knew he would have his man shortly —righthander Johnny Sain to help in a pennant race or a shortstop named Tony Kubek to move in as Phil Rizzuto was phased out.

They would sit there, these old friends of four decades, and talk about everything except the business at hand. It would be "Case" and "George," with the manager drinking Scotch and sodas and smoking, the general manager staying away from cigarettes. Each was a veritable encyclopedia: the front-office genius who had started by managing a

The muscle-grinding power of Mickey Mantle's righthanded home-run swing

374 Feet

108 Ft. 1 In.

The trajectory of his most famous lefthanded homer, off the Stadium's top façade

high school team in New Haven, then moved to a semipro club that ran the minor league team out of town; the grizzled ex-ballplayer who began on a farm team in Kankakee, Illinois, in a league briefly known as the Northern Association.

When the Northern Association was extinguished in midseason, Stengel wrote home to Kansas City for carfare. His father could afford it; he was a contractor who watered down the city's dusty roads, most of which were dirt. Years later Stengel was to hear some old guy yell jeeringly from the Kansas City seats, "G'wan, Stengel, your old man took free water and sold it to the city."

Kankakee was also the site of Illinois' state mental institution, which overlooked the tiny ballpark. As the centerfielder, Stengel was closest to these nonpaying spectators and received their advice in a steady stream. After watching some of his antics, someone would occasionally drop a note inviting him to join the fun inside. On his team's final out Stengel would take his glove, fling it as far as he could toward center field, dash madly toward it and slide into it.

"Whaddya mean, nuts?" he demanded when someone suggested a certain eccentricity in his conduct. "I'm practicin'. I'm throwin', runnin' and slidin', ain't I?"

After a couple of additional seasons in the bush, fighting off family suggestions that he become a dentist, he was picked up by Montgomery in the Southern League. In 1912 he was sent up to Brooklyn, got into his first World Series with Uncle Wilbert Robinson's 1916 club and made it again in 1922 and 1923 with John McGraw's Giants. He was no baby, and the story of a thirty-three-year-old outfielder staggering around the bases for an inside-the-park homer got headlines. Out in California the father of Edna Lawson read it and wondered why his daughter had picked a worn-out old man to marry. For a half-century Edna herself sought the answer.

Casey hit .393 in his three World Series, and if the All-Star Game had been held in those years he probably would have been picked for two or three. And along the way he picked up a lot of baseball savvy.

He also had an overriding faith in baseball, something not too many participants then or now could say they have had with any degree of honesty. He believed in the game as a sort of ultimate reason for existing. When he put together a nest egg, he didn't invest it in real estate or oil wells (though he did well there, too). He put his money back into baseball. In 1925 he bought into the Worcester, Massachusetts, club in the Eastern League, where he first met Weiss, who had the New Haven club.

Stengel was president and player-manager of the Worcester club when an excellent offer arrived from an old pal who was operating the Toledo club in the American Association. Half a century ago there was stature in managing minor league baseball (playing it, too) that is unknown now. Stengel was in a quandary. He had signed himself (as president) to a contract (as manager and player). The manager sat down with the president and argued successfully for his release.

"What'll I do with my interest in the Worcester club?" asked the president.

"Sell it to the Boston Braves," suggested the manager.

Stengel returned to the major leagues in 1932 as a Dodger coach. But the Brooklyn club was a bank-held joke. When it finished sixth in 1934 under Max Carey, there were gags about three baserunners on third, about the Daffiness boys, about lit cigar butts in jacket pockets and about a newspaper line that "over-confidence could cost the Dodgers seventh place." The trouble was, people were laughing outside Ebbets Field, not inside. The Brooklyn Trust Company, the bank that had the Dodger mortgage and a worried look, suggested a change. The bankers came to Stengel, who told them he wanted a shot at managing a big-league team even if it had won only sixty-five games the previous year. But he didn't want to knock an old friend out of a job.

"Take it," Max Carey told him. "If you don't, someone else will."

Stengel took it. But what Carey couldn't do with mediocre talent, Stengel couldn't do, either. At the end of the 1935 season the Dodgers told him not to bother to return; they would mail him his 1936 salary. They offered the job to Burleigh Grimes, the last of the spitball pitchers permitted to work at his job in the majors without the cops being called.

Grimes, a friend of Stengel's, didn't like the idea of replacing him, but Casey, with a feeling of having heard these words before, said: "Take it. If you don't, someone else will."

Stengel then served another purgatory in Boston with the Braves, another hopeless team. In his sixth year there he was the victim of an automobile accident that caused him to walk with a slight hop the rest of his life. One rainy April night he was struck by a car. The leg fracture occurred above the ankle where the shin starts. It left an awesome bump.

"Get hit there once more," a doctor told him, "and it's goodbye leg."

Stengel was trying to clown his way through the Boston mess, but certain sportswriters were not laughing. They blamed him for the cheapness of a moribund front office. When he never got the Braves out of the second division, he was held personally responsible by men who should have known better.

One columnist chose Stengel as his particular target. Albert Camus has written that by age forty everyone has the face he deserves. Dave Egan, of the Boston *Record,* deserved the face he presented to the world on the infrequent occasions he ventured out. Mostly he sat in front of his office typewriter thinking of unpleasant things to write about Ted

Williams, the Red Sox and Casey Stengel. He is remembered best for
a line in a column in which he distributed imaginary "Christmas gifts."
He gave man-of-the-year honors in Boston to the "taxi driver who ran
down Stengel and broke his leg."

During a Yankee pennant drive years later Stengel was in Kansas
City in the lobby of the Muehlbach Hotel when someone walked in with
the next morning's paper. Dave Egan was dead in Boston.

Asked to comment, Stengel thought a bit, then said, "The fella drank
a lot. They wanted to fire him, but I went to the owners." He never
explained which owners—the club's or the newspaper's. Then he
added, "He sure was wrong. It wasn't a taxi driver that hit me. It was
a Spanish fella, and he didn't have any insurance."

Stengel was discharged by the Braves after the 1943 season, when he
went to Milwaukee, then in the American Association. His major
league days appeared to be over. He had a job with the Yankees' farm
team in Kansas City, working for George Weiss, then he handled the
Oakland club in the Pacific Coast League for Brick Laws, a movie-
house owner who enjoyed baseball more than he did the flicks. And
that's where Stengel was in 1948 when the Yankees needed someone in
a hurry after Bucky Harris had been fired.

But there's a footnote to the choice of Stengel that might well have
changed baseball history.

Billy Meyer, a strong Weiss man and a fine strategist though not too
robust physically, had been the 1947 manager of the Kansas City farm.
After the Pirates finished dead last that year with a lineup that included
Hank Greenberg, Ralph Kiner and Wally Westlake, the team's new
owners hired Meyer through a Yankee connection. He moved the club
up to fourth in 1948 and was named National League manager of the
year.

But when George Weiss had to choose a new Yankee manager,
Meyer was unavailable.

As it turned out, Casey Stengel supervised an unprecedented decade
of Yankee dominance to the day in 1960 when he was fired in the
Crystal Ballroom of the Savoy-Plaza Hotel, to be replaced by Ralph
Houk, one of his coaches. Stengel was bounced for two reasons—his age
and the management's reluctance to lose Houk to another organization.
Houk had several bids. Eventually, he figured to be Casey's successor.
Why not now?

Stengel's tenure was marked by records, excitement and adjustment
to such profound changes as night games, coast-to-coast travel and
television. His five straight World Series victories bear analysis. He beat
the Dodgers three times, the Phillies once and the Giants once. He
always had the extra pitcher that the Dodgers somehow missed. But
that was largely because of Weiss's wheeling and dealing.

Billy Martin saves the 1952
World Series by catching
Jackie Robinson's pop-up

Sometimes the Yankees would get burned, but usually they would come up with a pitcher who won big (Johnny Sain) or just enough (Ray Scarborough, Tom Ferrick, Bob Kuzava). And once there was the dizzying transfer of several surplus players to Baltimore for Bob Turley, the 1958 Cy Young winner, and Don Larsen, the 1956 World Series perfect-game pitcher.

The Turley-Larsen deal came after the end of the first season in which the Yankees did not win the pennant under Stengel. He had won his fifth pennant in 1953 with ninety-nine victories. Not much room for improvement there, but Stengel did improve in the 1954 season. His team won 103 games even though the pitching was beginning to be slightly frayed. Whitey Ford was back from the army and won eighteen games, but Vic Raschi and Allie Reynolds were coming to the end of their careers, winning only thirteen games each.

Still the Yankees topped 100 victories for the first and last time in Stengel's managerial career. The trouble was that in Cleveland one of Stengel's old pupils, Al Lopez, was winning 111 games with the Indians. When the Indians finished second in 1952 and 1953 under Lopez, the Old Man observed, "I better watch that fella. He was a pretty good catcher for me, and he knows what it's all about." Lopez was not only "pretty good"; he was durable. His Hall of Fame credentials include having caught more games than anyone else in baseball history.

In 1954 it was Lopez's time. He had enough hitting with sluggers like Al Rosen, Larry Doby and Vic Wertz; he had more than enough pitching in Bob Lemon, Early Wynn, Mike Garcia, an aging Bob Feller and a pair of superb relievers, Don Mossi and Ray Narleski. Mossi had a big beak of a nose, a lot like Warren Spahn's. The Indians memorialized it when they commissioned someone to draw the stylized Indian head that would represent the club. It came out with a big hook and protruding ears. There was no doubt as to the model, and it's still in use.

There was no doubt, either, that the Yankees were in a tough race in 1954, even though they had been the universal pick to repeat for a sixth flag. They were in first place for a few hours in mid-July when they won the first game of a doubleheader from Detroit, but they lost the second. They were only three games out in early September, but they wilted before the Indians' finish.

Stengel disliked losing to Cleveland. He made frequent sarcastic references to mysterious money connections and couldn't conceal his distaste for being beaten by a lineup that was one-third black. It has to be remembered that for most of his life the only blacks Stengel had contact with were the maids who cleaned his hotel room or the porters who made up his Pullman berth. The Yankees had given him an all-white team, and there was no indication that it was going to change

Casey Stengel's crystal baseball had five consecutive Series titles in it

Wide World Photos

Arm in arm, Edna Stengel and Casey celebrate at the 1952 World Series party

even though Jackie Robinson, Roy Campanella and Don Newcombe were in Brooklyn and Monte Irvin and Willie Mays were at the Polo Grounds with the Giants. Yankee scouts were advised not to concern themselves with black players. "We have no policy on black players," the scouts said uncomfortably to newsmen they trusted.

Under inexorable pressure the Yankees' non-policy changed while Stengel was manager, but there was a lot of catching up to do. When Al Smith, Bobby Avila and Larry Doby were punishing American League pitching in 1954 in support of the Indians' pitching staff, the Yankees' first black star, Elston Howard, was a year away, polishing his credentials with Toronto in the International League.

For the life of him, Stengel couldn't understand why he couldn't do better than break even with Cleveland during the season. After they had made the Yankees look bad in a Stadium series in July, instead of accepting defeat gracefully, as he did 95 percent of the time, he scornfully described the Indians as a "bunch of plumbers," an old-fashioned equivalent of ineptitude.

"They ain't gonna beat me, neither," he snapped.

Maybe not, but his hitters certainly looked inept facing Lemon, Wynn and Garcia. And when a hasty series of purchases of pitchers such as Jim Konstanty and Tommy Byrne failed to plug the gaps on his fading staff, Stengel's baseball instincts told him he was a little over his head. In the final swing through the West that season the Yankees found themselves six and a half games behind after a weekend series in Chicago with a Sunday doubleheader in Cleveland next. It was a scheduling oddity, a Sunday doubleheader and that was all.

Stengel knew this to be the Yankees' last chance. On the train from Chicago to Cleveland he picked at his dining car meal and advised the newsmen he called "my writers" that "We're six behind"—he always junked the fractions—"and we go in there tomorra and we win two and we're only four behind, and then we go from there."

Those who saw that doubleheader will never forget it. The crowd of 86,563 (84,587 paid) is still baseball's biggest. The Indians had sold out during the week but turned down $75,000 for telecasting rights, a lot of money in those days. If you were back in New York, your lifeline was radio, with Mel Allen and Red Barber sharing the play-by-play.

Lopez had saved his Lemon-Wynn punch for the Yankees. Against them Stengel had Ford and Tommy Byrne, back from the minors after an earlier tour with the Yankees. It appeared a hopeless mismatch.

Ford and Lemon dueled through six innings at 1–1, but then Ford was forced out with a pain in his shoulder. Stengel brought in Allie Reynolds, and Al Rosen, later to resurface as the Yankee's president in 1978, doubled home two runs. Rosen had been the unanimous MVP in the American League the previous year. In 1954 he had slipped some, but for a valid reason. He played most of the season with the index finger on his throwing hand in a rigid splint, thanks to having stuck his hand into an errant toss early in the schedule. Even so, he was a formidable, if odd figure up there at the plate, one finger cocked a couple of inches away from the bat. His hitting dipped from .336 to an even .300, but he had 24 homers and drove in 102 runs.

Yogi Berra, the player ticketed to succeed Rosen as MVP, gave the Yankees hope in the second game when he cracked a two-run homer off Early Wynn in the first inning. In retrospect, it was a mistake. It merely made Wynn hate the Yankees that much more. He seemed to puff up out there on the mound like a disturbed water moccasin. He gave them one hit the rest of the way. And to get that hit, Hank Bauer had to bunt.

The Indians got three runs off Byrne in a big fifth, and suddenly the Yankees were eight games behind with the Indians headed for the Series.

When the Yankees assembled in 1955, their pitching staff had been retooled. Bob Turley and Don Larsen had been obtained from the Orioles to support Whitey Ford, the ace. Big things also were expected of Bob Grim, a righthander who had won twenty in 1954, the Yankees' first rookie of the year since McDougald in 1951. But what the Yankees didn't know was that Grim, who tended his family's Brooklyn bar in the off-season, had wrecked his arm. He would never have another big year. His best was a 12-8 record in 1957 before he drifted to Kansas City the next season.

Even with Grim slipping to 7-5 in 1955, the Yankees had enough pitching and more than enough hitting. Homers off the bats of Mantle, Berra and Hank Bauer settled arguments in a hurry. Moose Skowron, Joe Collins and Eddie Robinson shared first base and combined for forty-one homers. The Yankees simmered the Indians' succotash nicely and found themselves back in the World Series with the Dodgers again.

It was no longer the "nickel" series, meaning that for a nickel you could ride the subway between the two ballparks, one in Brooklyn, the other in the Bronx; nor was it a "dime" series, either. The rate had gone up to 15 cents.

The Dodgers had a new senior patrol leader, quiet Walt Alston, then in the second year of what was to prove an amazing string of twenty-three single-year contracts. His team had trailed the Giants by five games in 1954, his first campaign as manager. But in 1955 the Dodgers won by thirteen and a half games.

Like several other Dodger teams, they took the Yankees to seven games. But unlike the others, they won the World Series.

They won when a pale Polish kid from the Adirondack mountain town of Witherbee, New York, a lefthander named Johnny Podres, pitched an eight-hit shutout, 2–0, in the decisive seventh game that featured the famous Sandy Amoros catch. And there was dancing in the Brooklyn streets after a World Series for the first time—and the last.

Sandy Amoros was the Dodgers' sometime leftfielder, a small, smiling Cuban who spoke virtually no English. He had come up through the extensive Dodger organization and proved to be the right man in the right place. In his case, the right man was lefthanded.

The Dodgers had scored once in the fourth and felt they had to have more runs. In a bases-loaded, two-out situation, Alston sent George Shuba to pinch-hit for Don Zimmer, the second baseman. Shuba grounded out, and now some rearranging was necessary.

Jim Gilliam, who had been playing left field, moved to second base, and Amoros went to left. There were two on and none out in the sixth when Yogi Berra lifted a long fly down the leftfield line. Amoros raced over, seemed to disappear from the view of half the people in Yankee Stadium, then reappeared holding the ball, but only for a split second before he fired it to Pee Wee Reese, the Dodger shortstop. Gil McDougald had rounded second and now had to hurry back to first, but Reese relayed accurately to Gil Hodges for a double play.

And the next day Johnny Podres drove off in the first car presented by *Sport* magazine to the World Series' most valuable player.

That fall Yogi Berra was voted the American League's MVP for a third time, the first Yankee so honored. Mantle had led the league with thirty-seven homers. Ford had an 18-7 record; Turley was 17-13; the new righthander, Don Larsen, was only 9-2. But in another Yankee-Dodger World Series the following year Don Larsen would pitch a perfect game.

Many people are under the impression that the perfect game occurred either in Larsen's first appearance in that Series or in the seventh game. Neither. Whitey Ford started the Series, as he was to do a record total of eight times in his distinguished career, but he was gone by the fourth inning after home-run blasts by Jackie Robinson and Gil Hodges produced four runs in a 6–3 victory at Ebbets Field.

The next day the Yankees sent Larsen to the mound to try to get even. But the big fellow was wild, issuing four walks in less than two innings. He came out, and the Yankees went on to lose, 13–8—the most runs ever scored against them in a Series game.

Ford came back to win the third game at the Stadium, then Sturdivant took the fourth game. Now it was Larsen's turn again in an October 8 matchup with Sal Maglie, once a Dodger nemesis when he was the Giants' ace. Pitching without a windup, a style he had adopted late that season, Larsen needed only ninety-seven pitches to record his perfect game in a 2–0 victory—the first game in which no runner

Don Larsen hurls the final pitch of his perfect game, then catches Yogi Berra

Mickey Mantle and Billy Martin primp shortly before the Kansas City trade

reached first base in the major leagues since April 30, 1922, when Charley Robertson of the White Sox stopped the Tigers, 2–0. It was also the first World Series no-hitter after 307 games, beginning in 1903.

Larsen's control was so sharp that he went to three balls on only one batter—Reese, in the first inning.

Mantle made the best defensive play, racing into deep left center at the Stadium for a backhanded catch of Hodges' long line drive in the fifth. The previous inning Mantle had hit a homer. The other run developed in the sixth on Andy Carey's single, Larsen's sacrifice and Hank Bauer's single. With two out in the top of the ninth, Dale Mitchell, an extra outfielder recently acquired by the Dodgers from the Indians, hoped to break the spell as a pinch-hitter. But with two strikes he half-swung at a close pitch. Babe Pinelli, the plate umpire, called him out for Larsen's seventh strikeout and the perfect game.

"In that kind of a game," Pinelli said later, "it would have had to be a lot closer for me to go the other way on that pitch."

Twenty years later, in an official Bicentennial poll conducted by Commissioner Bowie Kuhn's office, Larsen's performance was voted the third most memorable moment in baseball history. Ahead of it were (1) Hank Aaron's 715th home run and (2) Bobby Thomson's pennant-winning homer for the Giants in the 1951 playoff. Behind it were (4) Babe Ruth's "called" homer in the 1932 World Series and (5) Joe DiMaggio's fifty-six-game hitting streak. Note that three of the most memorable moments were Yankee moments.

Larsen's perfect game put the Yankees ahead, 3–2, in the Series, and they went back to Brooklyn, seeking to end it. Instead they suffered a tenth-inning setback when Jackie Robinson singled off Turley for a 1–0 victory. Turley gave up four hits, compared to seven off Clem Labine, the Dodgers' sinkerball righthander. Now there was a seventh game with Don Newcombe, the first Cy Young Award winner with a 27-7 record, facing Johnny Kucks, a youthful righthander whose big strength was keeping his pitches low. It proved to be no match, or at least Big Newk proved to be no match for the aroused Yankee bats.

Berra nicked the huge righthander for successive two-run homers in the first and third. Elston Howard started the fourth with another round-tripper, and Big Newk was gone. In the seventh a grandslam homer by Moose Skowron off Roger Craig completed a 9–0 rout. Things had returned to normal; Casey Stengel again was a winning World Series manager. He was to have three more shots—at the Braves in 1957 and 1958, and at the Pirates in 1960—but he was to beat only the 1958 Braves.

It would be pleasant to report that Larsen, who had a 11-5 record in 1956, went on from his perfect game to become a big winner and a Hall of Famer, but the next year his record was 10-4. When he dipped to 6-7 in 1959, George Weiss put him on the shuttle to Kansas City, where he promptly came up with a 1-10 record. When Larsen finished up in 1967 after playing with five other clubs, he had an overall 81-91 won-lost mark.

Apparently, there was always someone willing to take a chance on a pitcher able to retire twenty-seven men in succession on a hazy World Series afternoon.

Larsen presented Stengel with several difficult moments. High on the list was the night he wrapped a car around a light pole in St. Petersburg during spring training. Fortunately it was his own car, and fortunately he was barely scratched. But what was the big guy doing out at five in the morning?

"He went out to mail a letter," Stengel said.

St. Pete was also the site of the only occasion when a Yankee manager was arrested. The manager? Charles Dillon Stengel. Bank robber? Embezzler? Indecent exposure? Don't be silly. The charge was kicking a photographer. In some quarters in baseball that infraction of the civil code is regarded about as bad as refusing to give an autograph. The photographer from the St. Pete evening paper was trying to make some interesting shots of the Yankees in their dugout before a 1957 game at Al Lang Field down by the bay. But he was blocking Stengel's view of first base. The manager considered his view more important than the pictures the photographer hoped to take and told him, "Take that camera and get the hell outta here." The photographer, however, was intent on trying to get a group in his rangefinder. Stengel advanced on him menacingly. The photographer still had his head down, focusing. And then Stengel did—or didn't—kick him in the shin.

The photographer limped away in a hurry, found the Yankee press agent and complained. Since both knew Stengel, they decided to forget it. On his way back to the office, however, the photographer decided this wasn't much of a way to be treated. When he got there, he told his managing editor about the incident. Midway during the story he decided to brush it off with "Aw, he's a silly old man, forget it."

"Did he kick you hard?" demanded the managing editor.

The photographer mumbled, "Well . . ."

But now the publisher also was listening. He was a Canadian, no great admirer of the Yankees, or of baseball. "Swear out a warrant," he ordered. "Make it aggravated assault."

"Wait a minute now," the photographer said.

"Better do it," he was told. "He kicked you, didn't he?"

Soon the photographer was down at the police station giving the desk sergeant the details. That evening Stengel was having dinner at the Soreno Hotel, trying to outtalk the three-piece orchestra, when two strangers walked up and introduced themselves to Stengel as detectives. Stengel shook hands very friendly-like and reached for his ball-point pen to sign a couple of autographs.

"Casey," one said, "we have a warrant for your arrest. Better come down to the station house with us."

When they got there, Casey Stengel was booked, fingerprints and all. Then he was told he could post $50 bail and leave. Stengel rummaged through his pockets. He had a couple of fives and some change. "Lemme use the phone," he said. He called the club's public-relations director, Bob Fishel.

"I'm in jail," Stengel announced. "Y'gotta come down and bail me out. It's $50, but bring more because they might change their mind."

The publicity man promptly aged several years. "Don't talk to anyone down there," he shuddered. "I'll be there in ten minutes."

He made it in five. He arrived to see Stengel sitting at the sergeant's desk telling Yogi Berra stories. The publicity man peeled off five $10 bills, got his receipt, promised to leave some tickets for the cops at the gate the next afternoon and hustled Stengel into the car.

"Don't talk to anyone when we get back to the hotel," he warned. "No one."

When they got back, Fishel went to the front desk to check on messages. He had tried to reach Weiss and Topping before going over to the police station, but both were out. Suddenly he heard Stengel; there was no mistaking that gravelly voice. Some newspapermen had just come through the door and the manager had collared them.

"Guess what happened to me tonight. I was arrested. They'll probably put me away and throw away the key and Yogi'll be managing the club. Let's see what kind of stories you'll get from him."

There were some frantic phone calls that evening—from the Yankees to the Chamber of Commerce contact man, to the St. Pete newspaper, to the police, and back. To that Florida city the Yankees represented several million dollars' worth of annual tourism. It could all be blown because of a bruised shin. Meanwhile, some self-appointed advisers were telling Stengel to apologize.

"For what?" the Old Man demanded.

"Well, you kicked him, didn't you?"

"You don't see any marks on him, do you?"

He finally agreed to sign something to the effect that he didn't kick the photographer or anyone because he always had excellent relations with the press wherever he went (which of course he did) and he wanted to keep it that way.

"Put it in there," demanded Stengel, "that I couldna kicked him because he's a veteran. I have great respect for veterans, having been one myself from the Navy in World War I, and you can look it up."

The charges were ultimately dropped. Bob Fishel got his $50 back. The Chamber of Commerce people stopped sweating, and Stengel's fingerprints presumably went on to Washington to go into the FBI files along with those of Al Capone, Pretty Boy Floyd, Ma Barker and Lee Harvey Oswald.

The high point of Mickey Mantle's career occurred in 1956, the year he won the Triple Crown. He hit .353 to Ted Williams' .345; his 52 homers were far ahead of Vic Wertz's 32 for the Indians; his 130 runs batted in topped Al Kaline's 128 for the Tigers.

Whitey Ford emerged as the earned-run average leader that year with 2.47 (his record was 19-6), and Billy Martin, the third member of the axis that was dabbling a little extra gray into George Weiss's temples because of their antics off-field, hit a respectable .264 at second base.

But it would be Martin's final full season in pin stripes. Weiss was firmly convinced by now that Billy had the potential to wreck his club through his not-so-shining example. And waiting in the wings was Bobby Richardson, who would be one of the finest second basemen in Yankee history. Then, early in the 1957 season, an incident at the Copacabana nightclub assured Martin's departure. The evening started out innocently enough—a party, with wives, to celebrate the Martin and Berra birthdays. Mantle and Ford also were there, as were Hank Bauer, Gil McDougald and Johnny Kucks.

It's important to remember that several wives were along; the players weren't looking for any trouble.

They found it anyway. A scuffle developed in the passageway outside the men's room at the Copacabana. Bauer was involved. The cops were called. And a delicatessen owner from the Bronx, the Yankees' borough, filed a big suit for damages. He claimed Bauer had belted him. Bauer, an ex-Marine with a face like a clenched fist, claimed he didn't; if he did, he said, the guy wouldn't be around filing damages suits.

Basically, there was nothing wrong with the Yankee people being in a nightclub. Wives get tired of neighborhood movies, and there they could see Sammy Davis Jr. in person.

Weiss, however, took it personally. After conferring with Dan Topping, who had been in more nightclubs than any of the players involved, Weiss slapped all but one with $1,000 fines, a brisk sum in those days. Kucks' lowly status on the payroll got him off with a $500 fine. To the front office the scandal was deadly serious, but it turned into a laugh when a newsman asked Yogi what had happened.

"Nuthin'," advised Yogi. "Nobody did nuthin' to nobody."

Weiss was now convinced that Martin was somehow responsible. The general manager had one of his newspaper friends ask Mantle casually how come he was always doing things that Martin suggested and getting into trouble. Mantle answered, "Some people are leaders and some are followers. I'm a follower." At the June 15 trade deadline Martin found himself on the shuttle to Kansas City, now a major league club, along with Ralph Terry, Woody Held and Bob Martyn.

In return, the Yankees got Ryne Duren, a pitcher who wore glasses that looked like the bottoms of soda bottles, along with Jim Pisoni and Harry Simpson.

That was the start of Martin's travels—from the A's to the Tigers to the Indians to the Reds to the Braves to the Minnesota Twins, before embarking on a stormy managing career. For a long time Billy blamed Stengel for his exile to the A's, claiming the Old Man hadn't stood up for him. Eventually they had a tearful reconciliation. And eventually the Copacabana incident was settled. The case of the dented delicatessen owner was thrown out of court. Bauer was advised by the Yankee lawyers that he now could sue in turn.

"Forget it," the ex-Marine snapped. "What would I do if I won? Take the guy's delicatessen?"

Now for a word about that shuttle bus to Kansas City which Bauer, too, eventually made. Actually, they all traveled by plane, but the impression of a bus that left on schedule was implanted strongly in the minds of those close to baseball then.

When the A's moved to Kansas City from Philadelphia in 1955, the Yankees relinquished the territorial rights of their American Association franchise. They retained certain perquisites, however, like Del Webb's construction company getting the contract to enlarge the old stadium to major league proportions. They also approved the new owner, Arnold Johnson, a Chicago businessman, who didn't know too much about baseball. But he was wealthy and he had wealthy associates.

"Don't worry," Johnson was told, "we'll give you someone who knows baseball better than most."

Johnston installed Parke Carroll, who had been the general manager of the Kansas City Blues, as the A's general manager. Anytime George Weiss got on the phone to Parke Carroll, the man in Kansas City naturally paid attention. Weiss had hired him in his first baseball job.

And so Kansas City emerged alternately as a Yankee staging area and a rest-and-recuperation area for such players as Enos Slaughter, Bill Renna, Clete Boyer, Art Ditmar and Roger Maris—enough to have had the Commissioner blowing the whistle as hard as he could, had he been able to find one. But the incumbent, Ford C. Frick, wasn't going to tangle with Del Webb; not in his right mind, he wasn't. Instead, the Commissioner got even in 1961 when Roger Maris cracked his sixty-one homers to break Babe Ruth's record. Frick insisted that an asterisk accompany Maris' name in the record book, indicating he had 162 games in which to do it compared to the 154 in the 1927 schedule.

Meanwhile, the Athletics weren't going to say no to any Yankee suggestions. One-third of their entire home attendance could be traced to visits featuring Mickey Mantle in those years. And they might even get lucky with a player the Yankees might be palming off on them.

Maris was to become a Yankee after Stengel had enjoyed his last World Series triumph. He did play for the Old Man in the 1960 World Series that the Pirates won on Bill Mazeroski's homer off Ralph Terry in the ninth inning of the seventh game, but it was under Ralph Houk that he was to hit his sixty-one home runs in 1961.

Maris had come up through the Cleveland organization, making it to the Indians in 1957. His rookie year, he was more impressive as an outfielder than as a hitter. When an opportunity developed in 1958 for a deal with the A's for Vic Power, a slick first baseman whom the Yankees had rejected as their first black player in favor of Elston Howard, the Indians considered him expendable.

Maris adjusted to big-league pitching in Kansas City, hitting twenty-eight homers that year, eighteen the next. With the Yankee outfield in a state of flux, Weiss decided to gamble. Another factor was that Maris' lefthanded swing would take advantage of the Stadium's close rightfield stands. In the deal, the last big one of the hundreds negotiated by George Weiss for the Yankees, Maris and a couple of spear carriers were acquired in exchange for Don Larsen, Marv Throneberry, Hank Bauer and Norm Siebern.

The only one of those four former Yankees subsequently heard from was Bauer, who turned up as a winning World Series manager in 1966 for the Baltimore Orioles.

As hoped, Maris' big swing was ideal for the short shot into the rightfield stands. He cracked thirty-nine homers in his first year as a Yankee, one less than Mantle, and was voted his first of two successive MVP awards. He didn't win it by much. Mantle got more first-place votes, 10 to 8, but Maris had more backing in the other spots on the ballot. He won, 225 points to 222, with Brooks Robinson of Baltimore third.

Now for the sixty-one homers Roger Maris hit in 1961—go look in the record book, and only there. The notorious asterisk ordered by Ford Frick, once a ghostwriter for Babe Ruth, is gone. But the then Commissioner's hand is still in there with a home-run breakdown separating 154-game seasons from 162-game seasons, to wit:

American League (162-game season)—61, Roger E. Maris, New
    York, 161 games, 1961.

American League (154-game season)—60, George H. Ruth, New York, 151 games, 1927.

National League (154-game season)—56, Lewis R. Wilson, Chicago, 155 games, 1930.

National League (162-game season)—52, Willie H. Mays, San Francisco, 157 games, 1965 and George A. Foster, Cin., 158 games, 1977.

The asterisk was sprung on Maris and the Yankees when it became evident that he had a better-than-even shot at breaking the Babe's record. Egged on possibly by the Babe's voluble and highly visible widow, a constant attendant at Stadium games in a front-row box, Frick proclaimed that no one could break Ruth's record unless it was done in 154 games. The Yankees, foolishly, said nothing. One phone call would have sent the Commissioner scurrying back to his stamp collection. If not Dan Topping, then certainly Del Webb had handled men a lot tougher than the Commissioner of Baseball, whose salary they helped pay.

And so the Yankees said nothing, but Maris did.

Maris wanted to know what the hell was going on. He didn't get a homer in the first eleven games that season. So did Frick mean the first 154 games, the last 154 games, the middle 154 games or what? And how about those thousands of other baseball records—pitching, fielding, base-stealing? Were they going to have asterisks, too?

Maris also didn't like the silence from his employers.

Many years later, long after Webb and Topping had gone to their reward, a one-time Yankee official explained that the front office never meant any harm to Maris.

"Really," the one-time Yankee man said, "we actually thought the asterisk was good for the game and the attendance. It kept things stirred up."

It kept Maris stirred up, too. And when the "bandwagon" sportswriters showed up—those who covered the Yankees while scrutinizing every aspect of Maris' life—he just couldn't deal with the situation. He found himself answering the same questions dozens of times a day. He knew the New York sportswriters assigned regularly to the Yankees, but why were a bunch of whisperers asking questions like "What would you rather do, break Babe Ruth's record or hit .300?" Maris, who had never hit .300 and never would, answered that question with one of his own.

"What," he asked, "would you rather do?"

The questioner, who wouldn't know what end of a bat to pick up, answered, "Hit .300."

"Well," responded Maris, "it takes all kinds."

Then there were those hotshot sportswriters who resented Maris'
seeming indifference to their questions which they translated into a
disregard for their eminence in the world of daily letters. They berated
Maris in print as a vain, pompous ass and uncooperative. They wanted
to know who the hell he thought he was just because he could hit a
baseball a little harder than anyone else.

One afternoon Ralph Houk was sitting in his office off to one side of
the Yankee clubhouse. He had been an infantry Ranger in World War
II, rising from enlisted man to major. He was tough and thought he had
seen everything. He hadn't. Roger Maris came in, shut the door, sat
down on the couch against the wall and burst into tears.

The New York Yankees

Roger Maris

"I can't handle this," sobbed Maris, a fellow powerful enough to be
able to punch a hole in the nearby wall. "They keep asking the same
questions. It never lets up."

"It will," Houk said with more hope than conviction.

Usually Houk was exceedingly capable of protecting his players in
their relationship with the media. Sometimes he would even pick a fight
and threaten some unfortunate writer with physical harm just to divert
his attention from a player's poor performance. But the Maris phenom-
enon was beyond him.

"Look at this," said Maris, bending to display the top of his crew cut.
"My goddam hair is coming out." He grabbed it, pulled, and sure
enough there were some blond hairs, short but obviously the real thing,
in his grasp. "Did your hair ever fall out from playing baseball?"

"No," said Houk, perhaps wondering what the departed Casey Stengel would have done, but then he grew stern. "You gotta handle this
all by yourself. Just get your hits and everything will take care of itself."

Not quite. The pressure increased. Now the TV crews had latched
on, waiting for the big moment, the sixtieth homer. The fifty-ninth had
come in Baltimore off Milt Pappas, and half-filled Memorial Stadium
rocked as though the Orioles were clinching the pennant that evening
instead of the Yankees. He certainly had the fans rooting for him even
if his own management, as he claimed, was indifferent.

Now the Yankees were back in the Stadium for the final week of the
season. Everyone was relaxed; the pennant had been clinched. Everyone except Maris.

But on Tuesday he shook off some of the tension with a sharp single
up the middle off Jack Fisher of the Orioles in the first inning. Then,
on a 2-2 count, he slammed his sixtieth homer into the upper rightfield
seats.

Wednesday was freaky. You'd think the fans would be storming the
gates to see Maris break Ruth's record, but only about 7,500 showed.
Maybe they knew something. Neither Maris nor Mantle was in the
lineup. Maris had asked for a rest; Mantle had a virus.

The swing and trajectory of Roger Maris's historic home run in 1961, followed by a locker-room inquisition. Sal Durante, who caught the ball, stands beside Maris.

Maris returned against the Red Sox, but Bill Monbouquette blanked him. Now it was Saturday afternoon. Again, surprisingly, there were only about 19,000 customers. Maris was held to a single by Don Schwall.

For the season's final game on Sunday only 23,154 gathered in the famous ballpark that then had more than 60,000 seats. But many crowded into the rightfield stands, hoping to catch the ball if Maris hit his sixty-first homer there. Out in California a restaurateur was offering $5,000 for the ball. He paid it to Sal Durante, a nineteen-year-old truck mechanic who outscrambled everyone else when Maris' fourth-inning homer off young Tracy Stallard landed in the lower rightfield stands.

The historic homer won the game, put Maris' name in the record book and made a sort of celebrity of Stallard, who was to join the Mets later. During his seven years in the majors Stallard had a career 30-57 record. But in addition to being the only pitcher ever to serve a sixty-first homer to anybody in the major leagues, he gained a bit of notoriety as a radio guest of Howard Cosell when he was unaware that the microphone was alive.

"What'll it be tonight, Howard?" he said cheerfully. "Do you bullshit me or do I bullshit you?"

Roger Maris hit one more homer that year—in the ninth inning of the third World Series game against Bob Purkey of the Reds, for a 3–2 victory. Fred Hutchinson, the Reds' manager, called that homer "the most damaging blow of the Series" as the Yankees went on to win it in five games.

1961 was not a good year for Babe Ruth. Just as Maris had surpassed the Babe's season record for homers, Whitey Ford knocked him out of the World Series record book. As a Red Sox pitcher, the Babe once had pitched twenty-nine and two-thirds consecutive scoreless Series innings. But, including two shutouts of the Pirates in 1960, Ford extended his streak to thirty-two consecutive scoreless innings. The little left-hander had a 25-4 record during the season, his first 20-victory year, and won the Cy Young Award.

Ralph Houk, meanwhile, became only the third rookie manager to win the World Series; the others were Bucky Harris with the 1924 Senators and Eddie Dyer with the 1946 Cardinals.

With his big cigar and hearty laugh, Ralph Houk had been groomed to succeed Casey Stengel by the Yankee front office and by Stengel himself. As a kid catcher out of Kansas, he had entered the Yankee organization before World War II and got as high as Class A before entering the army. He earned a battlefield commission as a Bastogne hero. Discharged as a major, he resumed his baseball career, but like several other catchers he found his way blocked by the chunky figure of Yogi Berra.

UPI

Ralph Houk's familiar pose as the 1966 Yankees finished an unfamiliar last

Ford breaks Ruth's scoreless-inning Series streak UPI Bob Turley

Yogi Berra and Elston Howard The New York Yankees

Houk, who never hit a homer with the Yankees, did not rate as highly as the others who couldn't get past Yogi—people like Gus Niarhos, Charlie Silvera, Lou Berberet and Clint Courtney, each traded for other talent. Houk stayed. Gradually his ability in terms of strategy and handling players impressed Stengel to the point where the Old Man made him a coach in 1953.

Then in 1955 the Yankees needed a manager for their Denver farm. Houk was chosen. He proved to be eminently successful, with a Junior World Series victory thrown in.

Houk's teams also were spirited, unlike their haughty big brothers. They fought, cursed and chewed tobacco along with their mentor. If things were dull, Houk didn't have to call for volunteers to pick a fight with the opposition to shake things up. There were always two or three players making the suggestion on their own. Houk once sent Tom Lasorda, later the Dodgers' manager but then a Denver pitcher, to pick a fight with the opposition's third baseman. Lasorda did the job so well that both teams became embroiled.

Houk returned to the Yankees as a coach in 1958 at the suggestion of the owners, who felt that Stengel's regime was drawing to an end. The previous year the Yankees had lost the World Series to the Milwaukee Braves in seven games. Lew Burdette's three victories (twenty-four consecutive shutout innings) for the Braves was a reminder that he had originally been in the Yankee organization. He was at spring training in 1951 at Phoenix, in Mantle's rookie year, but he was dealt to the Braves for Johnny Sain, who helped win a couple of pennants and stayed for a long time as the Yankees' pitching coach.

Burdette wouldn't have pitched the final Series game except that Hall of Fame lefthander Warren Spahn had the flu. With only two days rest, the suspected spitballer hurled his second shutout, the first time since 1920 that a pitcher threw three complete-game victories in the Series.

The following year the Yankees won the Series rematch from the Braves after losing the first three games. Hank Bauer had ten hits, including four homers, and Bob Turley, the Cy Young winner that year, won the fifth game, saved the sixth and won the seventh after relieving Don Larsen in the third inning.

That proved to be the last World Series that Stengel's teams won, although he probably would have won in 1960 against Pittsburgh if a bad-hop grounder hadn't hit Tony Kubek in the throat, helping the Pirates to a five-run eighth inning that canceled the Yankees' 7–4 lead in the final game. The Yankees tied it in the ninth, but Mazeroski's homer off Ralph Terry sailed over Yogi Berra's head in left and Stengel was gone.

After his World Series victory in 1961 as a rookie manager, Houk guided the Yankees to another Series triumph in 1962 over the San

Francisco Giants in seven games. With the tying run on third base and the winning run on second in the ninth inning, Willie McCovey drilled a line drive directly at Bobby Richardson, and Ralph Terry had a 1–0 victory. That also was Mantle's third MVP year—.321, 30 homers and 89 runs batted in during only 123 games.

Houk now was the first manager to win the World Series in each of his first two seasons. But in 1963 his spell ended when the Dodgers, notably Sandy Koufax, swept the Yankees in four. That year Elston Howard was the American League's MVP—.287, 28 homers, 85 runs batted in.

Instead of remaining in the dugout where he belonged, Houk moved into the front office as general manager in 1964, with Yogi Berra taking over as manager. Somehow the Yankees won the pennant by one game but lost the Series to the Cardinals in seven. Mantle hit three homers to complete his Series record total of eighteen—three more than the Babe, six more than Yogi.

But that Yankee loss set all kinds of things in motion, particularly Johnny Keane, the Cardinal manager.

Keane had been given to understand he was through in St. Louis, but how do you fire a World Series winner? You don't. You shake his hand enthusiastically and talk about more money. Keane, however, already had talked with Houk about succeeding Yogi as the Yankees' manager. Yogi was bounced and eventually wound up with the Mets under Casey Stengel, then moved to the role of a World Series manager in 1973 with that club before rejoining the Yankees in 1976 as a coach.

Keane's tenure with the Yankees was a disaster. He was in a different city and a different league. He had to adjust to different media conditions. He finished sixth. And in 1965 Ralph Houk had to come out from behind his desk to take charge in the dugout. Keane was not only discharged; he was ill with a bad heart and was to die shortly.

Houk watched the club finish tenth, the worst finish in Yankee history. Then he held the reins through 1973 before he moved to Detroit, where he tacked a final five years onto his managerial career.

During the disastrous 1965 season, the Yankees had a Mickey Mantle Day; they also retired his "7" in 1969 ceremonies. Already retired, of course, were the Babe's "3," Lou Gehrig's "4" and Joe DiMaggio's "5"—the rights of heritage that the Yankees have been famous for in projecting their "family" atmosphere.

Berra and Howard are dugout fixtures as coaches. Phil Rizzuto is still a cheerleader in the radio booth, his "Holy cow" as commonplace as Mel Allen's "How about that?" when he was the Yankees' voice. And at Old-Timers Days now, Allen gets a bigger hand than anybody except DiMaggio and Mantle—how about that?

Of all the Yankee royalty, only Roger Maris had to adopt another baseball family. He was traded to the Cardinals after the 1966 season for a journeyman infielder. Maris wanted to leave the Yankees, who were relieved to be rid of his $75,000 salary. He hit only eight homers in 1965, only thirteen the next year. He had damaged ribs and a damaged hand. Some ballplayers can look good and get sympathy nursing a hangnail; Roger Maris couldn't.

CBS gave Mike Burke, the new president, and Houk the go-ahead to deal Maris—but only to the National League, where he wouldn't have a chance to haunt them. It sounds peculiar, getting approval from a network to deal a ballplayer, but many teams were on the threshold of a new era of conglomerate ownership and the Yankees were among the first.

The people at CBS, who bought the Yankees from Dan Topping and Del Webb after 1964, would probably have failed to recognize Maris if they bumped into him in the hallway. They didn't know too much about the Yankees or about baseball, either, except that there was a lot about them in the papers most of the time.

Like a number of other Top 500 corporations, CBS was into an expansion era, going conglomerate with such subsidiaries as publishing houses and toy companies. Why not a ball club? The network had close

Whitey Ford officiates, with Joe DiMaggio in the background, at the retirement of Mickey Mantle's No. 7 uniform; clubhouse man Pete Sheehy later puts it in mothballs

The New York Yankees

to $100 million sitting around waiting for an attractive investment. They bought the Yankees for $14.4 million and sold it ten years later for $10 million. Some investment.

If the Yankees had been a CBS situation comedy, the network bosses would have ordered it canceled after the third installment.

Roger Maris, meanwhile, left this atmosphere of big business for another, dominated by the Busch brewery. But in St. Louis he finally found peace. He played in two World Series outfields alongside Lou Brock and Curt Flood as the Cardinals beat the Red Sox in 1967 but lost to the Tigers in 1968. Now he had two more World Series rings to go along with five as a Yankee.

For special occasions, it's invariably the Redbirds' jewelry he selects. That's because he was something special with the Cardinals and their fans.

No longer did Roger hear the boos, both home and away, questioning his assorted ailments. No longer was there a Mickey Mantle for the crowd to call for with "We want Mantle"—the man who had hit seven fewer homers than he that memorable 1961 season.

"They were really rooting for Mantle to break the record that year, not me," Maris said a decade later. "Not just the fans, but the ball club itself. How could I have any respect for them? I could only respect what respected me. I was an outsider to them."

But the "outsider" appealed to Gussie Busch, baron of the vast Budweiser beer empire. Busch liked the way he played and what he did for the club. And when Maris was done, Busch juggled his empire's Florida territory to give him a lucrative beer distributorship. And that's where Roger Maris disappeared after his playing days. Occasionally there would be a story when someone bumped into him in Gainesville or Jacksonville.

No, he hadn't heard from the Yankees. Why would he?

Would he be going to their Old-Timers gathering that summer? No, why should he?

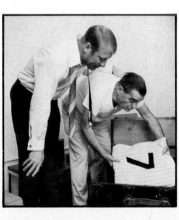

His attitude was straightforward, direct. As always. "Baseball was great," he often said, "and I loved playing. But it's over. I'm a business-man now. I have my family. And I have other interests."

Yankee officials would whisper, "He turned it down again. Guess he'll never come to an Old-Timers game."

But they turned out to be wrong. He did come. No, there had been no reason for a change of heart. Or had there?

"I have six children," said Maris a little thinly. "People talk. They hear things."

In the spring of 1978 they heard that their father had been invited to the Yankees' Opening Day ceremonies. That was a switch. Usually it was the Old-Timers Day invitation that he ignored. It was something special, thought up by George Steinbrenner, the dynamic and mercurial chief partner of the group that had bought the club in 1973 from CBS.

"I'm going," said Maris in a sudden snap judgment, and the family applauded. "Mickey'll be there too. He was sick last winter."

Mickey Mantle was there, in an open-throated sports shirt. Roger Maris was dressed more formally. He looked exactly like a successful beer distributor in a double-breasted suit that covered the fifty pounds he had picked up in a decade behind a desk. Mickey's hair was longer than when he was swinging that big bat, but Maris' privet-hedge crew cut still looked as though a fighter plane could land on it.

Billy Martin, a winning World Series manager, gazed at Maris and asked, "Where'd you park your truck?"

The voice on the public-address system was that of Mel Allen, who had no peer at introductions. His re-creation of homer sixty-one gradually awakened the crowd to the fact that Maris had come back. His appearance had not been advertised, and suddenly Mel Allen shouted, "There he is, Roger Maris!"

There he stood, alongside Mickey Mantle, the sluggers of 115 homers on a championship team seventeen years earlier. The team had hit 240 homers, a record that grows more impressive each year. Their two-man total is superior to that of any other one-two punch in the history of baseball, better than Ruth and Gehrig, better than Kiner and Greenberg, better than Foxx and Simmons, better than any other tandem.

Slowly, a maintenance cart took the pair out to the centerfield flag-pole for the traditional raising of the American flag and the World Series banner while opera star Robert Merrill sang The National Anthem. Behind them the plaques honoring Yankee greats could be seen with a quick glance to the left. In the old Yankee Stadium, when Mantle and Maris roamed the outfield, the bronze plaques were on stone markers on the field itself in front of the centerfield wall. And the other plaques were up on the wall.

Now there was a new "memorial park," off the field, where the fans could come and look.

Babe Ruth, Lou Gehrig, Miller Huggins—their monuments were there. And the plaques were there honoring Jake Ruppert, Ed Barrow, Joe DiMaggio, Joe McCarthy, Casey Stengel, Mickey Mantle and even Pope Paul VI, who had celebrated a Mass for peace in 1965 at Yankee Stadium on his American visit.

But there was nothing out there to remind people that Roger Maris had sixty-one home runs in the 1961 season.

It had taken an invitation from a new owner, George Steinbrenner, to appear in a new ball-park built for the Yankees by the City of New York to persuade Roger Maris to return to Yankee Stadium to honor

At last, Roger Maris returns to bask in applause; that's Mantle clapping

a new championship team. And now he was basking in the applause that honored him. Nearby, the man who had dominated his era, Mickey Mantle, was applauding, too. Roger Maris was a member of the Yankee family again. He had been away too long. Better get his measurements for a set of pin stripes for Old-Timers Day.

Or was he a member of the Yankee family?

"His number," an observer mentioned that day, "is still being worn."

"Whose number?"

"Maris' number."

"What about it?"

"Well, he used to be number 9, didn't he? All those other guys' numbers are retired—Ruth, Gehrig, Mantle, Ford, Berra, Dickey, even Stengel. But did you notice that Graig Nettles is wearing Roger Maris' number?"

Isn't there a bit of unfinished business?

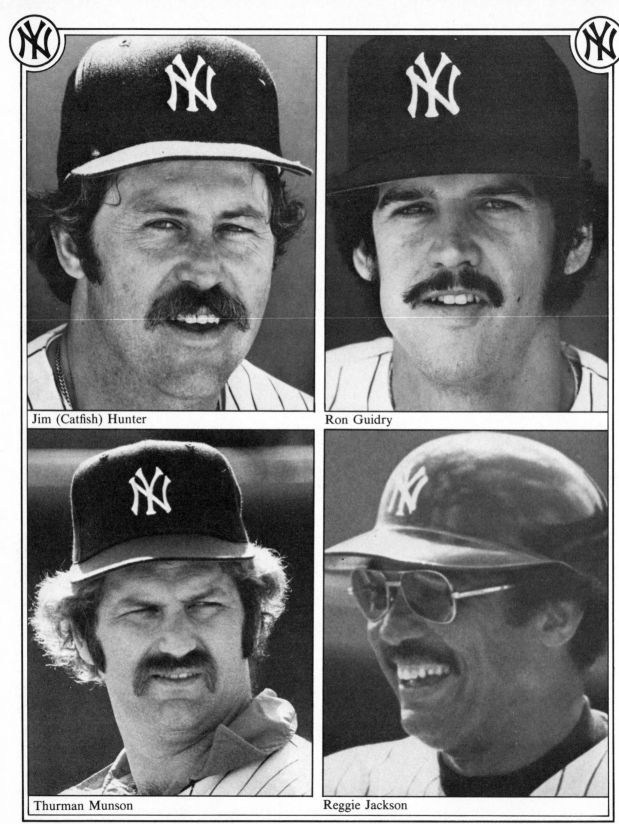

Jim (Catfish) Hunter

Ron Guidry

Thurman Munson

Reggie Jackson

The New York Yankees

The Money Players
by Murray Chass

"REGGIE! REGGIE! REGGIE!"

The tumultuous throng of 10,000 pushed toward the platform in front of City Hall and chanted their hero's name.

"Reggie! Reggie! Reggie!"

They pushed harder and yelled louder.

"Reggie! Reggie! Reggie!"

Reggie Jackson was, after all, the epitome of the new Yankees, the "money" players lured to New York by the appeal of the big city and by the aggressive, free-spending manner of George Steinbrenner. And now Jackson and some of his teammates were surrounded by a tiny percentage of their zealous fans who crammed into the space in front of City Hall. Earlier an estimated two million fans had squeezed onto the sidewalks of lower Manhattan to salute their heroes during a ticker-tape parade in honor of the Yankees' second straight World Series championship.

Not since V-E Day, marking the end of World War II in 1945, had more people gathered in those streets for a celebration.

People leaned out of office windows in the concrete canyon and showered the Yankees with a torrent of confetti. Down on the street other people threw Reggie candy bars onto the flatbed truck where Jackson stood at the rear with Governor Hugh Carey of New York. Carey was running for reelection; he knew how to be in the right place at the right time. Jackson, fielding the candy better than he does baseballs at times, scooped up the bars and tossed them back into the mob of Yankee fanatics.

Riding with Jackson on the first flatbed, among others, were Ron Guidry, the pitching wizard of 1978, and Lou Piniella, the popular outfielder who always is greeted with cries of "Lou! Lou! Lou!" Among the heroes on the second truck were Bucky Dent, Rich Gossage, Chris Chambliss and Willie Randolph. Graig Nettles and Roy White had remained in California after the team defeated the Los Angeles Dodgers for the second consecutive year. Thurman Munson had gone home to Canton, Ohio, and Sparky Lyle was at home in Demarest, New Jersey. Mickey Rivers was in his hotel room in Hasbrouck Heights, New Jersey, asking a Yankee official who would pay his cabfare if he went to the celebration—typical of the team that perhaps is more famous for what happened *off* the field.

The city's salute to the Yankees was supposed to culminate in a ceremony at City Hall that would be presided over by Mel Allen, the radio voice of the old Yankees. But the enthusiastic crowd was too loud ("Reggie! Reggie! Reggie!") and too intent on pushing closer to allow the ceremony to begin. Finally, Reggie himself stepped to the microphone.

"We want to talk to you, we want to talk to you," Jackson said, speaking calmly but earnestly. "We want to talk to you, but you have to be quiet or you won't be able to hear us."

Once again, Reggie was the center of attention, the man on whom all eyes were focused, the man who held center stage and appeared so natural in the role that it seemed likely that he had been born before a standing-room-only crowd at Yankee Stadium.

Six months earlier, on April 13, 1978, many of the 44,667 fans at Yankee Stadium for the team's home opener stood and tossed flat orange projectiles onto the field. In his first time at bat there since he hit three home runs on three consecutive pitches in the last game of the 1977 World Series, he had swung his thirty-three-ounce, thirty-four and one-half-inch bat at a Wilbur Wood knuckleball and catapulted it over the centerfield fence.

For an instant, just an instant, the stadium was still, like a stop-action photograph. Click. Then the fans erupted. They had Reggie bars—chocolate and caramel 25-cent candy bars—in their hands, and they began flinging them onto the field.

The first few Reggie bars had soared into the air from somewhere behind home plate. Then the candy with the orange wrapper and the picture of the Yankees' slugger cascaded down from the stands behind home plate, from the stands behind first base and third base, from the stands in left field and right field.

When the people from Standard Brands, the manufacturer, handed out the bars before the game with the Chicago White Sox, one to each fan, they supposedly expected the candy to wind up in stomachs, not on the field. The fans, however, had other thoughts, and Reggie came through.

Reggie, of course, always comes through. As if he were Sir Laurence Olivier or Richard Burton, he performs as though his lines and actions were written in a script. If it's the last game of the World Series and a home run is to be hit, Reggie will hit it. If thousands of fans clutch candy bars eagerly waiting to toss them onto the field, Reggie will give them a reason to toss them.

Reginald Martinez Jackson's *raison d'être* was not obvious immediately when he was born in Wyncote, Pennsylvania, a Philadelphia suburb, on May 18, 1946. He was one of six children of Clara and Martinez Jackson, who separated when Reggie was four years old. They later were divorced. Reggie lived with his father, who was a tailor, in the mostly white suburb of Cheltenham, and began to blossom as a baseball and football player. It was on a football scholarship that Jackson attended Arizona State University, but it was as a baseball player that he attracted attention.

When Charles O. Finley, whose A's were then in Kansas City, selected him in the free agent draft in 1966, he left school after his sophomore year and began a professional career that was to travel through conquests and controversy and lead him to another kind of free agent draft in 1976.

On November 29, 1976, the Yankees staged a coronation at the Americana Hotel in Manhattan. Roy White, who had been a Yankee for eleven years, served as part of the coronation party. At the appointed hour White placed a Yankee baseball cap atop the Afro on Reggie Jackson's head, officially merging baseball's most dynamic figure of the '70s with baseball's most dynamic team.

White, however, served as another symbol, one neither he nor the Yankees derived any satisfaction from or cared to dwell on. Having first played for the Yankees in 1965, White had suffered without playing on a pennant-winning team longer than any other Yankee. From 1965 through 1975, the Yankees wandered aimlessly through the league, finishing in nearly every position except first. They even wound up tenth and last during the 1966 season. It was their most forgettable period since they began winning pennants in 1921.

The New York Yankees

Roy White

There was nothing glamorous about the Yankees in that barren period. No one won any home-run titles; no one won any Most Valuable Player awards. The legendary Yankees—Babe Ruth, Joe DiMaggio and Mickey Mantle—were replaced by Horace Clarke, Jerry Kenney and Frank Tepedino. Bobby Murcer was supposed to replace Mantle, but that turned out to be a publicity man's fantasy.

Like Mantle, Murcer came from Oklahoma, and like Mantle, he began his career as a shortstop, then became a centerfielder. Murcer also played third base briefly, only long enough to make three wild throws in a game in Seattle, then, when another grounder was hit to him, hear one fan sitting in the stands behind third yell, "Look out, he's got it again!"

The Yankees, however, soon learned that they could not boast, "Look out, we've got another Mantle."

Murcer was a solid hitter but not a spectacular hitter who could power a team to a succession of pennants—not even when he had help from a young catcher named Thurman Munson, who joined the Yankees in 1969, or from Ron Blomberg, a Georgia gourmand who was the popular Jewish player for whom the Yankees long had yearned, or from Mel Stottlemyre, a fine pitcher who might have been a perennial twenty-game winner in another Yankee era.

As a rookie in 1964, Stottlemyre was a blood transfusion for the Yankees, winning nine games in the final two months of the season and starting three games in what was to be the team's last World Series for twelve years. He later was to win twenty or more games three times, but he was not to last long enough to experience the Yankees' new pennant-winning era. When a torn shoulder muscle ended his career in 1975, he was thirty-three years old.

The New York Yankees

Mel Stottlemyre

George Steinbrenner knew only a handful of people at this Manhattan cocktail party, but it was as if he were a one-man receiving line.

"George? George Steinbrenner?" one man asked tentatively. "I thought it was you. I just want to meet you and shake your hand. Your team did so much for New York this year. I've been waiting more than ten years for this."

The Yankees had won the 1977 World Series two months earlier, but the congratulations were still pouring in. Another man approached.

"Mr. Steinbrenner," he said, "I want to thank you for one marvelous season. I've been a Yankee fan since I was ten years old."

When Steinbrenner was ten years old, he was a Cleveland Indian fan because he lived in Cleveland. But he always looked forward to the arrival of the Yankees.

"When the Yankees came to town, it was like Barnum and Bailey coming to town," he explained. "I don't mean that they were like a circus, but it was the excitement. They had these gray uniforms, but there was a blue hue to them. I'll never forget them. Watching them warm up was as exciting as watching the game. Being in Cleveland, you couldn't root for them, but you could boo them in awe."

Steinbrenner began rooting for the Yankees in 1973 when he and a group of friends, mostly from Cleveland, purchased the Yankees from the Columbia Broadcasting System for $10 million.

Several years earlier Steinbrenner had made a bid to buy the Indians but didn't get them. Then one day during the 1972 season Steinbrenner was chatting with Gabe Paul at Municipal Stadium in Cleveland. Paul was vice president and general manager of the Indians, and Steinbrenner, who was at the ballpark that day on other business, asked him if he knew of any major league clubs that might be for sale. No, said Paul, but not long afterward the Yankees were placed on the market.

Paul himself met twice with Michael Burke, the Yankee president, before he brought Burke together with Steinbrenner at the Carlyle Hotel in New York for a breakfast meeting. Two months later Steinbrenner and Burke met with William S. Paley, chairman of the board at CBS, and the transaction was concluded.

George Mitchell Steinbrenner III long had been involved in sports. The son of a collegiate champion hurdler, Steinbrenner, who was born July 4, 1930, ran the low hurdles at Williams College from 1948 to 1952 and was a halfback on the football team in his senior year. He later coached high school football and basketball in Columbus, Ohio, then spent a year each at Northwestern and Purdue as an assistant college football coach before entering the family's ship business in 1957. It wasn't long, though, before he jumped back into sports, this time as owner of the ill-fated Cleveland Pipers professional basketball team that was to cost him at least $250,000.

Despite the financial setback, Steinbrenner raised enough money to buy the family firm, Kinsman Marine Transit Company, from his father and proceeded to parlay the company's five Great Lakes ore carriers into the American Ship Building Company. Because American Ship was a large concern, doing more than $100 million in annual business when Steinbrenner became the Yankees' general partner, he said he would leave daily operation of the baseball team to others.

"I won't be active in the day-to-day operations of the club at all," he said the day the sale was announced at Yankee Stadium. "I can't spread myself so thin. I've got enough headaches with my shipping company."

There are those who insist that Steinbrenner meant that when he said it. But the excitement of owning baseball's best-known team soon enveloped the new boss. His deep involvement sometimes created awkward situations. There was, for example, the incident surrounding the acquisition of Pat Dobson, a journeyman pitcher, from the Atlanta Braves.

Attending a luncheon in Tampa, Florida, one day in June, during his rookie season as owner, Steinbrenner said to a Chamber of Commerce friend, "We've traded Mike Kekich for Pat Dobson." The friend then told a television sportscaster, "The Yankees have traded Mike Kekich for Pat Dobson." Later on, the sportscaster was doing an interview with Steinbrenner.

"Congratulations," the sportscaster said, "on getting Pat Dobson for Mike Kekich."

Steinbrenner, thinking the trade had been announced (otherwise how would the sportscaster know?), replied, "Yes, we've traded Mike Kekich for Pat Dobson. It's the shot in the arm we need. We needed a lefthanded pitcher"—Dobson was righthanded—"and we got one in Dobson."

The Yankees, to be sure, obtained Dobson the righthander, but not for Kekich. Nevertheless, the premature report upset Kekich, already

George Steinbrenner, the Yankees' principal owner

The New York Yankees

a distraught pitcher, and Ralph Houk, the longtime Yankee manager who had no use for Steinbrenner. Kekich and Houk were not to be the last player and manager whom Steinbrenner upset. There were to be many uniformed Yankees who would mutter and curse and rebel at the owner's words or actions.

Some would see Steinbrenner's words and actions as interference and harassment, others would concede that it was his team and therefore his right to do whatever he wanted. Most of the players, though, saw many of Steinbrenner's ideas as annoying and much of his behavior as disruptive.

They thought it was demoralizing that, like a fan, Steinbrenner should scream at them from the stands when they struck out. They thought it was absurd that, in the middle of a heated pennant race, he should order some of the players to wear different baseball socks because he didn't like the length of the ones they had been wearing. They thought it was ridiculous that at all times he should harass them about the length of their hair.

There was the day in spring training one year when this note appeared on the bulletin board in the clubhouse:

"Attention—All personal [*sic*] locker inspection 9:45 A.M. Tuesday March 23rd. Be neat!! G.S. III."

Then there was the young catcher up from the Yankees' minor league camp just for the day. Drinking from the water cooler in the dugout, the youngster had just caught batting practice and his hat was still backwards, the way catchers wear their caps under the straps of their masks.

Noticing the youngster, Steinbrenner walked over to him and turned the cap around.

"I like to see a player look neat," Steinbrenner explained, sitting in the dugout, master of all that he surveyed. "Maybe I'm wrong, but we'll see. I have nothing against long hair per se, but I'm trying to instill a certain sense of order and discipline in the ball club because I think discipline is important in an athlete. I want to develop pride in the players as Yankees. We're starting it in our minor league system. The Yankee system isn't what it used to be, and we've got to get it back to what it was."

Forget about hair. Forget about socks. Even forget about discipline. To Steinbrenner's credit, he restored the Yankee system to what it used to be—not a short-haired system but a winning system.

With Gabe Paul as president to provide a baseball education, Steinbrenner approved wholesale trading and spending that resulted in a pennant in his fourth year as owner and a World Series championship in his fifth. It was a more successful five-year plan than Stalin or Khrushchev ever concocted.

Along the way Steinbrenner was accused of owning "the best team money can buy," but he answered his critics by saying he merely was playing by the new rules of the game, which every team had the right to do.

Unlike some other club owners, notably Charles O. Finley of the Oakland A's and M. Donald Grant of the New York Mets, the Yankees' boss adapted quickly to the new rules. Established by an arbitrator's decision, enforced by two federal courts and implemented in the collective bargaining agreement, the new rules had created free agents. In baseball's past a free agent signified a youngster who never had signed a professional contract or an older player who had been released by one team and therefore was free to sign with any team. Under the new rules a free agent also was a player who actually had become *free* of his own volition and who placed himself in a seller's market, offering his services to the highest bidder or to the team that, in that particular player's viewpoint, made the most attractive offer.

If George Steinbrenner is to receive credit for resurrecting the Yankees, in no small part by using the new rules to his advantage, Peter Seitz must also be recognized for his role in the resuscitation.

Peter Seitz never put on a major league uniform; he never even traded a player from one uniform to another. But he did make the decisions that allowed players to take off one uniform and put on another—at their choosing. Seitz is the arbitrator who ruled on the two most famous arbitration cases in baseball history. He declared Catfish Hunter a free agent in a breach-of-contract case. He declared Andy Messersmith and Dave McNally free agents in their challenge to the renewal clause in the uniform players' contract.

Seitz actually didn't make those rulings all by himself. He was only one member of baseball's three-man grievance panel. But his vote was decisive because Marvin Miller, the executive director of the Major League Baseball Players Association, voted for the players' side, and John Gaherin, the owners' labor relations representative, voted for the owners' side.

Three days after James Augustus (Catfish) Hunter became baseball's wealthiest player a visitor from New York knocked on the door of his house in Hertford, North Carolina, a quiet community of 2,300 tucked away in the northeastern corner of the state, about seventy miles south of Norfolk, Virginia.

Helen Hunter, who had been Jimmy's childhood sweetheart and now was his wife and mother of their two young children, opened the door and said, "He's out mowing the ditches."

At 9:30 in the morning Helen Hunter's husband could have been inside, still lounging in bed, a servant bringing him his breakfast and the morning newspaper and any number of hired hands working on the farm. But Hunter, up since 7, was out mowing ditches. Fresh from drastically changing his economic status, Hunter remained as unpretentious as ever, and he would remain that way in years to come.

The case that made Catfish a millionaire was in no way related to the ensuing free-agent struggle. It was a unique situation made significant by the player who was involved.

Hunter, the Hertford farmer, spent the first ten years of his major league career pitching for the A's of Kansas City and Oakland, winning from twenty-one to twenty-five games in each of his last four seasons with them. His final season in Oakland turned out to be 1974 because of a dispute with his boss, Charles O. Finley, over the method of payment of half of his $100,000 salary.

Finley, according to the contract, was to have paid $50,000 on a deferred basis to an insurance company. But he failed to make the payment by the stipulated time. Hunter, who like many of his teammates had battled Finley in previous confrontations over money, filed a grievance, and the Seitz-Miller-Gaherin panel ruled, two to one, that Finley indeed had breached the contract.

The decision created an unprecedented situation: here was a twenty-eight-year-old star pitcher in the prime of his career, winner that season of twenty-five games and the Cy Young Award as the best pitcher in the American League, and he was free to sign with any team in the major leagues.

Twenty-three clubs sought Hunter's services. Only the San Francisco Giants declined to make an effort to entice this attractive pitcher into their uniform; representatives of the other clubs either spoke with Hunter and his lawyers by telephone or met with them in Ahoskie, another small North Carolina town about sixty miles west of Hertford.

The law firm of Cherry, Cherry and Flythe, situated on Main Street in a red-brick building that once housed one of the first banks to go under in the Depression, served as the command center for an auction that was wilder than the Sotheby Parke-Bernet galleries ever had for a Rembrandt.

"People think I demanded a lot of money," Hunter said. "I didn't. I just said I wanted security for my wife and my children when I get out of baseball. The owners went from there. They made their proposals."

Each day during the last two weeks of that December, Hunter would get into his steel-gray pickup truck and drive the one hour and fifteen minutes to his lawyers' office to listen to the offers of two or three or four general managers, depending on how many visited or telephoned that particular day.

There was no time for hunting, the pitcher's favorite winter pastime.

Nor was there time to work the peanut, corn and soybean fields that stretched out for 113 acres behind the Hunters' ten-room red brick colonial on Route 1.

Hunter's success with the A's, all those twenty-victory seasons and three consecutive World Series championships, had not changed his life style. He still lived only half a mile from his parents' home (and was on their telephone party line) and three miles from the frame house where he grew up. The youngest of eight children of Lillie and Abbott Hunter, Jimmy (as he is known to the townfolk) was born April 8, 1946, only forty days before Reggie Jackson. But unlike the man who was to be his teammate in Oakland and New York, Hunter grew up in farming country in the "land of beautiful women" (the Indian meaning of Perquimans, the county name). As a child Hunter played some form of ball whenever he could.

If it rained, he and his brother, Pete, would go into the barn and break up corncobs and bat them around with sticks. Eventually, the corncobs gave way to real baseballs and Jimmy became a pitcher for Perquimans High School. One of his teachers told him he could never earn much money playing baseball, but upon graduating in 1964 he signed with Kansas City and received a $75,000 bonus.

Clyde Kluttz, a one-time major leaguer whose highest salary as a catcher was $10,000, was the A's scout who signed Hunter, and their ensuing relationship was to play a pivotal part in Hunter's decision ten years later. Hunter was especially fond of Kluttz because the scout was one of the few who remained confident of the pitcher's potential after he had the little toe on his right foot shot off in a hunting accident in 1964. Unable to play baseball during the 1964 season, Hunter won a spot with Kansas City in 1965 and never played in the minors.

Not long after he joined the A's, Hunter received a new name. Finley wanted his expensive prospect to project a more colorful image so he labeled him Catfish—a nickname that became as much a part of him as his strong right arm.

When Peter Seitz ruled that the A's no longer owned that right arm, Finley was enraged. Commissioner Bowie Kuhn also was less than ecstatic. Not that the Commissioner had formed a mutual admiration society with the A's owner. He did not like an outsider, even if the arbitrator had been hired by baseball people, dictating the destiny of players. In an effort to retain some control over this unique event Kuhn told the clubs they could not begin bidding for Hunter until he said ready, get set, go. Bowie fired his starter's pistol on December 18, and, like the homesteaders of the Old West, the clubs were off and running toward Ahoskie.

Not all sent representatives to the law offices of Cherry, Cherry and Flythe in the North Carolina town. Eleven chose to bid by phone. But whether by phone, telegram or face-to-face contact, the clubs threw money at Hunter like rice at a wedding. The bidding quickly took off into a stratosphere that baseball salaries never had approached.

Not too long ago a few players had climbed above the $150,000 plateau. Dick Allen, then with the White Sox, had soared to $250,000 for the 1974 season. But the Catfish auction rocketed higher and higher. When one club offered a $2 million package, one of Hunter's lawyers said, "That figure won't even get you into the ball park."

As a North Carolina hunter, Clyde Kluttz knew what a bird dog was. He knew, too, what a bird dog was in the scouting vernacular. He bird-dogged Hunter in 1964 for the A's, and now the old scout was bird-dogging him again—this time for the Yankees.

But on Monday, December 30, the Hunter attorneys told the Yankees they were turning down their offer. Gabe Paul, the Yankees' chief negotiator, returned to New York, but before he left he instructed Kluttz to stay in Ahoskie and not leave until he had succeeded in changing Catfish's mind.

The next morning Kluttz dutifully had breakfast with his friend and fellow hunter. Then he made his fourth visit to the red-brick office building with the off-white columns on both sides of the front door. No other bidder had appeared there more than twice.

But the San Diego Padres had been the other most persistent chaser. Peter Bavasi, the youthful general manager of the Padres, had arrived in Ahoskie with brochures depicting beautiful San Diego ("It's a good place to raise your family") and a blank check from Ray Kroc, the McDonald's hamburger millionaire who owned the club. That check included an offer of two McDonald's franchises.

"When you think about the franchises," Bavasi told Hunter, "keep in mind that the worst store in the chain netted $200,000 for the owner last year."

Catfish reflected momentarily on that inducement, then responded, "I don't know anything about the hamburger business. I'm a farmer."

Bavasi also had not signed Hunter to his first professional contract a decade earlier. Nor had Bavasi ever gone hunting with him. Neither Bavasi nor Kroc's check, in the end, possessed the persuasive power that Kluttz exerted on the Yankees' behalf.

By Tuesday afternoon, December 31, Jimmy Hunter, the country boy, had decided to play baseball in the big city.

Edward Greenwald, one of the bevy of Yankee owners who also was a tax attorney, had been in his Cleveland office that was otherwise closed in anticipation of New Year's Eve. Wearing only a sweat shirt and slacks, Greenwald hurriedly bought a sports jacket at a nearby store, drove to the airport and left by private jet at about 2 o'clock.

The plane descended on a small landing strip in Suffolk, Virginia, where Hunter and his four lawyers waited with Kluttz, the bring-'em-back-alive bounty hunter. En route to New York, Greenwald wrote out in longhand a ten-page contract. The plane landed in New York at 5:30, and the group of negotiators proceeded to the Yankee offices-in-exile at the Parks Administration Building in Flushing, Queens, across from Shea Stadium (Yankee Stadium was undergoing a $100 million renovation).

But the negotiating was not over. The lawyers, each trying to get the best for his side of the bargaining table, argued back and forth, sometimes loudly.

"No way you can put that in there," one said.

"Yes, you can," countered another attorney.

Frustrated and exasperated by the endless discussions, Hunter doubted the deal would be concluded that day. He would rather have spent the previous two weeks hunting. And tonight he and his wife had planned to go to Elizabeth City, North Carolina, with friends for New Year's Eve dinner.

New Yorkers, meanwhile, were preparing for their own New Year's Eve celebration. But several newsmen were missing the parties or shows they had planned to attend that evening because the Yankees had summoned them to a news conference at 8 o'clock.

The appointed hour, however, slipped by without the principals appearing in the appointed room. They were still locked in another room working out the fine print of the contract. One or two of those details even threatened, as late as 8 o'clock, to kill the whole deal. That would have ruined a lot of New Year's Eve celebrations—in New York and in Elizabeth City.

Finally, at about 8:30, Hunter signed Greenwald's historic handwritten contract. It provided for the following payments:

**$500,000 in salary at $100,000 a year for five years.

**$250,000 in deferred salary at $50,000 a year.

**$100,000 signing bonus.

**$1,500,000 deferred bonus, to be paid at the rate of $100,000 a year for 15 years, from 1980 through 1994.

**$750,000 in life insurance, payable at the rate of $50,000 a year for 15 years.

**$50,000 in insurance for his children, Todd and Kimberly ($25,000 each).

**$200,000 in lawyers' fees.

Catfish Hunter's unique
New Year's Eve party—a
$3.35 million contract

The total value to Hunter, who also would receive a new car each year of the contract, was $3,350,000, or an average of $670,000 a year. Baseball had never seen anything like it.

Wearing a blue long-sleeved sport shirt, blue-and-black checked slacks and a blue Yankee cap, Hunter sat behind a table in front of the bright lights of the television cameras, the popping flashes of 35mm cameras and the scribbling pens and pencils of reporters who had gathered on that snowy night. But he was as unpretentious and as low-key as ever in explaining his decision.

"Clyde never lied to me then, and he never lied to me now," he said, giving credit to the old scout. "If it hadn't been for him, the Yankees would've had a little more trouble signing me. To be a Yankee is a thought in everyone's head and mine. Just walking into Yankee Stadium, chills run through you. I believe there was a higher offer, but no matter how much money is offered, if you want to be a Yankee, you don't think about it."

But in LaPorte, Indiana, Charlie Finley was not enjoying such a prosperous New Year's Eve. "It is my opinion," the Oakland owner said, "that Hunter still belongs to the A's." But Hunter, as the courts were to confirm, now belonged to the Yankees and George Steinbrenner.

George Steinbrenner has a head of perfectly obedient hair. Every strand stays in place just like its owner wants it to. His hair is symbolic of his personality. Look at the rest of the man and you see apple pie and motherhood, Knute Rockne and Vince Lombardi. The Yankees' principal owner is immaculate and patriotic (he's a Yankee Doodle Dandy, born on the Fourth of July), an authoritarian and a disciplinarian. In another time and another arena his uniformed men might have called him General Patton.

But one day Steinbrenner made a mistake that would prevent him from being a visible Yankee negotiator in Ahoskie, North Carolina.

On the opening day of the 1974 baseball season, April 5, Steinbrenner, the chairman of the American Ship Building Company, became the first company executive ever indicted on felony charges in connection with illegal corporate contributions to political campaigns.

Specifically, the charges stemmed from contributions to President Richard Nixon's reelection campaign, which placed Steinbrenner under the scrutiny of the office of the Watergate special prosecutor.

Steinbrenner pleaded not guilty to the fourteen counts of the indictment, but later in the year, on August 23, he pleaded guilty to lesser charges—one count of illegal campaign contributions and one count of aiding and abetting obstruction of an investigation. He could have been sentenced to six years in prison on these charges, but he was punished only with a $15,000 fine. The worst, however, was yet to come.

On November 27, 1974, less than a month before the Yankees began their pursuit of Hunter, Commissioner Bowie Kuhn suspended Steinbrenner for two years. Steinbrenner was just beginning to adjust to operating a major league baseball franchise, but now he had been unceremoniously banished. He was unable to exert his charm on Hunter as he would on other players in later free-agent pursuits.

Steinbrenner can be a charming man. But in his Yankee Stadium office he sometimes appears to be a modern Jekyll and Hyde.

Yankee front-office employees have two collective personalities themselves: relaxed and cheery when the boss is away, uptight and on guard when he is there. In his first few years as owner, Steinbrenner watched nearly two dozen employees leave Yankee Stadium, including general manager Lee MacPhail, vice president Bob Fishel and executive vice president Tal Smith.

"They say I'm tough to work for," Steinbrenner acknowledged. "Well, I am, but I'm not trying to win any popularity contest. I know only one way, and that is to work my butt off and demand everybody else do the same."

Steinbrenner generated genuine fear among nonuniformed Yankee personnel, but he did not terrify his players. For one thing, he generally treated them like human beings. For another, the players who had confidence in their abilities ignored or replied to Steinbrenner's bark. Sometimes they even growled at him first. Graig Nettles, for example, was having no success in negotiating a new contract during the 1976 season. So he erupted at Steinbrenner.

"The owner wants to give everybody else in the league money except his own players," the third baseman charged. "It doesn't look like he wants to give out any money to the guys who have proven they've done the job in the past. I guess he doesn't think that way."

There also was Steinbrenner's confrontation with Hunter over a television commercial. Early in his second season in pin stripes Catfish was at Yankee Stadium one morning to film a chewing-tobacco commercial. That night he pitched against the Orioles and lost, triggering a tirade from Steinbrenner about how Hunter had no business doing the commercial on a day he was pitching, how he was being paid enough money that he didn't have to do that.

Hunter is among the mildest-mannered of men. He sometimes feigns agitation when his good friend, Lou Piniella, needles him sharply and unmercifully on team bus rides to and from airports and ball parks, but he rarely becomes upset by anything that is said or that happens. This time, however, he snapped back at Steinbrenner's remarks.

"If he's going to tell us what to do and when to do it," Hunter said disdainfully, "why doesn't he pay for our rent in New York City and then we could all stay in one place and he could put a guard outside and keep us in all the time. He called the trainer and got on him. He called the pitching coach and got on him and he called the manager and got on him. He got on the clubhouse men, he got on the groundskeepers and he got on the stadium manager. Why? Because they were here. That was it. Why doesn't he call me like a man? I'd be glad to talk to him and tell him what I think like a man. I'd rather him come to me than getting on guys who didn't have anything to do with it."

Steinbrenner was around to comment on Catfish's commercial because his suspension had been lifted. Originally the suspension had been scheduled to last through November, 1976, but Commissioner Kuhn terminated the suspension on March 1, 1976, nine months early, presumably for good behavior.

When the suspension was imposed, Kuhn said Steinbrenner was "ineligible and incompetent" to have "any association whatsoever with any major league club or its personnel. . . . an essential element of a professional team sport is the public's confidence in its integrity. If the public does not believe a sport is honest, it would be impossible for the sport to succeed. Attempting to influence employees to behave dishonestly is the kind of misconduct which, if ignored by baseball, would undermine the public's confidence in our game."

One year after he read those words Steinbrenner applied for reinstatement. He originally had considered fighting the suspension in court but then decided against it. His willingness to accept his punishment apparently helped lead to an early parole. So might have his decision to switch the pivotal Yankee vote from no to yes the previous July on the owners' ballot to renew Kuhn's contract as Commissioner.

In granting Steinbrenner's application for reinstatement, Kuhn offered three reasons for his decisions:

"1. My November, 1974, decision placing Mr. Steinbrenner on the ineligible list for two years was designed to assure public confidence in the integrity of professional baseball. I think that purpose has been achieved." (There were no Black Sox type scandals, if that's what he meant.)

"2. Nearly two years have elapsed since April, 1974, when Mr. Steinbrenner voluntarily removed himself from the daily affairs of the Yankees." (In body, perhaps, but not in spirit and tape-recorded messages to the troops.)

"3. The management and financial problems of the Yankees asserted in support of Mr. Steinbrenner's reinstatement would be significantly alleviated by his reinstatement with attendant benefits to the team and Yankee fans." (But not to Yankee front-office employees.)

If Steinbrenner's suspension prevented him from participating, at least in person, in the Catfish Hunter auction, the aggressive and persuasive owner would not miss out on any other free agent chases, including the one that triggered the free agent era.

The telephone rang in Andy Messersmith's home in Corona Del Mar, California. He had been waiting eagerly to hear from Herb Osmond, his agent. Messersmith, a righthanded pitcher who usually keeps his emotions hidden, was excited about the trip he was preparing to make. He had dyed his blue baseball shoes black and packed his suitcases for the flight to the Yankees' training camp.

"Forget it," Osmond told Messersmith from Tampa, Florida. "Don't come. The deal is off."

The deal was to have made Messersmith a Yankee for at least four years. If the Catfish Hunter case set no precedent for baseball, it certainly established a pattern that the Yankees would follow in ensuing years—spending money, huge sums of money if necessary, for players they felt would help make them or keep them champions. But the Messersmith case did establish a precedent for baseball.

Actually, the Messersmith case was the Messersmith–Dave McNally case, and it had been developing for several years. It could have been the Bob Tolan case or the Sparky Lyle case, but Tolan and Lyle chose to sign contracts at the end of the seasons through which they had played unsigned.

For several years the Players Association had tried to induce the owners to alter the reserve system so that players would have some freedom of movement. Under the existing rules a player was the property of a team until it traded, sold or released him. Not unlike "until death do us part." The marriages were not always happy, but the players never had the right to file for divorce.

But eventually, after exhausting the tactics available in collective bargaining, the players saw the renewal clause in the uniform players' contract as a possible weapon.

The New York Yankees

Andy Messersmith

The clause gave a club the right to renew a player's contract, if he chose not to sign a new one, at a salary no less than 20 percent below the salary stipulated in the original contract. During the 1975 season Messersmith pitched for the Dodgers under such a renewal, and Dave McNally pitched for the Montreal Expos under the same circumstances until he left the club midway through the season, convinced that he no longer could pitch effectively.

Although the Dodgers and the Expos tried repeatedly to induce the pitchers to sign new contracts and avoid a troublesome (if only they had known how troublesome) grievance hearing, the pitchers resisted. Instead they filed their grievances, contending that the clubs could not renew their contracts again. The clubs argued that the contract clause gave them perpetual renewal rights.

Just as they had done in the Hunter grievance, Peter Seitz, Marvin Miller and John Gaherin—baseball's arbitration panel—heard the Messersmith-McNally case. Seitz again would cast the decisive vote, but the respected arbitrator acted with one significant difference this time. Before issuing his decision, Seitz let Gaherin and Miller know virtually how he intended to vote. He didn't want to decide the issue; it was too important to the basic structure of baseball to be decided by an arbitrator. He urged them to settle the dispute at the bargaining table in their negotiations for a new labor agreement. When the current agreement expired in a few weeks, the reserve system would be a pivotal point for discussion.

Gaherin, a career labor-relations expert, related Seitz's message to his employers (the owners and their elected officials) and their lawyers with the recommendation that they heed the arbitrator's suggestion. Miller, an incomparable sports labor leader, was prepared to negotiate the issue. But the owners let Gaherin and his committee negotiate only so far, then let themselves be guided by their lawyers' thinking.

There was one problem with that strategy: based on cases won and lost, baseball's lawyers would finish below the old St. Louis Browns in the standings. In this case, they had not even let their labor lawyer, Barry Rona, argue the grievance. Instead, the league attorneys, Louis Hoynes and James Garner, took command, and their thinking, particularly that of Hoynes, still prevailed when Seitz extended his invitation to them to avoid suicide. They decided to let Seitz rule against them. Then they planned to take the case to court and win there.

But the lawyers should have known their case was in jeopardy for two reasons: one, they were going up against Richard Moss, the Players Association's brilliant counsel, and two, federal courts virtually never overrule an arbitrator.

Not long after Peter Seitz's ruling, judges in the U.S. District Court and the U.S. Circuit Court of Appeals quickly upheld it. The baseball establishment suddenly found itself immersed in quicksand. Its first reaction was to fire Seitz as the impartial arbitrator. But the structure of baseball had been altered drastically. The prevailing rule was now known as "one-and-one"—a player could sign a contract for one year, then play a second year without a new contract and be free to join the team of his choice.

While the establishment now attempted to dilute this disastrous turn of events at the bargaining table, Messersmith was available; McNally chose to remain a Montana auto dealer.

By late March the Yankees thought they had negotiated a deal with Messersmith for slightly less than $1 million. George Steinbrenner even had Pete Sheehy, the team's longtime clubhouse custodian, make up two uniform shirts with the number 47, Messersmith's number with the Dodgers and the California Angels.

But when the Yankees translated a handwritten memorandum of agreement into a formal contract, Messersmith's agent, Osmond, contended they had altered the terms significantly. That killed the deal and ignited a series of charges and countercharges as well as a hearing before Commissioner Bowie Kuhn.

Andy Messersmith, however, had helped create the new free agent structure. The Yankees would mine that structure more aggressively and more wisely than any other team in baseball.

Sitting behind his desk in the manager's office of the visiting club-house at Shea Stadium, Billy Martin lodged a complaint. It was July 7, 1975, less than four weeks before the Yankees' Old-Timers game honoring their pennant-winning teams of the fifties, and Martin, the Texas Rangers' manager, had not received an invitation. Martin had been on six pennant-winning teams in that decade, and he was miffed that he had been excluded from the gathering. When his complaint was reported in *The New York Times* the next day, he received an invitation.

Returning as manager, Billy Martin jokes with Mickey Mantle on 1975 Old-Timers Day

Three weeks later Martin received another Old-Timers Day invitation. This one was delivered personally by Gabe Paul in Denver, Colorado. The invitation was to begin managing the Yankees that day. George Steinbrenner, who had been declared "ineligible and incompetent" to operate the Yankees, had during his suspension decided to fire manager Bill Virdon and replace him with Martin, who had been fired by the Rangers on July 20.

When Steinbrenner bought the Yankees, he inherited Ralph Houk as manager. How long Steinbrenner would have retained Houk is debatable, but the man known as the Major resigned the day the 1973 season ended.

Houk's disenchantment with his new boss had begun on opening day. Steinbrenner, seated in his box seat next to the Yankee dugout, scrutinized the backs of his players' heads during the National Anthem and jotted down the uniform numbers of those players whose hair he felt was too shaggy. After the game he gave Houk the piece of paper with the offending numbers and instructed him to tell those numbers to have their hair cut.

Steinbrenner's original choice to succeed Houk had been Dick Williams, who had fled from Charlie Finley after the 1973 World Series despite the A's second straight championship. The Yankees even called a news conference to announce Williams' appointment, but they had acted prematurely.

Williams was still under contract to Finley, and the irrepressible A's owner wouldn't liberate him unless the Yankees gave the A's their two most prized minor league players, Otto Velez and Scott McGregor. The Yankees balked and chose Virdon, a former outstanding centerfielder who had been fired late in his second season as manager of the Pittsburgh Pirates.

Bill Virdon

Virdon, a totally honest and candid man—traits not often found in major league managers—directed the Yankees to a surprisingly strong second-place finish in 1974 and was, in Steinbrenner's view, "one of the finest men I've met in sports as a person and a competitor." Virdon, however, did not fit the owner's image of a manager, at least not a New York manager.

"In New York," Steinbrenner explained, "athletics is more than a game. You're in the Big Apple. The game is important, but so is the showmanship involved with the game important. You have to have a blend of capable, proficient players, but you have to have another ingredient in New York and that's color."

Steinbrenner had dabbled in the theater with James Nederlander, a theater owner and producer. They had produced the show *Applause* and won a Tony award. They produced another show, *Seesaw,* and it was not a hit. Steinbrenner attributed the difference in success not to the shows themselves but to the people who appeared in them. Lauren Bacall, he believed, made *Applause* a hit; Michelle Lee was an unknown at the time and couldn't do the same for *Seesaw.*

"That always stuck in my bonnet," Steinbrenner said. "Billy Martin is something more than just a baseball manager."

Even while serving the first year of his suspension, Steinbrenner began investigating the possibility of replacing Virdon with Martin as soon as the Rangers fired the one-time Yankee second baseman. He talked to owners who previously had hired and fired Martin, and they suggested he find another candidate. Gabe Paul, the Yankee president, also cautioned Steinbrenner that the chemistry of the owner and prospective manager would mix like a gas leak and a lit match.

"Your temperaments aren't compatible," the limited Yankee partner told the general partner. "There are going to be problems."

Steinbrenner acknowledged the potential problems but decided to defy them. He sent Paul off to the mountain streams of Colorado, where Martin was fishing. In a hotel room there Martin spoke first with Birdie Tebbetts, the Yankees' superscout, unaware that Paul was in the next room; later Paul completed the arrangements.

At 7:30 Saturday morning, August 2, about seven hours before the Old-Timers game was to be played, Bill Virdon arrived at Shea Stadium, temporary home of the Yankees, cleaned out his office and thanked Pete Sheehy, the clubhouse man, for "everything you did." About three hours later Billy Martin walked into the clubhouse.

It wasn't the Yankee clubhouse at Yankee Stadium, since Yankee Stadium was being renovated, but it was the job Martin had dreamed of for many years. Casey Stengel had been a father figure to Martin, and now he was following in his father's footsteps.

During a break in the filming of a television commercial Billy Martin was talking to the six-year-old boy who was his co-star. "My grandfather," the boy remarked to Martin, "told me to be very polite and nice, or you'll kick the crap out of me."

No one ever has caught Martin beating up on six-year-old boys or girls, but early in his baseball career he was thought of as a scrappy, brawling kid, and he never did anything as he grew older to erase that image.

Born on May 16, 1928, Alfred Manuel Martin grew up fighting in West Berkeley, California. "I didn't like to fight, but I didn't have a choice," he explained. "If you walked through the park, a couple kids would come after you. When you were small, someone was always chasing your ass. I had to fight three kids once because I joined the YMCA. They thought I was getting too ritzy for them."

Martin, of course, would sooner merit a line in *The Ring* record book, street division. He shattered the jaw of Jim Brewer, an opposing pitcher, when he was still a player; he knocked out Dave Boswell, one of his own pitchers, in defense of another of his players when he was a manager, and he hit the traveling secretaries of two teams he managed. More recently, he punched a sportswriter in Reno, Nevada, and he punched a marshmallow salesman in Bloomington, Minnesota.

"You wouldn't hold up Billy Martin to your sons as an example of what kind of person you'd want them to be," one of Martin's close friends has said, "except as an example of how to win."

In his first year as a major league manager, with the Minnesota Twins in 1969, his team won a division title. He was fired after the season. He won a division title in his next job, too, with the Detroit Tigers, but then the club fired him. After moving to the Texas Rangers, he manipulated a second-place finish for a young, inexperienced team and was fired there as well.

His general malady seemed to be that he wasn't satisfied with simply running the team on the field, which he could do brilliantly. He also liked to tell the front office—the general manager, the president, the owner—how to operate that end of the business.

"He was even getting after the organist if he didn't like the tunes," remarked Brad Corbett, who fired him at Texas but who has grown to like him so much personally that he calls him a "delightful rogue."

In summing up Martin's mercurial managerial career, baseball people would say that he achieved success in his first year on a particular job, then encountered trouble after that. In his first full year with the Yankees, 1976, he indeed enjoyed success because the Yankees scampered away from the rest of the teams in the Eastern Division by ten and a half games, then won the pennant in the playoffs with the Kansas City Royals—but not easily.

Just when the Yankees seemed to be on the brink of winning the decisive fifth game, George Brett, the Royals' third baseman, hit a three-run homer in the top of the eighth inning for a 6–6 tie. This was the Yankees' first year back in Yankee Stadium after the city's $100 million renovation, and there had been no more stunning or tense moment.

Chris Chambliss, however, removed that tension by creating an even more stunning moment. The quiet first baseman, who had been welcomed with something less than civility by his new teammates when he arrived from Cleveland in a 1974 trade, swung at Mark Littell's first pitch in the last half of the ninth inning and lofted it into the rightfield stands, making the Yankees league champions for the first time since 1964.

Now that they had returned to the October arena that once had been their second home, the Yankees next sought to win their 100th World Series game, not to mention their 101st, 102nd and 103rd.

But the Cincinnati Reds, who had won the Series in a stirring seven-game confrontation with the Red Sox the year before, embarrassed the Yankees by breezing to four straight victories and reducing a humiliated Billy Martin to tears. Martin, the tough-acting and tougher-talking street kid, wept in his office after the final game and wanted the world to forget, at least for the moment, that he was even there.

George Steinbrenner was humiliated, too, but he also was determined now to build a team that no one could beat in the World Series, let alone sweep in four games.

Under Steinbrenner and Gabe Paul, the Yankees already had transformed the team's personnel so that it bore virtually no resemblance to the impersonators who represented the Yankees the previous decade. Of the twenty-five players on the World Series roster, only four had come up through the farm system; only two of that group plus two others had played for the Yankees before the Steinbrenner purchase.

The trade the Yankees made for Chambliss and righthander Dick Tidrow early in the 1974 season typified the deals Paul made. Paul sent to the Indians, his old team, four pitchers—Fritz Peterson, Steve Kline, Fred Beene and Tom Buskey. When the other Yankee players learned of the trade after a Friday night game with Texas, they exploded in a tirade against the front office, accusing Steinbrenner and Paul of wrecking the team.

"That was the start of everything," Paul would recall later, after the Yankees had won three consecutive pennants and two World Series. "It broke up the country club. There was great camaraderie on those losing ball clubs."

Never satisfied, Paul constantly shuffled players, sending one or two here, grabbing two or three there. On the night of June 15, 1976, in the

Watching his 1976 pennant-winning homer, Chris Chambliss leaps for joy   The New York Yankees

last hours before the trading deadline, the Yankees made two deals—a ten-player swap with the Orioles, which brought Ken Holtzman among others to New York, and a cash transaction with the A's that was supposed to make Vida Blue a Yankee for $1.5 million.

The Yankees went so far as to print blue-ink inserts for their press guide detailing Blue's career, but the inserts were to be useless, except perhaps as collector's items. Commissioner Bowie Kuhn, placing himself across the battlefront from Steinbrenner again, voided the Blue purchase, ruling that the sale of a player for that much money with no other players involved was not in the best interests of baseball. Kuhn also canceled Finley's sale of outfielder Joe Rudi and relief pitcher Rollie Fingers to the Red Sox for $1 million each.

Finley fought Kuhn's ruling in court, and the Yankees threatened to fight it. "George Steinbrenner has tremendous attorneys, and he'll go after him," Billy Martin pronounced, sounding not unlike the child who boasts, "My father can beat up your father."

Steinbrenner, however, had his attorneys keep their briefs in their attaché cases. Instead of fighting the Commissioner, he tacitly accepted the decision. This very likely was Steinbrenner's first step in what evolved as his desire to become a powerful figure, perhaps the next Walter O'Malley, among the baseball owners. If he constantly battled Kuhn, he would be regarded by the other owners as a troublemaker, like Finley, and would never gain their respect. Or their votes.

About twenty-four hours after the Yankees and the Orioles exchanged ten players, members of both teams mingled in the lobby of the Executive House Hotel in Chicago. The Yankees had just arrived from Minnesota, the Orioles hadn't left for Texas and you couldn't tell the players and their teams even with a scorecard because they weren't wearing their uniforms.

Reggie Jackson, a tie hanging loosely from his neck over an open-collared shirt, still belonged to the Orioles. Finley had traded him just before the start of the season because, like several other Oakland players, Jackson planned to become a free agent at the end of the season under the new rules. But Jackson didn't become an Oriole immediately. The Orioles wouldn't give him the nearly $3 million contract he wanted, and he sat out a month, playing instead with his land-investment and automobile businesses.

Early in the morning of June 17, however, Jackson was with the Orioles as they joked about the mammoth trade with the Yankees and the number of gold bricks George Steinbrenner was paying for Vida Blue, Jackson's former teammate in Oakland.

"I'm not traded, but I'm not signed," Jackson told a reporter traveling with the Yankees. "Tell the man to save some money. I'll be there next year."

That remark was prophetic. His next was ironic. "Hey, Thurman," he called to Thurman Munson, the Yankee captain and catcher, "don't be too nasty, now. We might be teammates next year."

They would be, as it developed, in less than six months. But at the time Munson was on his way to becoming the first Yankee to win the Most Valuable Player award since Roger Maris, who earned it twice, Mickey Mantle and Elston Howard had produced four straight MVP awards from 1960 through 1963.

Munson was an unusually constructed baseball player from Canton, Ohio. His teammates referred to him affectionately as "squatty body," and others decided he was a munchkin because of his five-foot-eleven, 195-pound-frame. Others called him grouchy or grumpy.

One of the Yankees' few farm system products, Munson was the latest in a long line of outstanding Yankee catchers. Among baseball's best contact hitters, he also was a smart baserunner and a good defensive catcher—as long as he wasn't throwing to second base for an out, when the ball looked like a banana, curving as it neared the base and heading in the general direction of right centerfield.

In his eighth season Munson sparked the Yankees to their 1976 pennant along with Mickey Rivers, the fleet centerfielder who had arrived that year with righthander Ed Figueroa in a trade with the California Angels for outfielder Bobby Bonds.

Munson also played a significant role in the off-season, much to his eventual dismay. Opening their vault wide, the Yankees attacked the first free agent class with visions of a World Series championship and signed Don Gullett, a fragile lefthander who had just beaten them in the opener of the 1976 Series. The price on Gullett, a quiet Kentucky farmboy whom Steinbrenner later described as Jack Armstrong, the All-American boy, was $2,096,000, for six years.

That night, November 18, Steinbrenner had dinner with Munson. The owner was excited at the prospect of putting Jackson's dynamic bat and charismatic personality into Yankee Stadium, and he wanted to solicit Munson's views on how the players would accept the outfielder's outspoken nature.

"Go get the big man," Munson said. "He's the only guy in baseball who can carry a club for a month. And the hell with what you hear. He hustles every minute on the field."

Steinbrenner began hustling. He soon hosted Jackson in New York, turning his charm up to maximum. They had breakfast at the Carlyle Hotel and lunch at "21," then strolled around the midtown streets for a while before talking at Steinbrenner's apartment.

Two days later the owner flew to Chicago, where Jackson was holding final negotiations with the Montreal Expos, the Padres and the Orioles. Representatives of those other clubs conferred with Jackson,

Lou Piniella

Sparky Lyle

The home-run swing of Graig Nettles

The New York Yankees

his agent and his lawyer, but Steinbrenner met alone with the slugger for an hour and a half. After the meeting Steinbrenner left for Culver, Indiana, where he was supposed to have Thanksgiving dinner the next day. His son Henry was a student at Culver Military Academy, and he was a trustee. That same night, however, fearing that one of those other teams might gain an edge (the Expos, their owner said, had offered "a king's ransom"), Steinbrenner returned to Chicago and had breakfast with Jackson on Thanksgiving morning. By that time Jackson's advisers knew he had decided to play in New York, where, he once said, they would name a candy bar after him.

Four days later, on November 19, the Yankees staged the coronation at the Americana Hotel. Only the throne was missing.

"For a day or so after the draft," Jackson explained to the assembled throng of newsmen, "I didn't think I would play for the Yankees. But then Steinbrenner took it on his own to hunt me down. He's like me. He's a little crazy, and he's a hustler. It was like trying to hustle a girl in a bar. Some clubs offered several hundred thousand dollars more, possibly seven figures more, but the reason I'm a Yankee is that George Steinbrenner outhustled everybody else."

The Yankees, not wanting anyone to know just how much they had committed themselves to Jackson for the next five years, leaked word that he would receive about $2 million. Unlike other teams that immediately reported their agreements with free agents, as required, to the league offices, the Yankees belatedly informed the American League office of the Jackson contract. Even then, they didn't include all the terms. Jackson would receive $332,000 a year for five years ($132,000 of it deferred), a $400,000 bonus and $40,000 a year for fifteen years for "public relations" duties—a $2,660,000 total. He also obtained a $250,000 loan at a low 6 percent interest rate, and the Yankees paid his lawyer's and agent's fees.

The Yankees spent the winter denying that Jackson would have difficulty with his new teammates, particularly Munson. But difficulty had already developed. The previous March, in spring training, Munson had surrendered his opportunity to be a free agent at the end of the 1976 season by signing a four-year contract. Omitted from the document but promised verbally by Steinbrenner, according to Munson, was the stipulation that except for Catfish Hunter no one would be paid a higher salary than the catcher. That's why, when Jackson signed with the Yankees, Munson was delighted; he believed it meant more money for him. Then a winter-long dispute erupted as the owner denied having made such a promise.

On January 6, 1977, Munson signed another contract that called for additional payments and added two years to his existing contract. But he was still unhappy. He contended the Yankees neglected to include

Jackson's deferred salary of $132,000 a year when they computed his own new contract. Apparently he knew this at the time of the contract but signed it anyway, figuring he would spring his "new-found" knowledge on the Yankees at an appropriate time. It wasn't until early in the 1978 season that the catcher and the front office settled their dispute, agreeing on a package that would make Munson's income equal to Jackson's.

But the long contract battle diluted Munson's desire to continue as the Yankees' catcher. He had been saying for several months that he wanted to be traded to Cleveland so he could be close to his home in Canton, Ohio. Also, by then he had experienced Reggie Jackson up close and didn't like what he saw or heard.

When Reggie Jackson arrived in the Yankees' training camp at Fort Lauderdale, Florida, on March 1, 1977, he knew exactly what to expect. He knew which players in the clubhouse would support him, and he knew which players would resent him. Jackson was that way, always sizing up his friends and his foes; generally, if you weren't a friend, he figured you were a foe.

As it developed, he wound up having only one friend on the team—Francis Xavier Healy, a sensitive, perceptive, diplomatic reserve catcher who later would serve as the Henry Kissinger of the Yankee clubhouse. Much of the turmoil in which Jackson was about to become embroiled would result from the instigation of others, but he committed his share of blunders that understandably antagonized his co-workers.

"I think Reggie Jackson on your ball club is a part of a show of force," he said upon arriving in the Yankee camp. "It's a show of power. I help to intimidate the opposition, just because I'm here. That's part of my role."

When he played in Oakland, where he was the league's Most Valuable Player in 1973, his teammates would listen to such pronouncements, chuckle to themselves and forget what they'd heard. That, they said, was Reggie. They knew Reggie because they had grown up with him in the A's organization. In other places, though, he was considered an arrogant interloper. Some of the Yankees figured they had won their division by ten and a half games—why did they need him? But his new teammates, perhaps to their discredit, could not ignore him.

At times, of course, he was difficult to ignore. He would sit in an aisle seat on the team bus, take out his hefty roll of bills and count them. One day early in the 1977 season he stood outside the Sheraton Royal Hotel in Kansas City talking with three reporters. As they talked, he nonchalantly took his wallet from the back pocket of his slacks and began counting $100 bills. He also mentioned that he had just gone shopping with Catfish Hunter and Lou Piniella and that only Piniella had bought anything, some shirts and a $50 pair of shoes.

"I wouldn't wear $50 shoes," Jackson remarked.

Reggie is obsessed with money. Amateur psychologists view him as a tremendously insecure person who feels that money gives him instant status and importance far beyond his standing as a baseball player. That attitude irritates people who otherwise might become his friends. But what really irritated the Yankees was a statement Jackson made during spring training but which didn't appear in *Sport* magazine until May.

"I'm the straw that stirs the drink," Jackson said in one of his many metaphorical moments. ". . . Munson thinks he can be the straw that stirs the drink, but he can only stir it bad."

Until then Munson slowly had been building a relationship with Jackson; the Yankees needed a healthy bond between the two stars if they were to play in peace. At dinner one April night in Milwaukee two writers tried to cheer up a despondent Jackson and suggested he do something to change the atmosphere that had engulfed the team. The other players were avoiding Jackson, and he was reluctant to tread where he might not be wanted.

The next day Jackson burst to life in a studied animation in the clubhouse, mocking Munson's body (a popular Yankee pastime) and joking with Graig Nettles and Sparky Lyle, two players who had not and never would show any civility toward him. Jackson and Munson also chatted in the outfield during batting practice. The two stars clearly were growing closer and avoiding the expected fortissimo clash of egos.

Then the *Sport* article appeared, shattering their relationship.

Jackson's relationship with Billy Martin was no better. The manager was one of those who felt the team had done well enough winning the division title by ten and a half games. Martin wanted the Yankees to sign shortstop Bert Campaneris as a free agent and keep Oscar Gamble to platoon in right field, but the Yankees signed Jackson for right field and traded Gamble to the White Sox for shortstop Bucky Dent.

In Martin's opinion Jackson was not the player he believed he was. Furthermore, he was Steinbrenner's player, not his.

These feelings were embedded so deeply in the manager's mind that he was never able to view Jackson with objectivity. In the end Martin's obsessive hatred of Jackson led to his demise. And even when he had departed, he couldn't forget Reggie.

Sixteen days after he tearfully resigned in front of an antique shop in the Crown Center Hotel in Kansas City, Martin picked at a plate of spaghetti at Alex and Henry's restaurant in the Bronx and talked about Jackson. Two remarks in particular were telling.

"I never looked at Reggie as a superstar because he's never shown me he's a superstar," said Billy, tanned and relaxed on the outside but obviously still boiling on the inside. "I look at him as one of twenty-five players. I never put him above Chris Chambliss or Thurman Munson or Willie Randolph or Mickey Rivers or Roy White. There were times I put Fred Stanley above him."

If Martin's assessment could be faulted, his memory certainly couldn't be. "He said," Martin related, alluding to when Jackson joined the Yankees, "there would be no problems. 'George and I see eye to eye on everything.' He forgot one guy—Billy Martin."

It was a slight that Billy Martin would never forget, one that would influence his treatment of Reggie Jackson for a season and a half.

George Steinbrenner tried to influence Billy Martin's thinking. Sometimes he succeeded. He induced Martin to sign a three-year contract that included restrictive provisions the manager never would have considered agreeing to anywhere else. But the Yankees were the team Martin so eagerly desired to manage, and he allowed Steinbrenner to go further than any of his previous employers.

"A man would like to make his roots somewhere," Martin said a few days after turning fifty during the 1978 season. "I don't want to go around from club to club. I'm here where I started. I'd like to stay here as long as possible. Then someday I'd hope they would say, 'You've done a good job. Come upstairs; there's a job for you.' I'm not anxious to be a general manager, but I'd like to be something like assistant to the president, where I'd help talk about trades and coordinate things."

On September 11, 1976, with the Yankees leading their division by twelve and a half games, Martin signed a new three-year contract worth $302,000 ($92,000 the first year, then $100,000 and $110,000). In it he promised not to criticize Steinbrenner, not to question or criticize publicly any personnel moves made by the front office and to meet, when requested, with club officials.

Violations of these provisions would subject the manager to fines or, worse, to dismissal without being paid for the remainder of the contract. Martin agreed reluctantly, and the provisions, especially the one that commanded Thou shalt not criticize thy boss, later were to plague him as much as Reggie Jackson's presence.

The contract provisions, of course, did not prevent Martin from feuding with Steinbrenner privately. And those disagreements always surfaced, frequently bringing Martin to the brink of dismissal.

To be sure, Steinbrenner and Martin and Jackson—the triumvirate of turmoil—did not have a monopoly on controversy. Some of the other players contributed their share as the Yankees struggled toward their second straight pennant. Mickey Rivers, who had joined the Yankees in 1976, began 1977 by walking into spring training late the first day and announcing that he wanted to be traded.

"They're giving me a hassle already," the enigmatic centerfielder said in the clubhouse as the rest of the team worked out on the field. "I don't need that hassle. They're hassling me on every little thing. They're trying to pressure me. I don't need any pressure. I've had enough pressure."

Rivers, a man-child from Miami, did not have an ego problem, like some of his teammates. His problem was motivation. Although a good hitter and outstanding base stealer, Mickey hit and stole only when he felt like it. And he could pick the most exasperating times not to feel like it. During the 1977 playoffs and World Series it took private pep talks by Fran Healy, the reserve catcher and lay psychiatrist, to motivate him. Healy had retired before the 1978 Series, but after Rivers sat out the fourth game with an ailing leg and hip several teammates went to him separately before the fifth game and asked him if he could play.

Mickey Rivers

"It's hard," he said later, "to tell them no."

Rather than tell them no, Rivers went out and rapped three singles, scored two runs and drove in one. But when the unmotivated Rivers showed up late the first day of spring training in 1977, he set the tone for the season. Graig Nettles even walked out of camp briefly, unhappy that the front office would not renegotiate the contract he had signed halfway through the previous season—before he led the league with thirty-two homers. And when the season began, turmoil erupted regularly:

—Sparky Lyle and Ed Figueroa were fined $100 each for sleeping through a Steinbrenner address to the troops in Kansas City.

—Lyle and Rivers were fined $500 each for passing up an exhibition game in Syracuse.

—Catfish Hunter, on a Milwaukee radio show, criticized Martin's pitching rotation, or lack of same.

—Ken Holtzman called Steinbrenner "a fool" for paying him $165,-000 a year to sit in the bullpen.

—Mike Torrez, a new Yankee, criticized Steinbrenner for insulting him with a meager contract offer.

—Someone grew marijuana on Don Gullett's farm.

—Thurman Munson grew a beard in defiance of Steinbrenner's rules.

—Roy White, the team's elder statesman, refused to join in the World Series clubhouse celebration, dressing even more quickly than usual and leaving because he had been used only as a pinch-hitter.

These incidents were basically one-shot efforts by the players that added trouble to turmoil. But the primary confrontations of the swirling turbulence involved Steinbrenner against Martin and Martin against Jackson. Martin, by his own count, stood perched on the brink of dismissal five times. Jackson didn't become the everyday cleanup hitter, a prestige spot he coveted, until August 10, although Steinbrenner had wanted him to be the number four hitter—perhaps the real reason why Martin took so long in placing him in that role. Steinbrenner and Martin began clashing in spring training when, accompanied by Gabe Paul, the owner stormed into the clubhouse in St. Petersburg after a Saturday night loss to the Mets and ranted at Martin in front of the players.

"I ought to get rid of you!" the owner shouted.

"Why don't you fire me right now!" Martin screamed.

Inadvertently, the manager splattered ice water on both Steinbrenner and Paul, but the next morning the owner and his manager had a quiet breakfast together. Steinbrenner even apologized for initiating the skirmish in the clubhouse.

"As soon as he apologized," Martin said later, "I knew he'd spend the rest of the season getting my ass."

Martin was fined $2,500 in May for publicly criticizing the front office on personnel matters and failing to keep an appointment with Paul to discuss those matters. Later, in July, Steinbrenner and Paul met with newsmen and outlined the Seven Commandments by which Martin would be judged. They had been jotted down on a piece of paper by Paul; if they had been inscribed in stone, Steinbrenner might have broken the tablets over Martin's head. The commandments:

* Does he win?
* Does he work hard enough?
* Is he emotionally equipped to lead the men under him?
* Is he organized?
* Is he prepared?
* Does he understand human nature?
* Is he honorable?

If Martin had issued commandments for Jackson, perhaps Reggie would have found life more tolerable; as it was, he had to try to figure out from day to day how Martin would react to him. With the season only a week old Jackson had been benched in Milwaukee because he had told some writers his left elbow was ailing.

"He didn't know I don't allow players to tell the press about injuries," said the manager.

Martin informed Jackson of his idiosyncrasies in a long barstool session in the club's hotel, then returned him to the starting lineup the next night. Jackson was benched again in Oakland in May with no apparent reason. Then, when he hit a home run against the Red Sox a few nights later at Yankee Stadium, he deliberately avoided the near end of the dugout, where teammates generally gather to congratulate the home-run hitter. Instead, he ignored Jim Wynn, who had come to the top step, and headed for the far end. That way he would miss

Martin, whose hand he had no desire to shake. But he also was snubbing his teammates, already alienated by his "straw that stirs the drink" line about Munson.

Jackson's behavior also turned many fans against him, establishing a pattern for the rest of the season. There were still those who chanted "Reggie! Reggie! Reggie!" but others booed him constantly unless he hit a home run. No one cheered in the Yankee dugout June 18 at Fenway Park, unless they were cheering silently for Jackson and Martin to punch each other out. Martin had snatched him out of right field when, the manager believed, he loafed in getting to a hit. In the dugout both were fuming.

"You never liked me!" Jackson screamed at Martin in the nationally televised scene.

Martin screamed some things himself, all profane, and Elston Howard, one of the Yankee coaches, stepped between them. Moments later, when Martin started to follow Jackson up the runway leading from the dugout to the clubhouse, Yogi Berra and Dick Howser, two other coaches, held him back.

"I ask only one thing of my players—hustle," Martin said when he had calmed down. "It doesn't take any ability to hustle. When they don't hustle, I don't accept that. When a player shows the club up, I show him up."

Jackson was distraught. That evening he sat in his room at the Sheraton Boston sipping white wine and reflecting on the incident. His face wore a mask of pain, and his mouth uttered many expletives to be deleted.

"It makes me cry the way they treat me on this team," he said. "The Yankee pin stripes are Ruth and Gehrig and DiMaggio and Mantle. I'm just a black man to them who doesn't know how to be subservient. I'm a big black man with an IQ of 160 making $700,000 a year, and they treat me like dirt. They've never had anyone like me on their team before."

Then he thought of Steinbrenner and added, "I love that man. He treats me like I'm somebody. The rest of them treat me like dirt."

Steinbrenner had seen the dugout confrontation on television. Appalled, he flew to Detroit, the next stop on the Yankee trip, to meet with Gabe Paul, who had brought Jackson and Martin together for an unsatisfactory meeting in Boston that Sunday morning. By the next afternoon the Yankee hierarchy had concluded that Martin must be fired. At that point it would have been easier for Martin to free himself from chains and a padlocked trunk at the bottom of the Hudson River than to save his job. But strangely Jackson and Healy saved his job.

The calm, reasoned actions of Fran Healy, a quiet New Englander,

Martin and Jackson confront each other in the Fenway Park dugout

restored a peaceful coexistence. As soon as the dugout incident occurred, the six-foot-five reserve catcher rushed from the bullpen to the clubhouse. He persuaded Jackson to return to the hotel immediately, thus avoiding a possible post-game confrontation with the manager. And in the next two days he initiated a series of meetings with Steinbrenner, Martin, Jackson and Munson.

After speaking with Healy on Monday afternoon, Jackson met with Steinbrenner and appealed to the owner not to fire Martin. Healy met with Steinbrenner for some twenty minutes in the hotel lobby, providing the owner with an insight into what the other players were thinking, and later met with the manager for fifteen minutes. Then Martin phoned Steinbrenner, and during a short meeting, in painfully precise terms, the owner laid out for a genuinely shaken manager the changes he would have to make in his behavior. After the two met with Jackson, the storm subsided. Martin had escaped from the chains and the padlocked trunk.

After winning the pennant in 1976, then adding free agents Jackson and Gullett and shortstop Bucky Dent, the Yankees figured they would have no trouble coasting to the American League East title. But they had not figured that their intramural squabbles would represent a greater threat to their success than the teams they played. By midseason it was obvious that some problems had to be eradicated if the team were not to self-destruct.

Late on the night of July 13, after a game in Milwaukee, Thurman Munson and Lou Piniella decided to try and alleviate some of the intense pressure on the team. As captain and a longtime Yankee player, Munson felt a responsibility to help avert disaster. Piniella felt no inhibitions about confronting Steinbrenner; he was the Yankees' most candid player.

While others either declined comment on an issue or spoke anonymously to avoid reprisal, Piniella not only commented but also insisted that his name be used. He also possessed a fiery temper that often launched him into attacking dugout water coolers. Piniella had encountered the cooler in Kansas City's old Municipal Stadium so frequently that he took it home as a memento when the ballpark was to be razed.

The veteran outfielder, a hustler who was better than most baseball people gave him credit for, was playing right field in an exhibition game earlier in 1977 when Mickey Rivers, feeling unmotivated, misplayed two balls in center field. Piniella was asked later for his up-close account of what happened.

"I don't know; I have no idea," he barked, his voice rising in anger. "I'm not going to worry about Mickey, I'm not going to worry about

Reggie, I'm not going to worry about anyone other than me. I've got to get in shape. The hell with these guys. If they don't want to play, it's not my business."

And on an August night in Seattle he raged in the clubhouse about the players who had been saying publicly they wanted to desert the sinking ship.

"Why doesn't everyone speak up now?" he shouted as reporters entered the clubhouse. "Now's the time. Everybody wants to get traded. Talk about it now after you get beat 9–2 by a last-place team. How come nobody's saying anything now?"

When Piniella and Munson visited Steinbrenner in the owner's hotel suite in Milwaukee on July 13, Lou did not shout. But he was earnest. Finding Steinbrenner in his pajamas, the players told the owner to get it over with if he was going to fire Martin; if not, leave him alone and let him manage.

At about 1:30 A.M. Martin was heading for his room on the same floor and heard familiar voices as he passed Steinbrenner's door. He knocked, and the owner opened the door.

"What the hell's going on here?" Martin asked.

"Nothing's going on," Steinbrenner replied.

At which point Martin pushed open the door and discovered Munson and Piniella hiding in the bathroom.

"He was lying to me at the door," Martin was to say later. "He doesn't know what the truth is."

The owner, the manager and the two players talked for much of the night. At one point Steinbrenner asked Martin what was wrong with the team.

"You are," the manager replied. "You're meddling in the club and making things bad."

By the time the session ended Steinbrenner had agreed to relieve some of the pressure from Martin by guaranteeing his salary even if he were fired for violating those extra provisions in his contract. The meeting could have been constructive for the Yankees, but Steinbrenner proceeded to tell people about it. He also gave the impression that he was told at the meeting that a majority of the players did not support the manager.

The story of the meeting did not emerge publicly until the Yankees were in the middle of the World Series. Then *Time* magazine reported that Munson and Piniella had told Steinbrenner the team couldn't win with Martin as manager. The owner denied being the source of the story, but Martin and the players believed he was.

The morning of the sixth game of the Series, however, the front office called Martin to Yankee Stadium, told him he would be back in 1978 for the second year of his three-year contract and rewarded him for the job he did in 1977 by giving him a three-part bonus: about $35,000 in cash, a rent-free apartment and a new Diamond Jubilee Mark V Lincoln Continental.

Reggie Jackson received no bonus. More headaches and more adulation, but no bonus.

One of the headaches was a dugout confrontation with Sparky Lyle during a game in Kansas City in July. Jackson had misplayed a hit by Hal McRae to the right-centerfield wall, and Lyle, who was pitching, yelled at him, "Get your head out of your ass and quit loafing!" Another incident occurred after the All-Star game at Yankee Stadium, in which Jackson was accused (and later exonerated) of having knocked down and stepped on an autograph-seeking thirteen-year-old boy.

Even though Martin finally placed Jackson fourth in the batting order and Jackson responded with a productive hitting streak, the animosity that separated the two did not dissolve. Open warfare erupted once again during the playoffs and World Series.

The Kansas City Royals were the Yankees' playoff opponents for the second straight year. And for the second straight year the teams alternated winning through the first four games. The fifth-game result was also similar to the previous year, except this time the Yankees won, 5–3, with three runs in the ninth inning.

Paul Blair ignited the rally with a lead-off single, Mickey Rivers tied the game, 3–3, with a run-scoring single and Willie Randolph, quickly emerging as the best second baseman in the American League, drove in the go-ahead run with a sacrifice fly off Mark Littell, the same relief pitcher against whom Chris Chambliss hit his pennant-winning home run the year before.

"We shouldn't even have bothered to take our bats in the ninth," John Mayberry, the Royals' first baseman, reflected later. "All everybody was thinking was, 'It happened again.' We were dead."

But while the Royals were still alive, in the eighth inning, Reggie Jackson came to bat as a pinch-hitter and singled across an important run. Incredibly, the cleanup hitter whose bat had carried the Yankees during the previous seven weeks had been benched—removed from the batting order. The reason, Billy Martin explained, was that lefthander Paul Splittorff was starting for the Royals.

"Two players told me he didn't hit the ball off this guy," the manager said. "It's not a decision I'm happy making, but I have to do it. I probably wouldn't do it in the World Series, but I just have to do it now."

Martin did not tell Jackson himself that he wasn't playing. Martin seldom told his players anything directly; he had his coaches or even other players carry messages. It's something he learned from Casey Stengel. Players, at least the players of this era, resent that kind of communication.

"I've had two of his closest friends talk to him," Martin said.

"I got two friends?" Jackson retorted. "But it's not for me to say."

After his important pinch-single, Jackson figured he would be in the lineup for the first two games of the World Series against the Dodgers because two righthanders, Don Sutton and Burt Hooton, were starting. Asked about Jackson's status, Martin announced he would play because "Splittorff isn't pitching for them." Sarcasm tinged his reply; anger rose in Jackson when Martin's words were relayed to him.

"I know what I can do," Jackson countered. "If he did, we might be a lot better off."

Martin erupted the next day during a Dodger Stadium workout. In words meant for Jackson, he angrily told newsmen, "Play your position, do your job and if you can't do your job, shut up. He's got enough trouble playing right field without second-guessing the manager." Martin added that Jackson could "kiss my dago ass."

Jackson responded with a run-scoring single against Tommy John in the third game, then cracked a double and a homer the next day. The Yankees won both games, behind Mike Torrez and Ron Guidry, for a 3–1 lead. But the Dodgers won the fifth game, 10–4, as Jackson hit a harmless homer in the eighth inning. Then the Series returned to Yankee Stadium, the arena that Reggie would turn into a stage for the most dramatic performance of his career.

In the second inning he walked and scored on Chambliss' game-tying homer. He would take three more swings that night. On the first he lined Burt Hooton's pitch into the rightfield stands for two runs. On the second he smashed Elias Sosa's pitch into the rightfield stands for two more runs. On the third he lofted Charlie Hough's knuckleball deep into the unused centerfield bleacher area for the final run in an 8–4 victory.

"I must admit," Steve Garvey, the Dodger first baseman, said later, "when Reggie hit his third home run and I was sure nobody was looking, I applauded in my glove."

The Yankees had won their first World Series championship since 1962, and Reggie Jackson had put himself into the World Series record book as nobody else ever had. His five homers set a Series record; so did his three consecutive homers in one game, his four homers in four consecutive official at-bats over two games, his twenty-five total bases and his ten runs scored. His three homers tied the one-game Series record established by Babe Ruth in 1926 against the Cardinals and repeated by the Babe in 1928 against the Cardinals (both games were in St. Louis); his twelve total bases in one game also tied the Babe's record and his four runs scored in one game equaled a record shared by four others (the Babe in 1926, Earle Combs in 1932, Frank Crosetti in 1936 and Enos Slaughter of the Cardinals in 1946).

"I don't like the guy," one Yankee said afterward, "but I have to admire what he did. He's a great performer."

Reggie Jackson, meanwhile, spent the winter thinking about what a bad actor Billy Martin had been as manager.

One hundred members of the Hollywood Hills High School band, twenty-eight pompon girls and nine majorettes waited in the Delta Airlines lounge at the Fort Lauderdale airport, their instruments, pompons and batons poised for action the instant they got the signal. Delta Flight 137 had landed, and any moment now, a little after noon on this mild February day, Sparky Lyle would emerge from the jetway.

When the Yankees' publicity director, Micky Morabito, spotted Lyle and his wife, Mary, he signaled the band director, and the salute began. Lyle entered the lounge, heard the band playing "Pomp and Circumstance," saw the large blue-and-white sign that said "Welcome Sparky Lyle . . . finally" and exclaimed, his face red with embarrassment, "What the hell's going on?"

George Steinbrenner's show was going on, that's what. Three days earlier Steinbrenner had triggered a feud with the relief pitcher by criticizing him for not having reported to spring training with the other pitchers. This greeting was a way of defusing a volatile situation, but it also represented an edge for the owner in a game of one-upmanship with Lyle, the master practical joker.

In his distinguished career with the Yankees after being acquired from the Red Sox for infielder Danny Cater in a 1972 trade, Lyle had sat on birthday cakes in his birthday suit; he had risen from a coffin, his face powdered a ghostly white, in the middle of a team meeting; he had substituted "white heat" arm liniment for Yogi Berra's toothpaste; he had limped onto the field on the first day of another spring training with a cast on his left arm and a cast on his left leg when nothing was wrong with either.

But there was something wrong now, and it wasn't funny to Lyle, the devil-may-care pitcher who had registered more saves than any other active reliever. Lyle won the Cy Young Award in 1977 as the best pitcher in the American League, and Steinbrenner, in recognition of the lefthander's efforts, called him in after the season and rewarded him with an extra year on his contract and a bonus of $35,000. Lyle was pleased; the owner did not have a reputation for philanthropy.

Several weeks later Lyle learned the real reasons Steinbrenner had rewarded him. The Yankees, continuing their successful pursuit of free agents, gave a contract worth $2,748,000, including a $750,000 bonus,

Gabe Paul, Billy Martin and George Steinbrenner after the 1977 World Series

Firing his fastball, Ron Guidry struck out 18 Angels on June 17, 1978

Dick Tidrow

to Rich Gossage, a relief pitcher whose fastball appeared to come out of an M-16 rifle. Not long after that they also signed Rawly Eastwick, another relief pitcher (though not of Gossage's quality) for $1.1 million, including a $320,000 bonus.

Instantly, Lyle knew the bullpen was too crowded. In no way could Billy Martin, or any manager, find enough work for all those relief pitchers. Sensing trouble, Lyle asked to be traded. The Yankees refused: Lyle and Gossage would give them baseball's most awesome bullpen.

Lyle turned out to be a prophet (and a Texas Ranger; he was traded after the 1978 season). More and more, Martin used Gossage in the late innings—Sparky's time—and Lyle became an unhappy and ineffective middle-inning reliever.

That was only one of the problems the Yankees had with the staff that was supposed to be best in the majors. Catfish Hunter, whose twenty-three victories in his first Yankee season were reduced to nine in 1977, had developed diabetes and still had a bad shoulder. Don Gullett, who had fourteen victories and a bad shoulder in his first year, suffered with a bad shoulder beginning early in spring training (eventually he would undergo surgery for a double tear in his shoulder). Andy Messersmith suffered a shoulder separation in spring training and reinjured the shoulder in July.

Andy Messersmith? Wasn't he the righthander whom the Yankees courted as a free agent in 1976 but lost because of contract discrepancies? What was he doing here with the Yankees in 1978?

Steinbrenner, after admittedly gambling on Eastwick, purchased Messersmith and the remaining $333,333 of his three-year contract from the Atlanta Braves for $100,000. Steinbrenner was gambling here, too, because Messersmith had undergone elbow surgery the previous September; the Braves' doctors were predicting he wouldn't be able to pitch until July or August.

Messersmith, a determined athlete, surprised everybody with his pitching in spring training. No one on the staff looked better. But covering first base in an exhibition game he tripped over the bag while reaching back for the throw, fell and suffered a shoulder separation. He was to pitch in only six games, losing three, and then be released after the season.

At the other extreme Ron Guidry suddenly developed into baseball's most dominant pitcher. The twenty-seven-year-old Cajun from La-fayette, Louisiana, grew up in the Yankee farm system as a relief pitcher —a five-foot-eleven, 160-pound lefthander who could throw a baseball so fast it could probably knock out an alligator in his hometown bayous. Guidry's slight frame lends an aura of mystery to his ability to throw a ball so fast. Looking like he was in desperate need of a Charles Atlas body-building course, Guidry created a new game among Yankee Stadium fans. Whenever he got two strikes on a batter, the fans would begin cheering and clapping in anticipation of strike three, their hands and voices rising in a crescendo that would explode into a roar when he got the strike.

Guidry's reaction to the fans' behavior was typical of his low-key, unspoiled personality that makes him easy to like. "It's good for me," he said of the noise, "but I feel sorry for the batter. He's up there trying to hit the ball, and all those people are yelling."

Joe Rudi, the Angels' outfielder who played on Oakland's three consecutive championship teams with Jackson and Hunter, heard that yelling four times in one game and struck out all four times. "If you saw that pitching too often," the cleanup hitter said, shaking his head, "there would be a lot of guys doing different jobs."

Guidry, whose black hair and black mustache bring to mind a riverboat gambler, nearly quit baseball in 1976, when the Yankees wanted to send him to their Syracuse farm. He had actually started driving home from New York when his wife, Bonnie, pierced the silence.

"Ron," she said, "do you really want to quit? You know you won't be happy not playing ball. Don't do something you'll regret the rest of your life."

Minutes later the car was headed north, and Guidry was headed toward a role as a starting pitcher who would register performances and statistics unparalleled in Yankee history. Becoming a regular starter in May 1977, when Martin performed his magic act and made Ken Holtzman disappear, Guidry had a 16-7 record while earning $34,000 that season. Then he had a 25-3 record in 1978 with a 1.74 earned-run average and 248 strikeouts, a Yankee record. For that he was paid $38,500, but he had already signed a contract extension worth $600,000 over the next three seasons.

He won thirteen games in 1978 before he lost; he struck out a Yankee-record eighteen batters in a thrilling performance against the Angels; his .893 winning percentage was the best in baseball history by a twenty-game winner; he held opposing batters to a collective .193 batting average (the league batted .261 overall); he was credited with the victory in the playoff game against Boston for the division title; and he won one game each in the American League playoffs and World Series, duplicating his 1977 achievement.

Between August 10, 1977, and the end of the 1978 World Series he won thirty-seven games and lost four. Not surprisingly, he was a unanimous winner of the Cy Young Award.

Much of Guidry's incredible season went unchronicled in New York because of the newspaper strike that began August 9 and continued after the World Series ended. But he was not bothered by the lack of publicity. He expressed more concern for the newsmen who were out of work, unlike some of his teammates who hoped the strike would continue because they thought the absence of the city's three papers would help them avoid controversy.

There was no difference of opinion, however, on Guidry's value to the team. That value was captured in a remark Paul Blair made in September, just after the skinny lefthander had shut out the Boston Red Sox on two hits for the second time in seven days. Blair, the best reserve outfielder in the game, was looking for extra playoff tickets, and he asked Guidry if he would be using his entire allotment.

"I might not be here at the end of the season; they might trade me," Guidry said jokingly.

"No way, buddy," Blair replied. "You ain't goin' anywhere. You own the franchise."

The irony of that exchange was that the Yankees nearly did trade Guidry in the spring of 1977. Counting on him to replace Lyle as their lefthanded reliever, the front office was disappointed when he pitched poorly in the exhibition games. Steinbrenner was ready to include Guidry in the package for Bucky Dent because Bob Lemon, the White Sox manager, had asked for him. Lemon had been the Yankee pitching coach in 1976 and knew Guidry's potential. But then Gabe Paul stepped in and refused to let the pitcher be sent anywhere.

Gabe Paul, who opened the Yankees' door for George Steinbrenner, had now worked for him for five years. At times it seemed like a life sentence. Steinbrenner relied on Paul for his baseball education, but too often he treated the Yankees' president no differently from the way he did his secretaries. Paul, who could himself occasionally be ruthless, was sixty-seven years old, had worked in baseball for more than fifty years and was looking for a saner way to complete his career.

Steinbrenner, meanwhile, was becoming increasingly less tolerant of what he regarded as Paul's growing inefficiency. Paul generally was thought to have served as the pacifying buffer between Steinbrenner and Martin, but the owner refuted that image, suggesting instead that Paul felt every bit as strongly about Martin's shortcomings and furthermore, "because of conversations I had and what I was being told," perhaps magnified some of the problems between owner and manager.

Paul, Steinbrenner believed, was getting too old for his job. And Paul, Steinbrenner believed, received too much credit for the Yankees' successful personnel moves of the previous few years.

"He was in baseball for forty years, twenty-five as a general manager, and did he ever win a pennant before?" Steinbrenner commented after Paul had departed to become part-owner, president and chief executive officer of the Cleveland Indians for the 1978 season. "You think he made all those moves with this team himself? You think all of a sudden he got brilliant?"

In December 1977, a few weeks before Paul left, Steinbrenner named Al Rosen his executive vice president. By the time spring training began, Rosen had become president.

Rosen, a leap-year baby born on February 29, 1924, had been a star third baseman for the Indians in the early fifties, winning the 1953 Most Valuable Player award. Steinbrenner, six years younger, had watched Rosen play, admired him and later became a friend. Rosen, who had been a stockbroker in Cleveland and then director of branch offices for Caesars Palace of Las Vegas, became a limited partner when Steinbrenner and his group bought the Yankees.

Shortly after Rosen became the team's president, Steinbrenner declared that his new man would become the top executive in baseball within two or three years. The owner also felt that because Rosen had played the game he would have a better rapport with Martin. "It's not so easy," Steinbrenner said, "for Billy to look Al Rosen in the face and say what do you know about baseball, which he can do with me."

Baseball background, however, would not preclude any confrontations between the former second baseman and the former third baseman. The blowup occurred after Thurman Munson was forced to leave a game with the Orioles on May 31 because his chronically sore legs were aching more than usual. Even before the game was over, Rosen announced that the Yankees were recalling Mike Heath, a young catcher, from their West Haven, Connecticut, farm.

Martin didn't know about the move until a reporter told him about it after the game. The manager was furious—not as furious, though, as he was the next day when Rosen summoned him to his office to answer for a quote that identified Rawly Eastwick as "George's boy," meaning that the owner had signed him and the manager wasn't sure what he was going to do with him.

Steinbrenner was out of town when the quote was printed, but after a friend showed it to him two days later he instructed Rosen to find out why Martin had made what he considered a disparaging remark. Steinbrenner had been making a pretense of concentrating on his ship business while Rosen operated the team. But telephones are wonderful instruments. Steinbrenner used them frequently in guiding Rosen here and there.

Martin, right or wrong, had the distinct feeling that he was suffering from those telephone calls.

"I'm not going to take any more harassment," Martin asserted to a newsman that day before heading to Oakland with the team and staying in the hotel bar much of the night. "I had it last year and that's enough.

I'm not going to take it this year. You call Rosen tomorrow and tell
him Billy says he wants it known that Al Rosen and George Steinbrenner are running the club. He doesn't run it any more. He can't take it
any more."

Dutifully, the newsman called Rosen the next day and repeated
Billy's angry charge. "Billy Martin," Rosen said calmly, if a bit exasperated, "is the manager of this ball club, he has been the manager of
this ball club, he will be manager of this ball club."

Three weeks later that statement nearly became inoperative, to use
a White House word.

Because of a quirk in the scheduling, the Yankees would not play
their archrivals, the Red Sox, until June 19, but then they would clash
in three series beginning on three consecutive Mondays. By the time
they arrived in Boston for the first series they had skidded seven games
behind the Red Sox, and by the time they left they were eight games
out. They had lost two of the three games. The second loss, in the last
game of the series, was especially dangerous since that was the first road
game Steinbrenner had seen in the 1978 season. Jim Beattie, a twenty-
three-year-old rookie righthander, had been thrust into the starting
rotation because of the rash of injuries to the regular starters. The
red-haired Dartmouth College graduate had to be replaced in the third
inning. By the sixth he was on his way back to Tacoma of the Pacific
Coast League.

"That kid pitching looked scared stiff," Steinbrenner told reporters
after the game.

The owner made other inflammatory comments as well, and they
filtered back to Martin.

"It's Al Rosen's decision," Steinbrenner had said when asked about
Martin's fate, just as he had said the previous season that it was up to
Gabe Paul. No one believed him then; no one believed him now. "But
I'll tell you one thing," he continued. "I won't put up with this much
longer. I won't stand for what I see now."

For just a brief moment Martin viewed the situation with humor.

"Next year I'm not coming to Boston," he said as he walked out of
Fenway Park, recalling the dugout confrontation with Jackson 369
days earlier. "Every time I come here I get fired. Next year I'll let
Howser manage, and I'll go straight to Detroit. I like Boston. It's good
for seafood—but bad for my sleeping."

On his way to Detroit this time, however, the manager grew de-
pressed and angry and bitter.

"I'm sick and tired of hearing about being fired," he said to a reporter
he had asked to sit next to him on the plane. "I give George Steinbrenner 100 percent loyalty, and I expect it in return. If he doesn't think

I'm doing the job right, he should call Al Rosen and tell him to do something. All this talk about me being fired is disrupting me. My son reads about it, and it bothers him. My mother reads about it, and it bothers her. It hurts my family and my friends, and it's hurting my health. There are managers all over baseball who have never won, and you never hear about them being close to being fired."

As he talked, Martin became so enraged at the prospect of being fired that he mentioned ways in which he could retaliate against Steinbrenner if it happened—how he knew where the bodies were buried, so to speak, and how he would use that knowledge if necessary.

The next night, before the game in Detroit, a deeply troubled Rosen said, "Billy, being a professional manager, knows what happens to managers who are supposed to win who don't win." The ominous comment represented a far different stance from the one Rosen had taken earlier in the week, but it was obvious that Steinbrenner had made a few points clear to the club president, whose job, as well as the manager's, suddenly seemed to be something less than solid. Rosen also had disturbed Steinbrenner because he failed, before the June 15 trading deadline, to acquire an experienced pitcher who could fill one of the gaps in a rotation riddled by injuries.

Later that night Rosen acknowledged to friends that he had to make a change. He had talked with Steinbrenner and Martin had to go. Just how he was to go and who would replace him had not been decided.

Then, on Sunday, just before the last game of the weekend series, Rosen met with Martin in the closet-like manager's office in the visitors' clubhouse at Tiger Stadium and might as well have hit the old street fighter with brass knuckles. He told the manager that Art Fowler, the pitching coach, would be reassigned to work in the farm system.

Fowler was not a wizard as a pitching coach; he was not Johnny Sain or George Bamberger, each of whom cultivated twenty-game winners as if they were tomatoes. But he had been the pitching coach wherever Martin managed because he was Billy's drinking buddy and confidant.

Steinbrenner had been upset about the lack of progress of the young pitchers and ostensibly wanted someone else to work with them. But some of the players immediately saw the Fowler exile as an attempt to induce Martin to quit. If the Yankees fired Martin, the players reasoned, the move would be unpopular with the fans. If, on the other hand, Martin resigned, the Yankees would avoid a potential backlash from the fans.

Martin himself lashed out. "If I can't have the guys around me I want," he said after the team landed at Newark Airport, "then you might see something happen."

Downstairs, in Billy Martin's office at Yankee Stadium, the plaque lay on a table. "Extraordinary Achievement Award to Billy Martin," it read. "For having reached the age of 50 without being murdered by someone . . . to the amazement of all who know him."

Upstairs, the manager had entered the Yankee executive offices on June 26, the day after Al Rosen told him Art Fowler was going to be banished, and to the amazement of all who knew what was happening he emerged with his managerial life. Not only did he survive again, but he also resurrected Art Fowler, retaining him as his pitching coach and drinking buddy.

"This should end the speculation that has been developing of late concerning Billy's job," Steinbrenner said in announcing that Martin would "remain as manager of the Yankees this year."

For more than two hours Martin and his agent, Doug Newton, met with Steinbrenner and Rosen, but how had Martin saved his job this time?

The night before he was hotter than a pot of boiling oil over the Fowler incident, but his agent, who had become a stabilizing influence in Martin's life, calmed him to at least the simmering level. Rosen and Steinbrenner, meanwhile, had decided that Fowler could stay because it would have been embarrassing for them to banish him now that the players believed they were trying to force Martin out. They also decided that even if they wanted to fire Martin, no suitable replacement was available.

That day's session produced two other decisions. One, the addition of Yankee scout and troubleshooter Clyde King to the coaching staff, would have beneficial results for the young pitchers and therefore the team in general. The other, the switch of Reggie Jackson from right field to designated hitter, would have depressing results for Jackson and disastrous results for Martin.

The immediate result was not a winning streak that would carry the Yankees past the Red Sox into first place. Instead, from that meeting until the All-Star game break two weeks later, the Yankees lost another two games in the standings, toppling eleven and one half games behind Boston.

On the verge of surrender Steinbrenner snapped, "The mark of a team isn't winning the championship; it's how you defend the championship. We're playing horseshit. We're going to bite the bullet and go with the young guys." He ordered a statistical study—he was always ordering statistical studies—and called a meeting for July 13, the day after the All-Star break. He proposed some lineup changes to Martin, who uncharacteristically accepted them.

"I had a choice," Martin explained. "I listened to their proposal. It sounded reasonable so I'm willing to try it."

The meeting, Steinbrenner said, was the best he ever had with Martin. Then he met with the players—the first time he entered the clubhouse during the 1978 season, he insisted, "except to get candy bars when the team isn't in there." But in speaking to the players Steinbrenner did not sweet-talk them. "I'm not going to lie down and die like a dog, and neither are you," he told them. "I expect you to accept whatever role you're given without griping and do it the best you can. You're among the best-paid athletes in the world, and I expect something in return since I sign the paychecks. We're going to do it the way I want to do it and the way Billy has agreed is the proper way to do it. If you don't like it, I'll try and accommodate you elsewhere. I know no cure-all, but we're going to try it this way."

The Yankees did not win that day's game. In fact, they won only one of the next five games and plummeted fourteen games behind the Red Sox on July 17.

The day after the meeting that was supposed to revitalize the Yankees, Steinbrenner and Martin filmed a television commercial. In the commercial the owner and the manager disagree over their views of a beer. And finally Steinbrenner says with a smile, "Billy, you're fired." "Oh, no," Martin responds, "not again."

Reggie Jackson, who had tried to maintain a low-key existence where Billy Martin was concerned for the first three months of the season, was rapidly spiraling into a deep depression. He had become not just a designated hitter but a part-time designated hitter.

His fate, at least for the present, had been sealed at the June 26 meeting, when Martin, Steinbrenner and Rosen decided he and the team would benefit more by having him as a designated hitter rather than a rightfielder. Jackson also heard that Rosen was disturbed that he had attended, by invitation, a birthday party some of Steinbrenner's friends, including Rosen, had given the owner. None of the other players had been invited or had gone. Rosen believed this would be one more reason for the players to dislike Jackson, whom they disliked already.

The players didn't like Jackson's picture on the T-shirts the Yankees gave away on T-shirt day on July 1—the same day as the birthday party. But that didn't bother the front office because Standard Brands, the Reggie bar manufacturers, paid for the shirts.

Discussing the party, Jackson said, "Bill Fugazy and those people are my friends. They asked me to come." Moreover, a few days earlier, Jackson had made some nasty comments about Steinbrenner, and he thought it would be a nice gesture to go to the party and say happy birthday to the owner.

But no one was saying anything nice to Reggie, who had the idea, apparently initiated by Rosen, that the Yankees might trade him, espe-

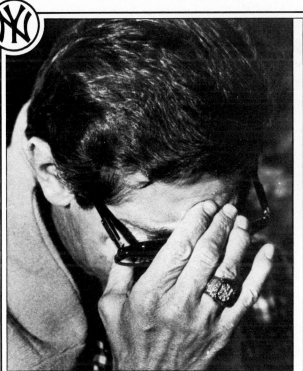

Haggard and tearful, Billy Martin announces
his resignation in Kansas City   Wide World Photos

Bob Lemon   The New York Yankees

Bright and smiling, Billy Martin is rehired by George Steinbrenner   The New York Yankees

cially if they could shore up their pitching staff. As the days plodded by, Jackson became more distraught. Finally, on July 16, after the regular Sunday morning clubhouse chapel that some players attend, Jackson spoke with Tom Skinner, who had preached at the chapel.

"Tom," Jackson told him, "I've had enough."

"Don't give up," Skinner counseled him. "Stick to it. God's preparing you for something. You can't do anything until you hear from God."

The next day something told Reggie that this was the day he would hear. Reggie made several telephone calls: to Steve Kay, his lawyer in California; to Gary Walker, his adviser, friend and business partner in Arizona; and to his business associates at both Standard Brands and the American Broadcasting Company. He solicited their thoughts, asked what they felt he should do. They suggested he talk with Steinbrenner, the man he always flattered by calling him "boss." Fran Healy, no longer a Yankee catcher but a Yankee broadcaster and still Jackson's only friend around the team, had advised him to do that a month earlier.

Jackson called Steinbrenner, who told him to call Rosen, who told him to call Steinbrenner.

Jackson again called Steve Kay, who called Steinbrenner and tried to set up a meeting for his client with the owner, Rosen and Martin because Jackson believed the only way he could resolve the rapidly deteriorating situation was to meet with all three simultaneously.

But in a phone call from Rosen he learned that he could meet with Steinbrenner alone or with Rosen and Martin together but not with all three.

Feeling somewhat defeated before he started, Jackson chose Steinbrenner—the man who had hustled him into joining the Yankees and who had been his biggest, perhaps only supporter. That afternoon he walked into Steinbrenner's office, where he had spent so many enjoyable hours. He made no demands, no threats. He did not ask to be traded.

"I'm afraid I'm losing control," he told the owner, "and I want to call your attention to it."

Steinbrenner, who does not waste time with small talk, told Jackson it was his idea to make the rightfielder a designated hitter. "I have listened to my baseball people, and they have convinced me that's the move," Steinbrenner said. "I agree that you should be the designated hitter. But you also should be hitting cleanup. I want you to bust your ass, and I want you to turn it on in the second half and make a pennant race of it, give the fans something to cheer about."

Jackson told Steinbrenner he would do what he could, but there was not much feeling or determination behind the words. After an hour and a half he left Steinbrenner's office, pushed open the glass doors of the executive offices, stepped into the elevator, rode down to the Stadium basement and walked slowly through the winding concrete corridors to the Yankee clubhouse. Once there, he was noticed by Martin, who thought he appeared to be mad at the world.

"He didn't talk to anybody," Martin was to say the next day. "He just went out for the team picture and didn't say anything to anybody."

Martin, at Steinbrenner's request, used Jackson as the cleanup hitter against the Royals that night, but Reggie failed to get a hit in his first four times up. His fifth appearance came in the tenth inning with the game tied 5–5, Thurman Munson on first base and none out. In controlling a game Martin flashes signs from the dugout to Dick Howser, the third-base coach, who relays them to hitters and runners with dazzling hand motions. And now, before Al Hrabosky's first pitch to Jackson, the manager flashed the sign for a sacrifice—a bunt, something Jackson had not been asked to do all season. But the fastball whizzed by Jackson's head, too high and too far inside for him to try to bunt.

The Royals' infielders, however, had seen that Jackson had intended to bunt. They moved in.

Noticing that, Martin removed the bunt sign. But the combination of his depression and the initial order for him to bunt with the winning run at first base was too much for Jackson—he intended to take it on his own to bunt. Not sure that Jackson had seen him flash the "hit" sign, Howser called time and walked down the third-base line. "Billy took the bunt sign off," Howser said. "He wants you hitting away."

"I'm going to bunt," Jackson said.

"He wants you to swing the bat."

But there were no swings in Jackson's bat. He tried to bunt Hrabosky's second pitch and missed the ball. He bunted the next one foul and then bunted the fourth pitch foul to Darrell Porter, the astounded catcher.

Martin was livid. Jackson returned quietly to the dugout, removed his glasses and placed them on the ledge behind the bench, anticipating a possible rerun of the Boston dugout scene. Martin, however, stayed away from him. Instead, the manager walked over to Gene Michael, the first-base coach, after the inning.

"Tell Reggie that Roy [White] is the designated hitter," Martin said. "He can shower and go home if he wants."

The Yankees went on to lose the game, 9–7, in eleven innings, but Jackson was still in the clubhouse when it ended. Martin again resisted the urge to confront him. This time he strode into his office, snatched the clock radio from the table near the door and flung it into the corridor outside the door. Then an empty bottle of Lowenbrau crashed against the wall opposite the door, pieces of green glass scattering along the floor. Martin drinks Miller Lite on television, but that night he threw Lowenbrau green. Moments later reporters walked through the broken glass and saw the manager standing in the corner diagonally opposite the door. His eyes were red, his body was shaking.

"No interviews right this minute," he mumbled, his voice quivering.

Howser, general manager Cedric Tallis and publicity director Mickey Morabito soon gathered in the office. The door was closed.

Meanwhile, across the clubhouse, Jackson stood at his locker.

"I was trying to advance the runner," he said calmly. "I figured I'd get him over the best way I could. I thought I'd be helping the ball club. How can they say I'm a threat to swing the bat? I'm not an everyday player. I'm a part-time player. If it was somebody else, there wouldn't be all this crap."

In Martin's office Tallis was on the phone with Steinbrenner and Rosen, who were in the owner's office upstairs. Eventually the manager's door opened.

"As of this moment," announced Martin, more composed but his voice and body still trembling slightly as he clutched a piece of note paper, "Reggie Jackson is suspended without pay, effective immediately, for deliberately disregarding the manager's instructions during his time at bat in the tenth inning. There isn't going to be anybody who defies the manager or management in any way. Nobody's bigger than the team. If he comes back again, he does exactly what I say. Period. I don't get paid three million dollars. I don't disobey my boss's orders. He tells me to do something, I do it."

Despite the intensely serious moment, some reporters in the room couldn't suppress a snicker.

About twelve hours later Martin had returned to his office. He was about to leave with the team for Minnesota on a road trip that would also include stops in Chicago and Kansas City over the next week. The broken green glass had been swept up. The clock radio with the shattered face lay on a trunk in an equipment room. But the manager was still fuming. "You have one person trying to dictate a situation; that's got to stop," he said. "I had a meeting with them two weeks ago, and I spelled out how I felt about the rules. I told them drastic measures would be taken if necessary. This is probably the best thing that's happened in a long time. It'll pull the team together. If you took a poll, I think you'd find the players were unanimous 100 percent."

Asked how long he would continue Jackson's suspension, which under baseball rules could not remain indefinite, he replied, "At least a week. I'll take a stand for at least that long."

But a few minutes later, in Rosen's office, Martin quickly agreed to the club president's recommendation that the suspension last five days. "I prefer that Reggie play some games before coming back to the Stadium next week," Rosen explained. "Let him get his feet on the ground."

And then the Yankees proceeded to win four consecutive games in Jackson's absence. Martin flourished.

Free of his personal albatross and buoyed by his firm action, the manager smiled and joked, told stories and generally enjoyed himself. He hadn't felt so good all season. He could even ignore the liver ailment that he privately had told friends about. But each night in Minnesota and Chicago he was asked about Jackson.

"I don't want apologies," Martin said Wednesday night in Minnesota. "I just want him to go to his locker, get dressed, go out on the field, and he'll be in the lineup."

Two nights later, in Chicago, the manager said, "I'll be putting him in the lineup Sunday. I hope he's done some hitting. If he hasn't, I don't want to send him out there and embarrass him." The next night, the eve of Jackson's return, Martin remarked, "If he hasn't hit in five or six days, I'm not going to stick him out on the field as a designated hitter, not with a lefthanded pitcher. It wouldn't be fair to him, it wouldn't be fair to the club. I can't see anyone sitting out five, six days, then coming back. You have to hit to be ready."

In his travels to California and Arizona that week Jackson had not found a batting cage. He had talked with several friends and advisers in an effort to straighten out his confused head, but he was reluctant to return. "I don't feel they feel he can play baseball any more," one close friend said. "It's affecting him."

Jackson's teammates, meanwhile, did not seem to think his suspension would change anything. One player, Chris Chambliss, foresaw additional trouble when Jackson returned. "I don't think he can come back and have things be rosy," the first baseman said. "If things don't change, something's going to happen. I just hope they do what's in the best interests of the team. The team should always come first. But if he comes back, something else has to happen. There will still be more problems."

The suspension, Chambliss believed, was not too drastic. "Not for him," he added. "He did it so obviously. I think he could've made his point a little more subtly. He didn't just hurt the manager. He hurt the team."

Chambliss had been quiet ever since Jackson became a Yankee; perhaps the quiet black man resented the arrogance of the loud black man. He also appeared to resent the commotion Martin encountered because of Jackson; aside from Graig Nettles, the first baseman might have been the only Yankee who cared about the manager.

And the manager's cheerful mood changed instantly on Sunday morning, the morning of Jackson's return.

Martin's obsessive hatred for Jackson, deeper perhaps than even he realized, had him agitated and impatient when he boarded the team bus shortly after 11 o'clock. Parked across the street from the Continental

Plaza Hotel, the bus was scheduled to leave for Comiskey Park at 11:15
sharp. The manager no longer was joking; he no longer was smiling.
He looked up quickly when Gerry Murphy, the young and efficient
traveling secretary, rose from his seat and moved toward the door.

"Where are you going?" Martin asked.

"I'm going to get Cedric [Tallis]," Murphy replied, referring to the
general manager. "He has his briefcase on the bus."

"I don't give a shit if he has his house on the bus—we go at 11:15."

Moments later Martin asked Murphy the time. He was clearly anxious to leave, as if he wanted to make sure the bus wouldn't wait even
an extra minute for Jackson if Jackson planned to take the bus. Jackson,
however, was not planning to take the bus. He was in room 1244,
having arrived from Phoenix the night before, and he intended taking
a cab with Fran Healy after the bus departed.

"I'm kind of apprehensive," Jackson had said. "I think it would be
better not to take the bus until I find out what happens."

Martin grew increasingly edgy. He noticed Frank Messer, a Yankee
broadcaster with leg and hip problems, starting across the street toward
the bus.

"If Messer's coming," Martin barked to no one in particular, "he
better walk faster."

Gary Thomasson, a Yankee outfielder, stood just outside the bus
talking with a friend. "Tell Gary to get on," Martin said. "We're
going." Thomasson stepped onto the bus. "We're going," Martin announced, but then someone yelled to hold the bus.

"We're going," Martin ordered emphatically. "We made those
rules."

When the bus arrived at Comiskey Park half an hour later, Martin
went directly to his office, sat down behind the desk and immediately
began writing out his lineup card. He did not know if Jackson had taken
any batting practice during his suspension, but he was not about to wait
and find out. He chose Roy White as his designated hitter. And as he
sat in his office he complained about all the newsmen who were disrupting his clubhouse. The newsmen were waiting, of course, for Reggie
Jackson, who arrived about ten minutes after the manager.

Now, against a backdrop of a dozen roses that had been delivered
with a card from "Andrea and Diane," the unsuspended Yankee stood
at his locker answering questions.

"The magnitude of me, the magnitude of the instance, the magnitude
of New York," he was saying. "It's uncomfortable, it's miserable. It's
uncomfortable being me, it's uncomfortable being recognized constantly, it's uncomfortable being considered something I'm not, an idol
or a monster, something hated or loved."

"If you had it to do over again," he was asked, "would you still try
to bunt?"

"I'd probably do the same thing, because I didn't realize what the consequences would be," he replied. "I didn't regard it as an act of defiance. I didn't know it would get people so upset. If I had known the consequences would have this magnitude, I would rather have swung and struck out and avoided the hassle. But the way I interpreted it, I don't think what I did was so wrong. I'm sorry I caused the guys on the club grief and uncomfort. I don't want to cause them any grief."

Jackson did not play that day as the Yankees extended their winning streak to five games—four without him around.

On his way to the team bus after the game Martin stopped in the Bard's Room, the press hangout at the ball park. He asked Jack Lang of the New York *Daily News* what Jackson had said on his return. Lang gave the manager his story to read. Martin instantly began burning over Jackson's refusal to admit he was wrong, his refusal to beg forgiveness. On the ride to O'Hare International Airport the manager sat in his customary window seat on the right side in the first row of seats facing forward. I was the only passenger on the double side-seat against the windows just inside the door.

"When we get to the airport, can I see you for a few minutes?" Martin asked me.

I did not know at the time that Martin was furious over Jackson's remarks; I didn't even know he knew what Jackson had said. Nor did I know that he was furious because the night before he had learned that the Yankees had considered trading him only a few weeks earlier to the White Sox for Bob Lemon in a midseason managerial exchange. When the bus arrived at the airport, Martin walked over to me inside the terminal.

"Jackson's refusal to admit he was wrong," he snapped. "Is that conduct detrimental to the Yankees?"

Only a few days earlier Martin had issued a written set of rules for the Yankee players in an effort to create more discipline. It was the front office's idea, not his. But one of the rules stated that a player could be suspended for conduct detrimental to baseball or to the team. Now he obviously was looking for a way to suspend Jackson another time. But before I could answer his question, he was snarling again.

"I'm saying shut up, Reggie Jackson," he said. "We don't need none of your stuff. We're winning without you. We don't need you coming in and making all these comments. If he doesn't shut his mouth, he won't play and I don't care what George says. He can replace me right now if he doesn't like it. We've got a smooth-running ship here, and I don't want him and his mouth coming along and breaking it up. If he wants to play ball, just shut up and play. I don't want to hear any more from him. It's like a guy getting out of jail and saying I'm innocent after he killed somebody. He and every one of the other players knew he defied me."

After making certain that Martin meant all of this to be on the record, I headed for a telephone and called my newspaper, *The New York Times*; about a half-hour later, after I had finished dictating my story, I was talking with another reporter when Martin walked by.

"Did you get all that in the paper?" he asked.

I assured him I had, and he grinned. Now the whole world would know what kind of guy Reggie Jackson was. But that wasn't enough for him. Now he was calling Jackson "a liar," then offering several examples to show how big a liar.

"He's a born liar," Martin said as we walked toward the gate where the Yankees' flight to Kansas City was boarding. "The two of them deserve each other. One's a born liar, the other's convicted."

George Steinbrenner's conviction in the Watergate-related case was the sorest subject of the owner's life. He resented writers who asked about it or wrote about it. "I didn't mean it about George," Martin would say a few weeks later. "How he came into it I don't know. I meant it about the other guy. I was mad at the other guy."

But the lava from Vesuvius does not pick its spots. It inundates everything in its way.

George Steinbrenner had just arrived home in Tampa, Florida, when the telephone rang at 10:30 Sunday night. Before he got to bed that night, there would be many phone calls—to and from reporters, to and from Al Rosen in his New York apartment. Steinbrenner and Rosen were stunned to hear Martin's intemperate remark.

"I . . . I just don't know what to say," Steinbrenner stammered. "I've got to believe that no boss in his right mind would take that."

Especially a boss who holds a contract that prohibits the employee from publicly criticizing him. The following morning, while Rosen was on an early flight to Kansas City to get a firsthand account of what had happened, the lobby of the Crown Center Hotel was buzzing with talk of Martin's remark.

"Oh boy," said Lou Piniella, putting down a newspaper.

"He's gone," commented Ken Clay, a young Yankee pitcher.

Martin was in room 1138. He had not slept much, and he had been in contact with Doug Newton, his agent. Newton, in New York, had spoken with Steinbrenner, still in Tampa. Martin had spoken with neither Steinbrenner nor Rosen, but by noon he had decided he would resign. If he had chosen otherwise, he would have been fired. There would have been no more last-second reprieves, no more escapes from padlocked trunks.

Mickey Morabito, the Yankee publicity director who had accompanied Rosen to Kansas City, went to Martin's room at 3 o'clock to bring him to Rosen's room. But by then Billy was preparing to go to the lobby and read a statement he had scribbled on a hotel note pad. With him was Bob Brown, a Kansas City friend.

In the elevator to the lobby Morabito looked at Martin's notes. The publicity director suggested that he rewrite the notes so they would be easier to read. They got off at the fifth floor. Martin returned to his room while Morabito went to 1639, Rosen's room. When the rewrite had been completed, Rosen, Cedric Tallis and Morabito went to Martin's room, not unlike the contingent of guards, warden and minister who go to Death Row to get the condemned prisoner.

Until then Rosen had not seen or talked with Martin about his comments. They shook hands, and Martin asked Rosen (all condemned men get a last request) to tell Steinbrenner, "I didn't say those things," a stand he would later take publicly, then recant.

Now the group headed downstairs. They got off the elevator on the balcony level and waited while Morabito summoned newsmen from the lobby. When the reporters had gathered in front of an antique shop, across from an indoor waterfall and weeping fig trees, Martin materialized from around the corner. No longer the pugnacious street fighter, Martin had his notes in his quivering right hand and a cigar in his left. He wore a World Series ring on each hand and dark glasses on his haggard face. With hotel guests as well as newsmen looking on, Martin announced he would answer no questions afterward.

"That means now and forever," he added, "because I am a Yankee and Yankees do not talk or throw rocks."

Then he began reading, fidgeting with his glasses as if that would dam up the tears in his eyes.

"I don't want to hurt this team's chances for the pennant with this undue publicity," he read. "The team has a shot at the pennant, and I hope they win it. I owe it to my health and my mental well-being to resign. At this time I'm also sorry about these things that were written about George Steinbrenner. He does not deserve them, nor did I say them. I've had my differences with George, but we've been able to resolve them. I would like to thank"—he started to cry—"the Yankee management . . . the press, the news media, my coaches, my players . . . and most of all . . ." Crying heavily now, he couldn't speak for nearly ten seconds before gasping almost inaudibly, ". . . the fans."

Led by Bob Brown, whose arms were around his sagging shoulders, Billy Martin walked quickly toward a door marked EXIT, his head bowed—an ex-manager for the fourth time.

Incredibly, five days later, on Old-Timers Day, three years after Billy Martin had been hired originally as the Yankees' manager, George Steinbrenner hired him again. "Managing the Yankees in the 1980 season," Bob Sheppard, the Stadium announcer, intoned imperiously to the crowd of 46,711 during the Old-Timers Day introductions, "and hopefully for many seasons after that will be Number 1 . . ."

He didn't have to say "Billy Martin." For seven minutes Billy Martin's fans cheered, their vocal cords erupting each time the former and future manager waved his cap or bowed. But what had happened in those five days?

Martin's agent, Doug Newton, was watching the Yankee game in Kansas City on Monday night, several hours after his client's tearful resignation, when Steinbrenner phoned him. Billy, the owner suggested, should be managing the Yankees. In the days that followed, Newton and Steinbrenner negotiated a deal by which Billy again would manage the Yankees beginning in the 1980 season. Crucial to the negotiations was Martin's apology to Steinbrenner for the "convicted liar" remark. Martin did apologize privately. But the agreement almost fell through when Steinbrenner believed Martin was telling people about his imminent return. Another conversation between the owner and the agent, however, solidified the new contract through the 1981 season.

"What he said to me," Steinbrenner commented the day of the announcement, "showed me that he was a man who realized he had made a small mistake, and it *was* small in the total picture."

The owner also acknowledged that there are times when a person has to be understanding and compassionate, and "I didn't feel that what happened was right." As for his political conviction, he realized it was "going to come up again and again and again, and I should live with it." Whether he was motivated purely by compassion or pragmatically by a desire to placate the unhappy fans, Steinbrenner was committing himself to bringing Martin back in 1980 if his health allowed it. Publicly, at least, both men were saying they could work together again.

"George and I in the past have had our indifferences," Martin said, in an unaccustomed reversion to Stengelese, "but we always found a way sometimes to solve them."

Still, not many baseball people believed that Martin would return. Their reasoning was that either Martin would find another job before then or Steinbrenner would find an excuse, such as health or public behavior, not to honor his commitment. By rehiring Martin during the 1979 season, the owner honored his commitment even before he said he would, but at that time Yankee-watchers believed Steinbrenner wanted to give Martin time to hang himself again. He knew Billy's tendency to self-destruct. He knew it so well that he was concerned it might happen on the very day Billy Martin was rehired. Riding the elevator up to his stadium office after the stunning announcement, Steinbrenner turned to an aide.

"Go stay with Billy," he whispered, "and make sure he doesn't say anything."

As the manager of the White Sox during the 1977 season, Bob Lemon enjoyed his view of the Yankees. "I can't wait to pick up the paper every morning to see what's happening," he joked one day. "It's like *Mary Hartman, Mary Hartman.*" Fourteen months later the joke was on him; he found himself directing the cast of baseball's hit soap opera. Hours after Bill Veeck fired Lemon on June 30, Al Rosen phoned his one-time Indians' teammate at his Chicago apartment.

"Keep yourself in cold storage," Rosen told him. "Sooner or later I want you in the Yankee organization."

Rosen and Lemon went back more than thirty years together. Lemon, whom Rosen affectionately called Meat, won twenty or more games seven times as an Indian pitcher and was elected to the Hall of Fame in 1976. The jovial, red-nosed, chain-smoker served as Yankee pitching coach in 1976 but departed to manage the White Sox, a job he handled so effectively he was named American League manager of the year in 1977. Now, the Sunday evening that Rosen was informed of Martin's remarks at O'Hare Airport, the Yankees' president phoned Lemon at his home in Long Beach, California. Rosen wanted to make sure that Lemon was available to be the Yankee manager. The next day Rosen called him back.

"How long," he asked, "will it take you to get to Kansas City?"

Billy Martin was out, Bob Lemon was in. His arrival was tantamount to turning off the fire under a pot of boiling water. The calm nature of the fifty-seven-year-old manager restored peace and tranquillity to the turbulent clubhouse.

To be sure, Lemon's takeover virtually coincided with the return to complete health of centerfielder Mickey Rivers, second baseman Willie Randolph, shortstop Bucky Dent and pitcher Catfish Hunter. But the change in managers was the most important factor in the Yankees' surge that saw them climb steadily toward the Red Sox, overtake them and then defeat them in a one-game playoff for the division title.

"Things are more settled," Roy White noted long after the change. "You don't have the expectancy of Billy being fired or him resigning as you had before, the uncertainty of whether he'd be the manager tomorrow or next week or whatever. Now that you don't have that, it's a relief. It's something you're not thinking about when you go to the ball park."

Sitting in the owner's box at Yankee Stadium one night, Rosen looked down at the Yankee dugout and said, "Lem might get up from that seat, but if he does, he'll go to get a drink of water. That's the extent of it." There would be, Rosen added, no dugout confrontations, no clubhouse confrontations, no front-office confrontations.

Not that Lemon didn't encounter potential troubles. He experienced

The New York Yankees

Al Rosen

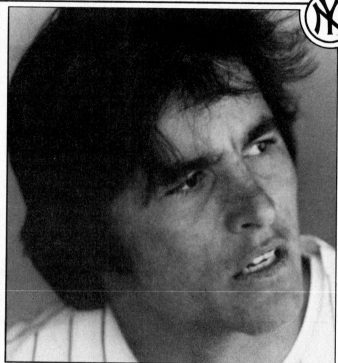

Bucky Dent returns to the Yankee dugout after Fenway Park playoff homer

Rich Gossage

Ed Figueroa

several but turned them aside as if he were flicking a fly off his arm.

Ed Figueroa once left the mound during a game before Lemon reached the mound to take him out. Lemon followed him into the clubhouse and chewed him out. When a reporter asked about the incident, the manager said, "Everything's all right."

His tone of voice suggested that the matter should be dropped.

Another time Jackson removed himself from the lineup just before a game in Baltimore, saying he was ill. Some of his teammates suggested his illness developed when he saw his name eighth in the batting order. Billy Martin surely would have had something to say if he were the manager. But not Lemon.

"All I know," he said, "is that he told Clyde King that he didn't feel too good. I'm not going to play a guy that isn't feeling good."

When he took command, Lemon often emphasized the importance of Jackson being in the lineup every day if the Yankees were to win. Jackson responded with a hitting surge similar to his comeback in 1977 once Martin made him the cleanup hitter.

Mickey Rivers, in one of his periodic states of unhappiness, arrived late for a game in Seattle after he had played lethargically the night before. Lemon fined him $250.

"I'm not looking to have any prolonged warfare," the manager said. "He was late and I fined him and that was it."

And that *was* it. The Yankees responded to their new manager's easygoing style, winning forty-eight games and losing only twenty. Playing with the ferocity of the Yankee teams of Ruth and DiMaggio and Mantle, the Yankees crushed the Red Sox in six consecutive games in September, rocketing three and a half games in front of the staggering Red Sox. Their four-game sweep in Fenway Park, where the Red Sox lose about as often as a Boston Republican wins, was awesome. The Yankees won by scores of 15–3, 13–2, 7–0 and 7–4, and left the Red Sox muttering.

"The Yankees are together, nine guys giving their all," said Rick Burleson, the Red Sox shortstop. "Us? We come to the ball park and one guy's dizzy, another guy's hand hurts. That's bull. They've got one guy who comes out of the hospital to play. That's how much this series meant to them."

Burleson was talking about Reggie Jackson, who had spent forty-eight hours in traction for a sore back. But by then Ron Guidry had the Red Sox thinking they might be better off in a hospital, shutting them out on two hits in the third game of the Fenway Park sweep. Six days later at Yankee Stadium he fired another two-hit shutout. That, however, was not the last the Red Sox would see of the Cajun left-hander. Winning their last game of the season while the Yankees were losing, the Red Sox forced a one-game playoff on Monday afternoon,

October 2, at Fenway Park—but was a one-game playoff fair? Wouldn't three games be better?

"One's enough," Guidry replied. "I can only pitch one game."

Accustomed to four days off between starts, Guidry started the American League's first playoff game since 1948 on only three days' rest. He didn't overwhelm the Red Sox, but he pitched well enough for the Yankees to have a 4–2 lead when he departed during the seventh inning. It wasn't Jackson or Munson or Nettles who gave Guidry that lead; rather, it was Bucky Dent, the light-hitting shortstop, who socked a startling three-run homer off Mike Torrez, a Yankee free agent defector, in the seventh. To preserve that lead, the Yankees were counting on Rich Gossage, whose father "almost but not quite" struck it rich in the gold fields of Cripple Creek, Colorado, in the 1940's. But the husky twenty-seven-year-old righthander struck gold on his own when he signed with the Yankees as a free agent for $2,748,000. While supplanting Sparky Lyle as the relief pitcher, he had performed spectacularly well and spectacularly poorly.

In his first Yankee appearance Gossage gave up a game-losing home run to Richie Zisk of the Rangers on opening day. In his second outing he gave up a game-tying homer to Larry Hisle of the Brewers; later in the season he gave up two consecutive homers to Hisle that resulted in another loss.

"I was just trying to do too much," Gossage explained. "The pressure of the contract, the free agency, playing in New York, proving myself on a new team—I just wanted to come in here and do so well and prove myself when I didn't have anything to prove. People knew I could pitch."

In his final thirty appearances the man they call Goose pitched the way people knew he could pitch. He didn't allow a home run, and he registered fifteen saves and six victories while absorbing only three losses, twice on unearned runs. Now he had to protect the Yankees' 4–2 lead to win the Eastern Division title. Soon he had a 5–2 lead on Reggie Jackson's homer into the centerfield bleachers in the eighth. But then Gossage allowed the Red Sox two runs, to narrow the lead to 5–4 going into the ninth. With one out, Rick Burleson walked and Jerry Remy singled. Lou Piniella lost Remy's low liner in the glare of the late-afternoon sun, but the rightfielder stabbed the ball with his glove, holding Burleson, the tying run, at second.

To protect the lead, Gossage now had to face Jim Rice, who would be chosen the American League's Most Valuable Player because of his 46 homers and 139 runs batted in, and Carl Yastrzemski, the Red Sox patron saint.

Rearing back, Gossage fired his fastball, which has been clocked at 98 mph. Rice lifted a soft fly to Piniella, and then Yaz popped a high

Virtually upside down, Graig Nettles turns the Dodgers inside out

foul that Graig Nettles caught near third base. The Yankees won the game, 5–4, and the division title after having been fourteen games behind the Red Sox on July 19—one of the most remarkable team comebacks in baseball history.

But now the Yankees had to play the Royals again for the American League pennant, this time with the first two games in Kansas City.

In the opener Reggie Jackson—who was being called Mr. October—collected a single, a double and a three-run homer in the 7–1 victory behind two young righthanders, Jim Beattie and Ken Clay. After a 10–4 loss, the Yankees returned to the stadium for the third game.

Jackson drove in three of the Yankees' first four runs with a homer, a single and a sacrifice fly, then Thurman Munson clouted a mammoth homer into the monument area in left-centerfield for two eighth-inning runs and a 6–5 victory.

If the pattern of the previous two pennant playoffs was to hold, the Royals would have to win the fourth game—but this time Ron Guidry was pitching.

After a triple by George Brett led to a first-inning run, Guidry was flawless. Graig Nettles, meanwhile, hit a home run in the second, Roy White hit a home run in the sixth and the Yankees had a 2–1 victory, their third straight pennant and the thirty-second pennant in their history.

"I was hoping it would hold up as the winning run," White said of his homer. "That was one I wanted to have."

The year before, White had nothing. After being a leftfielder or designated hitter most of the season, he started only one of the five playoff games and pinch-hit twice in the six Series games. He was especially embarrassed in Los Angeles during the Series because he has many relatives there. "The only time they got to see me," he said, "was during the introductions when the announcer would say, '. . . and now all the other Yankees.' "

White, at thirty-four, was the senior Yankee in point of service; a true gentleman with a mellifluous voice, he first played for them in 1965 and served as the bridge between championship eras. The bridge didn't lead to a pennant for him until 1976, but the outcome that year was disappointing. The Yankees lost the Series, and the next year he was neglected.

"I just didn't feel I was part of it," the outfielder said. "It was like having a full-course meal and not getting a chance to have the dessert. This year I didn't get much of a meal, but I got a helluva dessert."

White had played irregularly until Lemon replaced Martin, so irregularly that there were "a couple of times I felt like taking my uniform off and going home." Back in May, when Martin still was the

Willie Randolph

manager, White became so frustrated by his inactivity that he uncharacteristically exploded in the dugout.

"Get me the hell off this team!" he screamed. "Get me anywhere, but get me the hell off this team. I can't play two days a week."

But after Lemon's arrival White flourished once more, proving what he had been saying all along: if he played regularly, he would produce as he always had. And the Yankees continued producing when they had to. As George Brett, one of the dejected Royals, remarked, "We're the best team money can't buy, and they're the best team money can buy. Maybe we've resigned ourselves to their superiority. They have a lot of players who play their best under pressure."

Pressure. Fourteen games from first place on July 19—that's pressure. Playing in Fenway Park in Boston in a one-game playoff—that's pressure. And then losing the first two games of the World Series to the Dodgers—that's pressure.

In the Series opener Ed Figueroa, the first Puerto Rican pitcher to be a twenty-game winner in the major leagues, failed to last two innings as the Dodgers won, 11–5; then Reggie Jackson failed against rookie righthander Bob Welch in a theatrical ninth-inning confrontation before the Dodgers won again, 4–3. Ron Cey had driven in all four Dodger runs with a single and a homer. Jackson had produced all the Yankee runs with a double and a run-scoring grounder. But in the ninth the Yankees had runners on first and second when Jackson strode to the plate against Welch, a cool twenty-one-year-old fastball pitcher.

For six minutes the drama built—Welch firing his fastball, Jackson swinging mightily and fouling off several pitches.

With a 3-2 count Jackson swung and missed another fastball. As the Dodger fans shouted in ecstasy, Jackson fumed. He flung his bat against the dugout wall and, head down in the runway to the clubhouse, angrily tried to push past Bob Lemon, who turned and pushed him back.

The Yankees clearly were an endangered species. Ron Guidry hadn't been able to pitch in the first two games because he had started the fourth playoff game, Mickey Rivers was ailing and Willie Randolph was out with a hamstring pull.

The season had not treated Randolph kindly. He had suffered torn cartilage in his left knee in June and had to miss the All-Star game after he was voted the starting second baseman for the second consecutive year. He had come to the Yankees from the Pirates in 1976, and he was improving steadily as a hitter and a wide-ranging fielder. But the front office was wondering if he was a malingerer or a hypochondriac. They were particularly suspicious when his knee injury was diagnosed as a bruise, only to have him contend the ailment was more serious.

As it developed, Randolph was correct. Tests by an independent orthopedist determined that he had torn cartilage, although even then

Thurman Munson, 1947–79

The New York Yankees

Tommy John

Al Rosen referred to the injury as "slight damage" to the knee. After resting and then strengthening the knee by exercise, Randolph returned just after the All-Star break. Again he was one of the team's most productive hitters, but he pulled a hamstring muscle on Friday night before the end of the regular season. Suddenly he was a dugout cheerleader. But he and the rest of the Yankees had much to cheer about in the third game as the Series returned to the Stadium and Graig Nettles, diving and spinning, turned the Series around.

The box score showed that Ron Guidry had stopped the Dodgers, 5–1. The game may not have been one of Guidry's most artistic—he walked seven—but Nettles never was more artistic.

Nettles saved at least five runs with spectacular plays on three wicked grounders—Reggie Smith's in the third with one on and two out, and Steve Garvey's in the fifth and Davey Lopes' in the sixth, each with two out and the bases loaded. Nettles made twisting, diving stops on each grounder and ended the inning, throwing Smith out in the third and getting force plays at second in the fifth and sixth.

"That," Dodger manager Tom Lasorda said, "was one of the greatest exhibitions of playing third base I've seen in all my career."

Nettles' uncanny style is not merely his diving stops. Even more impressive is the way he instantly jumps back to his feet (no jack-in-the-box ever popped up faster), whirls and throws unerringly to first or second. His sense of direction is unsurpassed.

Off the field Nettles has an uncanny wit. Viewing Sparky Lyle's season, he remarked how the relief pitcher had gone from "Cy Young to sayonara." Talking about himself and the Yankees, he said, "When I was a little boy, I wanted to be a baseball player and join a circus. With the Yankees, I've accomplished both."

But he has another side. He treats fans with contempt and sportswriters even worse, firing his most vulgar shots at official scorers who call plays or hits the way they see them, not the way he sometimes sees them. His wit also is tainted at times with cruel humor. Wit and cruelty aside, Nettles emerged as the best third baseman in baseball, and he was clearly that in the Series' third game. If anything turned the Series around, it was his glove with the self-deprecating "E5" inked on it— the scorer's symbols for error, third baseman.

In the fourth game Jackson was involved in another controversy, but this time his teammates did not complain. Attempting to complete an inning-ending double play, Dodger shortstop Bill Russell's throw hit Jackson's right thigh and bounded away as an important run scored. The Dodgers argued that Jackson deliberately interfered with the ball. Asked about it later, Jackson denied all but later implied that maybe he had turned his leg ever so slightly.

"Something odd always happens around him," Bob Lemon observed.

Whatever, the umpires allowed the run and the Yankees eventually won, 4–3, on a walk, Jackson's single and Piniella's single in the tenth inning. The next day the Dodgers committed three errors and several of omission, Munson drove in five runs with two singles and a double and the Yankees romped to a 12–2 triumph and a 3–2 lead. Jim Beattie was the winning pitcher, scattering nine hits—the same Jim Beattie who four months earlier had looked "scared stiff" to George Steinbrenner in a Fenway Park loss. After watching the Dodgers crush the Yankees in the Series opener, Beattie had thought he might be scared stiff if he got a chance to start.

"Damn," he said to himself, "I don't know how to pitch to these guys."

But his wife of one month, Martha, came up with a scouting report that bolstered his confidence. "After one of the games in Los Angeles," Beattie related, "she told me she heard people in the stands saying that hard-throwing righthanders gave the Dodgers trouble so a guy like Beattie could do well against them." Beattie did so well the Yankees now had an opportunity to do what never had been done before—win the World Series with four straight victories after having lost the first two games. And the Yankees did it, winning, 7–2, as Bucky Dent and Brian Doyle, substituting for Randolph at second base, drove in the first five runs.

Dent, the heretofore unheralded shortstop who struck the vital homer in the division playoff at Fenway Park, was voted the Series Most Valuable Player. He had ten hits in twenty-four times at bat, he knocked in seven runs with six hits and he had four runs batted in in the last two games.

Dent, a Georgian by birth and a Floridian by residence, joined the Yankees as the 1977 season opened. Rather than lose him as a free agent after the season, White Sox owner Bill Veeck had traded him for outfielder Oscar Gamble, two minor league pitchers and $400,000— and the Yankees declared their search for a shortstop to be over.

Dent, who does a verbal imitation of Donald Duck so well he probably could converse with Mickey Mouse, shied away from the clubhouse turbulence. But he mentioned occasionally that he was unhappy at being removed for a pinch-hitter in the late innings. He appreciated Lemon's arrival because the new manager didn't pull him as much as Martin did.

As a handsome, black-haired favorite of teenage girls and older women as well, the twenty-seven-year-old Dent became even more popular after the World Series—a folk hero of sorts. He portrayed a football player in a television movie, he co-hosted a New York television show for a week, he worked on a television sports program, he did commercials and he emerged as a poster rival of Shaun Cassidy and Andy Gibb.

But with all the attention he received and the time he had to spend on being a hero, Dent also almost had his marriage wrecked. His personal problems, which were to affect his performance the following season, served as an omen of the ill fortune that was to engulf the Yankees in 1979.

The New York Yankees

Dick Howser

The season's most tragic moment occurred on August 2, an off-day in the schedule. Most of the team returned to New York after a mid-week series in Chicago, but Thurman Munson decided to go home to Canton, Ohio, where he could spend some time with his family and also test his newly purchased $1.4 million Cessna Citation, a twin-engine jet. While practicing takeoffs and landings at the Akron-Canton airport that Thursday afternoon, Munson was at the controls when the jet crashed short of the runway. Munson died in the flaming fuselage, although two other pilots accompanying him were able to escape.

Along with baseball, Munson's family and flying commanded his primary attention. One of the reasons he learned to fly was that it enabled him virtually to commute to and from Canton, where his wife Diana and their three young children stayed.

"He was like a little boy about flying," says Richard Moss, the noted baseball lawyer who negotiated Munson's last Yankee contract. "He talked about getting up in the air alone, being with nature, able to think. And of course, he was able to get home to his family. It was a marvelous thing to him."

Flying was so important to the Yankees' captain and catcher that it had been part of Moss' contract negotiations. Unlike virtually all other guaranteed baseball contracts, Munson's did not have a clause absolving the Yankees from paying the remainder of the contract if he were killed while piloting a plane.

Munson's death devastated his teammates, especially the pitchers. "He made me a pitcher," Ed Figueroa said. "He taught me how to pitch to the hitters."

Reluctantly, the Yankees resumed their schedule the night after their captain was killed. Before the opener of a weekend series with the Orioles, the fans saluted Munson's memory with an eight-minute standing ovation while the catcher's area behind home plate remained vacant in the tradition of the riderless horse at a military funeral.

Munson's death was the nadir of the Yankees' season but it had no material effect on their failure to reach the World Series for the fourth consecutive year. By the time the Cessna Citation crashed, the Yankees had dropped 14 games out of first place.

At the start of the 1979 season, the Yankees had no reason to believe they would finish in fourth place. George Steinbrenner believed he had assured another pennant by plunging into the free-agent market again, adding Tommy John and Luis Tiant to the pitching staff.

John had been the Dodgers' lefthander with the "bionic" arm. His elbow had been repaired in a rare surgical procedure in 1974 that made him a better pitcher than before. He signed a $1,417,000 three-year contract. The cigar-smoking El Tiante had significantly aided the Red Sox with victories on the mound and laughter in the clubhouse. He signed a $740,000 two-year contract.

But the Yankees could not profit from their presence despite John's twenty-one victories and Tiant's thirteen. The Yankees' season, it developed, turned on the absence of Rich Gossage for twelve weeks, one week shy of half the season.

On April 19, following an afternoon game with the Orioles at Yankee Stadium, Gossage, the team's premier relief pitcher, became involved in a clubhouse fight with reserve catcher Cliff Johnson, a playful bear who justified his reputation as baseball's Joe Btfsplk, the Li'l Abner comic-strip character who was followed by a black cloud wherever he went.

The encounter between Gossage and Johnson, which began with good-natured needling, quickly escalated after Reggie Jackson asked Johnson if he could "handle Goose's smoke" when they were National League opponents two years earlier.

"Only when he heard it," Gossage replied.

Shortly afterward, the 6-foot-4, 225-pound Johnson and the 6-foot-3, 215-pound Gossage tangled in the shower room. When Gossage grabbed Johnson and tried to hold him back, the pitcher tore a ligament in his right thumb.

"They say you should walk away from things like that," Gossage said two days later, sitting dejectedly in his Mercedes in the players' parking lot, his thumb in a cast. "But what are you going to do? It's an instinctive thing. I don't know what happened. It just happened—boom boom. As quick as it happened, it was over. I feel awful about it. It's very depressing."

If the injury was depressing to Gossage, it was disastrous for the Yankees. Their bullpen collapsed. Ron Davis, a bespectacled young righthander, eventually provided some stability, but by then Dick Tidrow had been banished to the Chicago Cubs and Ron Guidry had volunteered for relief duty. Manager Bob Lemon gratefully accepted, using Guidry three times in relief before returning the lean lefthander to the rotation where he would have an 18-8 record and a 2.78 earned-

Luis Tiant

run average. But not even Guidry could save the Yankees—or Lemon's job.

By mid-June, the Yankees were floundering in fourth place and Steinbrenner, understandably unhappy, concluded that Lemon could not stir the team from its lethargy.

Billy Martin, meanwhile, was serving his penance, waiting patiently until he was to resume his Yankee managerial career in 1980, as decreed the previous year. Martin had stayed out of trouble since engaging in a fight with a Nevada sportswriter the previous November and he even had reached an out-of-court settlement with the newsman, Ray Hagar.

Steinbrenner had insisted that Martin would have to clear up the pending court action if he hoped to be the Yankees' future manager, so Martin publicly apologized. Hagar also received an $8,000 payment through a Reno minor-league basketball team, which Martin had been helping to promote when he allegedly punched Hagar during an interview. As his part of the settlement, Hagar dropped both the criminal charge of battery and his civil suit.

On June 17, Steinbrenner summoned Martin to Columbus, Ohio, where they met for several hours. Assured that Steinbrenner would attach no conditions to his employment, as the owner had done the first time around, Martin agreed to return immediately. He also received a contract for 1980 and 1981 at $120,000 annually plus certain expenses.

"I think if it can be turned around," Steinbrenner explained, "Billy is the guy to do it. Last year I needed someone 180 degrees from what Billy was. This year I need someone 180 degrees from what Bob Lemon was. I don't know if it's too late, but I think we can make a run."

Yankee fans greeted Martin's return June 19 with a thunderous ovation. Reggie Jackson, however, was not applauding.

The last time Reggie Jackson played for Billy Martin he bunted into a five-day suspension. But before he could play for Martin again, Jackson had to recover from a leg injury and a reluctance to rejoin his long-time adversary.

On the night Martin returned as manager, Jackson, who was on the disabled list, did not go to the clubhouse before the game. Instead, he went to the stadium executive offices where, in a meeting with Steinbrenner and other Yankee officials, he asked to be traded. Although the Yankees talked to some American League teams, they did not comply with his request.

Resigned to at least another half-season with Martin as manager, Jackson proceeded to play and, typically, play well. Despite missing four weeks, Jackson hit 29 homers and drove in 89 runs. His .297 batting average was the highest of his career.

Not that life proceeded smoothly for the controversial slugger. Although he achieved a state of peaceful coexistence with Martin, he developed a feud with George Steinbrenner, once his staunchest ally. From the right fielder's behavior in the last couple of months of the season, it appeared that he was intent on talking himself into being traded.

Typical was his reaction to Al Rosen's resignation as Yankee president in July; the front office had not remained quiet and stable either.

"Rosen left," Reggie remarked, "because he's a man who wants to be treated like a man and refused to be subservient to The Man. Why don't you write an editorial telling the fans what really goes on here? It's not easy to work here. Rosen was under pressure ever since he got here. He wasn't getting the respect he deserved. He was a good guy who got tired of taking all that bull from Steinbrenner."

In September, Jackson was quoted as accusing the owner of slurring him racially, calling him "boy," as in, "You better get your head screwed on straight, boy." Two weeks after that, Jackson disclosed that Steinbrenner would not let him present Catfish Hunter his gift of a replica of the World Series championship trophy during the Stadium retirement ceremony for this long-time teammate on the A's and Yankees.

Goaded sufficiently, Steinbrenner began replying publicly to Jackson's comments. The principal owner even persuaded Martin to join in, despite the manager's reluctance to become involved in something that, for once, was not his battle.

By that time, Al Rosen was ensconced in his new office in Atlantic City, New Jersey, far from the Yankees' lost season. He was executive vice president of the Park Place Casino-Hotel, working once again for his friend, William Weinberger of Bally Manufacturing Corporation, and he was free from the pressures and harangues to which his friend, George Steinbrenner, had subjected him. Other important members of the Yankees also were scattering.

Catfish Hunter, after a 2-9 record in the final season of his five-year contract, retired to his farm in North Carolina to plant soy beans and collect $100,000 a year for fifteen years.

Roy White, a Yankee for fifteen seasons, the quiet bridge between the championship eras, became a free agent, no longer wanted at age thirty-six.

Cedric Tallis prepared to return home to Kansas City and serve the Yankees in player personnel matters, giving way as general manager to Gene Michael, a former Yankee shortstop whom Steinbrenner had groomed for the new position by assigning him a variety of duties—coach, minor-league manager and administrative assistant in the front office.

Gene Michael

Then there was Alfred Manuel Martin, who chose his usual bizarre manner of escape, this time an incident with a marshmallow salesman. Not that he wanted to go anywhere, but Martin was fired even before he originally was to have been rehired.

The manager and the marshmallow salesman met by chance in the bar of the Chez Colette restaurant at L'Hotel de France in Bloomington, Minnesota, late on the night of October 23. Martin had just returned from hunting pheasant in South Dakota while Joseph W. Cooper of Lincolnshire, Illinois, was there selling marshmallows.

Their versions differed on what occurred but no one disputed the fact that when their confrontation ended, the fifty-two-year-old Cooper lay on his back on the floor of the hotel lobby, blood gushing from his lip.

The marshmallow salesman's bleeding lip was one bleeding lip too many for Steinbrenner; five days later he fired Martin. This time there were no tears and this time there would be no reconciliation and no triumphant return.

"How much can we take and still command any respect?" Steinbrenner explained. "How can the Yankees, as an organization, keep putting their head in the sand? The public, at some point, thinks we are part and party to it. Then there are the players, especially the younger ones. How can I stand up and talk to them about the Yankee tradition? I can't permit a dual standard to exist."

Earlier on the day that he fired Martin, Steinbrenner sent a private jet to bring Dick Howser from his home in Tallahassee, Florida, to the owner's horse farm in Ocala, Florida.

Howser, once a Yankee infielder, had served as their third-base coach for ten years but left after the 1978 season to become Florida State University's baseball coach. Howser, as quiet and unobtrusive as Martin was noisy and noticeable, had been the Yankees' interim manager for one game—a 1978 loss in Kansas City in the hours between Martin's tearful resignation and Bob Lemon's arrival. He had spurned an opportunity in 1977 to become the Yankee manager during one of Martin's several shaky periods that year. But when Steinbrenner offered him the opportunity now, the forty-two-year-old Howser accepted.

The managerial change, the fifth in seven years of Steinbrenner's stewardship, triggered a ten-day flurry of business in which Steinbrenner blitzed his competition. In whirlwind fashion, the owner:

—kept Bucky Dent and Jim Spencer from becoming free agents by signing them to new contracts for a total of nearly $3,000,000.

—signed free agents Rudy May, a lefthanded pitcher, for three years at $1,000,000 and Bob Watson, a first baseman and righthanded slugger for four years at $2,160,000.

—acquired Ruppert Jones from Seattle to fill the center-field vacancy that had been created in July when he tired of Mickey Rivers' erratic behavior and traded him to Texas.

—obtained, in a trade with the lowly Toronto Blue Jays, catcher Rick Cerone and lefthanded pitcher Tom Underwood in exchange for Chris Chambliss, who was disappointed at leaving the club.

"We wanted to get everything done so quickly that no one knew strategically what we were doing," Steinbrenner explained. "Once you reach the December meetings, you're in tough shape. There's nothing the other guys would like more than to have the Yankees at a disadvantage. That's why I was so determined to get it done quickly. I didn't want to go to the meetings vulnerable."

In their glittering history, the Yankees have seldom been vulnerable. When Steinbrenner took command, he vowed to restore the franchise to what he felt was its rightful place in baseball. He succeeded, then it slipped in 1979 but then he regrouped. His thinking was different from that of his predecessors, but the rules were different too. Then again, in acquiring the best players available, he was merely doing what Colonel Jacob Ruppoert had done back in 1920 when the Yankees obtained Babe Ruth.

The New York Yankees

Records and Rosters

Yankee Won-Lost Record, Year by Year

Year	League Position	Won	Lost	Pct.	Manager	Attendance	World Series Opponent	W-L
1903	4th	72	62	.537	Griffith	211,808		
1904	2nd	92	59	.609	Griffith	438,919		
1905	6th	71	78	.477	Griffith	309,100		
1906	2nd	90	61	.596	Griffith	434,700		
1907	5th	70	78	.473	Griffith	350,020		
1908	8th	51	103	.331	Griffith-Elberfeld	305,500		
1909	5th	74	77	.490	Stallings	501,000		
1910	2nd	88	63	.583	Stallings-Chase	355,857		
1911	6th	76	76	.500	Chase	302,444		
1912	8th	50	102	.329	Wolverton	242,194		
1913	7th	57	94	.377	Chance	357,551		
1914	6th (tie)	70	84	.455	Chance-Peckinpaugh	359,477		
1915	5th	69	83	.454	Donovan	256,035		
1916	4th	80	74	.519	Donovan	469,211		
1917	6th	71	82	.464	Donovan	330,294		
1918	4th	60	63	.488	Huggins	282,047		
1919	3rd	80	59	.576	Huggins	619,164		
1920	3rd	95	59	.617	Huggins	1,289,422		
1921	**1st (+4½)**	**98**	**55**	**.641**	**Huggins**	**1,230,696**	**Giants**	**3-5**
1922	**1st (+1)**	**94**	**60**	**.610**	**Huggins**	**1,026,134**	**Giants**	**0-4**
1923	**1st (+16)**	**98**	**54**	**.645**	**Huggins**	**1,007,066**	**Giants**	**4-2**
1924	2nd	89	63	.586	Huggins	1,053,533		
1925	7th	69	85	.448	Huggins	697,267		
1926	**1st (+3)**	**91**	**63**	**.591**	**Huggins**	**1,027,095**	**Cardinals**	**3-4**
1927	**1st (+14)**	**110**	**44**	**.714**	**Huggins**	**1,164,015**	**Pirates**	**4-0**
1928	**1st (+2½)**	**101**	**53**	**.656**	**Huggins**	**1,072,132**	**Cardinals**	**4-0**
1929	2nd	88	66	.571	Huggins-Fletcher	960,148		
1930	3rd	86	68	.558	Shawkey	1,169,230		
1931	2nd	94	59	.614	McCarthy	912,437		
1932	**1st (+13)**	**107**	**47**	**.695**	**McCarthy**	**962,320**	**Cubs**	**4-0**
1933	2nd	91	59	.607	McCarthy	728,014		
1934	2nd	94	60	.610	McCarthy	854,682		
1935	2nd	89	60	.597	McCarthy	657,508		
1936	**1st (+19½)**	**102**	**51**	**.667**	**McCarthy**	**976,913**	**Giants**	**4-2**
1937	**1st (+13)**	**102**	**52**	**.662**	**McCarthy**	**998,148**	**Giants**	**4-1**
1938	**1st (+9½)**	**99**	**53**	**.651**	**McCarthy**	**970,916**	**Cubs**	**4-0**
1939	**1st (+17)**	**106**	**45**	**.702**	**McCarthy**	**859,785**	**Reds**	**4-0**
1940	3rd	88	66	.571	McCarthy	988,975		
1941	**1st (+17)**	**101**	**53**	**.656**	**McCarthy**	**964,722**	**Dodgers**	**4-1**
1942	**1st (+9)**	**103**	**51**	**.669**	**McCarthy**	**988,251**	**Cardinals**	**1-4**
1943	**1st (+13½)**	**98**	**56**	**.636**	**McCarthy**	**645,006**	**Cardinals**	**4-1**
1944	3rd	83	71	.539	McCarthy	822,864		
1945	4th	81	71	.553	McCarthy	881,846		
1946	3rd	87	67	.565	McCarthy-Dickey-Neun	2,265,512		
1947	**1st (+12)**	**97**	**57**	**.630**	**Harris**	**2,178,937**	**Dodgers**	**4-3**
1948	3rd	94	60	.610	Harris	2,373,901		
1949	**1st (+1)**	**97**	**57**	**.630**	**Stengel**	**2,281,676**	**Dodgers**	**4-1**

Yankee Won-Lost Record, Year by Year

Year	League Position	Won	Lost	Pct.	Manager	Attendance	World Series Opponent	W-L
1950	1st (+3)	**98**	**56**	.636	**Stengel**	**2,081,380**	**Phillies**	**4-0**
1951	1st (+5)	**98**	**56**	.636	**Stengel**	**1,950,107**	**Giants**	**4-2**
1952	1st (+2)	**95**	**59**	.617	**Stengel**	**1,629,665**	**Dodgers**	**4-3**
1953	1st (+8½)	**99**	**52**	.656	**Stengel**	**1,537,811**	**Dodgers**	**4-2**
1954	2nd	103	51	.669	Stengel	1,475,171		
1955	1st (+3)	**96**	**58**	.623	**Stengel**	**1,490,138**	**Dodgers**	**3-4**
1956	1st (+9)	**97**	**57**	.680	**Stengel**	**1,491,784**	**Dodgers**	**4-3**
1957	1st (+8)	**98**	**56**	.636	**Stengel**	**1,497,134**	**Braves**	**3-4**
1958	1st (+10)	**92**	**62**	.597	**Stengel**	**1,428,438**	**Braves**	**4-3**
1959	3rd	79	75	.513	Stengel	1,552,030		
1960	1st (+8)	**97**	**57**	.630	**Stengel**	**1,627,349**	**Pirates**	**3-4**
1961	1st (+8)	**109**	**53**	.673	**Houk**	**1,747,736**	**Reds**	**4-1**
1962	1st (+5)	**96**	**66**	.593	**Houk**	**1,493,574**	**Giants**	**4-3**
1963	1st (+10½)	**104**	**57**	.646	**Houk**	**1,308,920**	**Dodgers**	**0-4**
1964	1st (+1)	**99**	**63**	.611	**Berra**	**1,305,638**	**Cardinals**	**3-4**
1965	6th	77	85	.475	Keane	1,213,552		
1966	10th	70	89	.440	Keane-Houk	1,124,648		
1967	9th	72	90	.444	Houk	1,141,714		
1968	5th	83	79	.512	Houk	1,125,124		
1969	5th	80	81	.497	Houk	1,067,996		
1970	2nd	93	69	.574	Houk	1,136,879		
1971	4th	82	80	.506	Houk	1,070,771		
1972	4th	79	76	.510	Houk	966,328		
1973	4th	80	82	.494	Houk	1,262,077		
1974	2nd	89	73	.549	Virdon	1,273,075		
1975	3rd	83	77	.519	Virdon-Martin	1,288,048		
1976	1st (+10½)	**97**	**62**	.610	**Martin**	**2,012,434**	**Reds**	**0-4**
1977	1st (+2½)	**100**	**62**	.617	**Martin**	**2,103,092**	**Dodgers**	**4-2**
1978	1st (+1)	**100**	**63**	.613	**Martin-Lemon**	**2,335,871**	**Dodgers**	**4-2**
1979	4th	89	71	.556	Lemon-Martin	2,537,765		

All-Time Yankee Top 10—Hitting

Games

Mantle	2,401
Gehrig	2,164
Berra	2,116
Ruth	2,084
White	1,881
Dickey	1,789
DiMaggio	1,736
Crosetti	1,682
Rizzuto	1,661
Lazzeri	1,659

Average

Ruth	.349
Gehrig	.340
DiMaggio	.325
Combs	.325
Dickey	.313
Meusel	.311
Chapman	.305
Mantle	.298
Schang	.297
Keeler	.295

Runs

Ruth	1,959
Gehrig	1,888
Mantle	1,677
DiMaggio	1,390
Combs	1,186
Berra	1,174
Crosetti	1,006
White	964
Lazzeri	952
Rolfe	942

Hits

Gehrig	2,721
Ruth	2,518
Mantle	2,415
DiMaggio	2,214
Berra	2,148
Dickey	1,969
Combs	1,866
White	1,803
Lazzeri	1,784
Rizzuto	1,588

Doubles

Gehrig	535
Ruth	424
DiMaggio	389
Mantle	344
Dickey	343
Meusel	338
Lazzeri	327
Berra	321
Combs	309
White	300

Triples

Gehrig	162
Combs	154
DiMaggio	131
Pipp	121
Lazzeri	115
Ruth	106
Meusel	87
Henrich	73
Mantle	72
Dickey	72

Home Runs		Runs Batted In		Stolen Bases	
Ruth	659	Gehrig	1,991	Chase	248
Mantle	536	Ruth	1,970	White	233
Gehrig	493	DiMaggio	1,537	Chapman	184
DiMaggio	361	Mantle	1,509	Conroy	184
Berra	358	Berra	1,430	Maisel	183
Maris	203	Dickey	1,209	Mantle	153
Dickey	202	Lazzeri	1,154	Clarke	151
Keller	184	Meusel	1,005	Rizzuto	149
Henrich	183	Pipp	825	Lazzeri	147
Nettles	181	Henrich	795	Daniels	145

All-Time Yankee Top 10—Pitching

Games		Innings		Wins	
Ford, Whitey	498	Ford, Whitey	3,171	Ford, Whitey	236
Ruffing	426	Ruffing	3,169	Ruffing	231
Lyle	420	Stottlemyre	2,662	Gomez	189
Shawkey	415	Gomez	2,498	Shawkey	168
Murphy	383	Shawkey	2,489	Stottlemyre	164
Gomez	367	Hoyt	2,273	Pennock	162
Hoyt	365	Pennock	2,189	Hoyt	157
Stottlemyre	360	Chesbro	1,953	Reynolds	131
Pennock	346	Peterson	1,856	Chesbro	126
Hamilton	311	Caldwell	1,718	Raschi	120

Pct.		Strikeouts		Shutouts	
Chandler	.717	Ford, Whitey	1,956	Ford, Whitey	45
Raschi	.706	Ruffing	1,526	Stottlemyre	40
Ford, Whitey	.690	Gomez	1,468	Ruffing	37
Reynolds	.686	Stottlemyre	1,257	Reynolds	27
Mays	.670	Shawkey	1,163	Chandler	26
Lopat	.657	Downing	1,028	Gomez	26
Ruffing	.651	Reynolds	967	Shawkey	26
Gomez	.649	Chesbro	913	Raschi	24
Pennock	.643	Turley	909	Turley	21
Byrne	.643	Peterson	893	Lopat	20

Complete Games		Earned Run Average		Saves	
Ruffing	261	Ford, Russ	2.54	Lyle	141
Gomez	173	Chesbro	2.58	Murphy	104
Chesbro	169	Orth	2.72	Page	76
Pennock	165	Bonham	2.73	McDaniel	58
Shawkey	161	Ford, Wh.	2.74	Gossage	44
Ford, Wh.	156	Chandler	2.84	Duren	43
Hoyt	156	Stottlemyre	2.97	Arroyo	43
Stottlemyre	152	Caldwell	2.99	Ramos	32
Caldwell	151	Warhop	3.09	Aker	31
Chandler	109	Peterson	3.10	Hamilton	28

Yankee Achievements and Awards

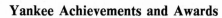

Batting Champions

Joe DiMaggio (2)	1939 (.381)
	1940 (.352)
Babe Ruth	1924 (.378)
Lou Gehrig	1934 (.363)
George Stirnweiss	1945 (.309)
Mickey Mantle	1956 (.353)

Runs Batted In Champions

Babe Ruth (5)	1920 (137)
	1921 (171)
	1923 (131)
	1926 (145)
	1928 (142)
Lou Gehrig (5)	1927 (175)
	1928 (142)
	1930 (174)
	1931 (184)
	1934 (165)
Joe DiMaggio (2)	1941 (125)
	1948 (155)
Roger Maris (2)	1960 (112)
	1961 (142)
Mickey Mantle	1956 (130)
Bob Meusel	1925 (138)

Home Run Champions

Babe Ruth (10)	1920 (54)
	1921 (59)
	1923 (41)
	1924 (46)
	1926 (47)
	1927 (60)
	1928 (54)
	1929 (46)
	1930 (49)
	1931 (46)
Mickey Mantle (4)	1955 (37)
	1956 (52)
	1958 (42)
	1960 (40)
Lou Gehrig (3)	1931 (46)
	1934 (49)
	1936 (49)
Joe DiMaggio (2)	1937 (46)
	1948 (39)
Wally Pipp (2)	1916 (12)
	1917 (9)
Roger Maris	1961 (61)
Bob Meusel	1925 (33)
Graig Nettles	1976 (32)
Nick Etten	1944 (22)

Most Valuable Player Award

Joe DiMaggio (3)	1939, 1941, 1947
Mickey Mantle (3)	1956, 1957, 1962
Yogi Berra (3)	1951, 1954, 1955
Lou Gehrig (2)	1927, 1936
Roger Maris (2)	1960, 1961
Babe Ruth	1923
Joe Gordon	1942
Spud Chandler	1943
Phil Rizzuto	1950
Elston Howard	1963
Thurman Munson	1976

Cy Young Award

Bob Turley (21-7)	1958
Whitey Ford (25-4)	1961
Sparky Lyle (13-5)	1977
Ron Guidry (25-3)	1978

Rookie of the Year

Gil McDougald	1951
Bob Grim	1954
Tony Kubek	1957
Tom Tresh	1962
Stan Bahnsen	1968
Thurman Munson	1970

Hall of Fame

Babe Ruth	1936
Lou Gehrig	1939
Willie Keeler	1939
Clark Griffith	1945
Jack Chesbro	1946
Herb Pennock	1948
Ed Barrow	1953
Bill Dickey	1954
Frank (Home Run) Baker	1955
Joe DiMaggio	1955
Joe McCarthy	1957
Miller Huggins	1964
Casey Stengel	1966
Red Ruffing	1967
Waite Hoyt	1969
Earle Combs	1970
George Weiss	1970
Yogi Berra	1971
Lefty Gomez	1972
Mickey Mantle	1974
Whitey Ford	1974
Bucky Harris	1975
Joe Sewell	1977
Larry MacPhail	1978

Joe DiMaggio's 56-Game Hitting Streak, 1941

Date	Opposing Team, Pitcher	AB	R	H	2B	3B	HR	RBI
May 15	Chicago, Edgar Smith	4	0	1	0	0	0	1
May 16	Chicago, Thornton Lee	4	2	2	0	1	1	1
May 17	Chicago, John Rigney	3	1	1	0	0	0	0
May 18	St. Louis, Bob Harris (2)							
	Johnny Niggeling (1)	3	3	3	1	0	0	1
May 19	St. Louis, Denny Galehouse	3	0	1	1	0	0	0
May 20	St. Louis, Eldon Auker	5	1	1	0	0	0	1
May 21	Detroit, Schoolboy Rowe (1)							
	Al Benton (1)	5	0	2	0	0	0	1
May 22	Detroit, Archie McKain	4	0	1	0	0	0	1
May 23	Boston, Dick Newsome	5	0	1	0	0	0	2
May 24	Boston, Earl Johnson	4	2	1	0	0	0	2
May 25	Boston, Lefty Grove	4	0	1	0	0	0	0
May 27	At Washington, Ken Chase (1)							
	Arnold Anderson (2)							
	Alex Carrasquel (1)	5	3	4	0	0	1	3
May 28 (n)	At Washington, Sid Hudson	4	1	1	0	1	0	0
May 29	At Washington, Steve Sundra	3	1	1	0	0	0	0
May 30	At Boston, Earl Johnson	2	1	1	0	0	0	0
May 30	At Boston, Mickey Harris	3	0	1	1	0	0	0
June 1	At Cleveland, Al Milnar	4	1	1	0	0	0	0
June 1	At Cleveland, Mel Harder	4	0	1	0	0	0	0
June 2	At Cleveland, Bob Feller	4	2	2	1	0	0	0
June 3	At Detroit, Dizzy Trout	4	1	1	0	0	1	1
June 5	At Detroit, Hal Newhouser	5	1	1	0	1	0	1
June 7	At St. Louis, Bob Muncrief (1)							
	Johnny Allen (1)							
	George Caster (1)	5	2	3	0	0	0	1
June 8	At St. Louis, Eldon Auker	4	3	2	0	0	2	4
June 8	At St. Louis, George Caster (1)							
	Jack Kramer (1)	4	1	2	1	0	1	3
June 10	At Chicago, Johnny Rigney	5	1	1	0	0	0	0
June 12 (n)	At Chicago, Thornton Lee	4	1	2	0	0	1	1
June 14	Cleveland, Bob Feller	2	0	1	1	0	0	1
June 15	Cleveland, Jim Bagby, Jr.	3	1	1	0	0	1	1
June 16	Cleveland, Al Milnar	5	0	1	1	0	0	0
June 17	Chicago, Johnny Rigney	4	1	1	0	0	0	0
June 18	Chicago, Thornton Lee	3	0	1	0	0	0	0
June 19	Chicago, Edgar Smith (1)							
	Lee Ross (2)	3	2	3	0	0	1	2
June 20	Detroit, Bobo Newsom (2)							
	Archie McKain (2)	5	3	4	1	0	0	1
June 21	Detroit, Dizzy Trout	4	0	1	0	0	0	1
June 22	Detroit, Hal Newhouser (1)							
	Bobo Newsom (1)	5	1	2	1	0	1	2
June 24	St. Louis, Bob Muncrief	4	1	1	0	0	0	0
June 25	St. Louis, Denny Galehouse	4	1	1	0	0	1	3
June 26	St. Louis, Eldon Auker	4	0	1	1	0	0	1
June 27	At Philadelphia, Chubby Dean	3	1	2	0	0	1	2
June 28	At Philadelphia, Johnny Babich (1)							
	Luman Harris (1)	5	1	2	1	0	0	0
June 29	At Washington, Dutch Leonard	4	1	1	1	0	0	0
June 29	At Washington, Arnold Anderson	5	1	1	0	0	0	1
July 1	Boston, Mickey Harris (1)							
	Mike Ryba (1)	4	0	2	0	0	0	1

Joe DiMaggio's 56-Game Hitting Streak, 1941

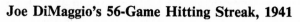

Date	Opposing Team, Pitcher	AB	R	H	2B	3B	HR	RBI
July 1	Boston, Jack Wilson	3	1	1	0	0	0	1
July 2	Boston, Dick Newsome	5	1	1	0	0	1	3
July 5	Philadelphia, Phil Marchildon	4	2	1	0	0	1	2
July 6	Philadelphia, Johnny Babich (1)							
	Bump Hadley (3)	5	2	4	1	0	0	2
July 6	Philadelphia, Jack Knott	4	0	2	0	1	0	2
July 10 (n)	At St. Louis, Johnny Niggeling	2	0	1	0	0	0	0
July 11	At St. Louis, Bob Harris (3)							
	Jack Kramer (1)	5	1	4	0	0	1	2
July 12	At St. Louis, Eldon Auker (1)							
	Bob Muncrief (1)	5	1	2	1	0	0	1
July 13	At Chicago, Ted Lyons (2)							
	Jack Hallett (1)	4	2	3	0	0	0	0
July 13	At Chicago, Thornton Lee	4	0	1	0	0	0	0
July 14	At Chicago, Johnny Rigney	3	0	1	0	0	0	0
July 15	At Chicago, Edgar Smith	4	1	2	1	0	0	2
July 16	At Cleveland, Al Milnar (2)							
	Joe Krakauskas (1)	4	3	3	1	0	0	0
	Total .408	223	56	91	16	4	15	55

Babe Ruth's 60 Home Runs, 1927

Home Run	Date	Yankee Game	Ruth Game	Inning	Opposing Team, Pitcher
1	Apr. 15	4	4	1	Philadelphia, Howard Ehmke
2	Apr. 23	11	11	1	At Philadelphia, Rube Walberg*
3	Apr. 24	12	12	6	At Washington, Hollis Thurston
4	Apr. 29	14	14	5	At Boston, Slim Harriss
5	May 1	16	16	1	Philadelphia, Jack Quinn
6	May 1	16	16	8	Philadelphia, Rube Walberg*
7	May 10	24	24	1	At St. Louis, Milt Gaston
8	May 11	25	25	1	At St. Louis, Ernie Nevers
9	May 17	29	29	8	At Detroit, Harry Collins
10	May 22	33	33	6	At Cleveland, Benn Karr
11	May 23	34	34	1	At Washington, Hollis Thurston
12	May 28	37	37	7	Washington, Hollis Thurston
13	May 29	39	39	8	Boston, Danny MacFayden
14	May 30	41	41	11	At Philadelphia, Rube Walberg*
15	May 31	42	42	1	At Philadelphia, Jack Quinn
16	May 31	43	43	5	At Philadelphia, Howard Ehmke
17	June 5	47	47	6	Detroit, Earl Whitehill*
18	June 7	48	48	4	Chicago, Tommy Thomas
19	June 11	52	52	3	Cleveland, Garland Buckeye*
20	June 11	52	52	5	Cleveland, Garland Buckeye*
21	June 12	53	53	7	Cleveland, George Uhle
22	June 16	55	55	1	St. Louis, Tom Zachary*
23	June 22	60	60	5	At Boston, Hal Wiltse*
24	June 22	60	60	7	At Boston, Hal Wiltse*
25	June 30	70	66	4	Boston, Slim Harriss
26	July 3	73	69	1	At Washington, Hod Lisenbee
27	July 8	78	74	2	At Detroit, Don Hankins
28	July 9	79	75	1	At Detroit, Ken Holloway
29	July 9	79	75	4	At Detroit, Ken Holloway
30	July 12	83	79	9	At Cleveland, Joe Shaute*
31	July 24	94	90	3	At Chicago, Tommy Thomas

Home Run	Date	Yankee Game	Ruth Game	Inning	Opposing Team, Pitcher
32	July 26	95	91	1	St. Louis, Milt Gaston
33	July 26	95	91	6	St. Louis, Milt Gaston
34	July 28	98	94	8	St. Louis, Walter Stewart*
35	Aug. 5	106	102	8	Detroit, George Smith
36	Aug. 10	110	106	3	At Washington, Tom Zachary*
37	Aug. 16	114	110	5	At Chicago, Tommy Thomas
38	Aug. 17	115	111	11	At Chicago, Sarge Connally
39	Aug. 20	118	114	1	At Cleveland, Jake Miller*
40	Aug. 22	120	116	6	At Cleveland, Joe Shaute*
41	Aug. 27	124	120	8	At St. Louis, Ernie Nevers
42	Aug. 28	125	121	1	At St. Louis, Ernie Wingard*
43	Aug. 31	127	123	8	Boston, Tony Welzer
44	Sept. 2	128	124	1	At Philadelphia, Rube Walberg*
45	Sept. 6	132	128	6	At Boston, Tony Welzer
46	Sept. 6	132	128	7	At Boston, Tony Welzer
47	Sept. 6	133	129	9	At Boston, Jack Russell
48	Sept. 7	134	130	1	At Boston, Danny MacFayden
49	Sept. 7	134	130	8	At Boston, Slim Harriss
50	Sept. 11	138	134	4	St. Louis, Milt Gaston
51	Sept. 13	139	135	7	Cleveland, Willis Hudlin
52	Sept. 13	140	136	4	Cleveland, Joe Shaute*
53	Sept. 16	143	139	3	Chicago, Ted Blankenship
54	Sept. 18	147	143	5	Chicago, Ted Lyons
55	Sept. 21	148	144	9	Detroit, Sam Gibson
56	Sept. 22	149	145	9	Detroit, Ken Holloway
57	Sept. 27	152	148	6	Philadelphia, Bob (Lefty) Grove*
58	Sept. 29	153	149	1	Washington, Hod Lisenbee
59	Sept. 29	153	149	5	Washington, Paul Hopkins
60	Sept. 30	154	150	8	Washington, Tom Zachary*

At Yankee Stadium: 28
On the road: 32
Off righthand pitchers: 41
Off lefthand pitchers: 19
Two-homer games: 8

Apr.: 4
May: 12
June: 9
July: 9
Aug: 9
Sept.: 17

*Lefthander.

Roger Maris' 61 Home Runs, 1961

Home Run	Date	Yankee Game	Maris Game	Inning	Opposing Team, Pitcher
1	Apr. 26	11	11	5	At Detroit, Paul Foytack
2	May 3	17	17	7	At Minnesota, Pedro Ramos
3	May 6 (n)	20	20	5	At Los Angeles, Eli Grba
4	May 17	29	29	8	Washington, Pete Burnside*
5	May 19 (n)	30	30	1	At Cleveland, Jim Perry
6	May 20	31	31	3	At Cleveland, Gary Bell
7	May 21	32	32	1	Baltimore, Chuck Estrada
8	May 24	35	35	4	Boston, Gene Conley
9	May 28	38	38	2	Chicago, Cal McLish
10	May 30	40	40	6	At Boston, Gene Conley
11	May 30	40	40	8	At Boston, Mike Fornieles
12	May 31 (n)	41	41	3	At Boston, Billy Muffet
13	June 2 (n)	43	43	3	At Chicago, Cal McLish
14	June 3	44	44	8	At Chicago, Bob Shaw

Roger Maris' 61 Home Runs, 1961

Home Run	Date	Yankee Game	Maris Game	Inning	Opposing Team, Pitcher
15	June 4	45	45	3	At Chicago, Russ Kemmerer
16	June 6 (n)	48	48	6	Minnesota, Ed Palmquist
17	June 7	49	49	3	Minnesota, Pedro Ramos
18	June 9 (n)	52	52	7	Kansas City, Ray Herbert
19	June 11	55	55	3	Los Angeles, Eli Grba
20	June 11	55	55	7	Los Angeles, Johnny James
21	June 13 (n)	57	57	6	At Cleveland, Jim Perry
22	June 14 (n)	58	58	4	At Cleveland, Gary Bell
23	June 17 (n)	61	61	4	At Detroit, Don Mossi*
24	June 18	62	62	8	At Detroit, Jerry Casale
25	June 19 (n)	63	63	9	At Kansas City, Jim Archer*
26	June 20 (n)	64	64	1	At Kansas City, Joe Nuxhall*
27	June 22 (n)	66	66	2	At Kansas City, Norm Bass
28	July 1	74	74	9	Washington, Dave Sisler
29	July 2	75	75	3	Washington, Pete Burnside*
30	July 2	75	75	7	Washington, Johnny Klippstein
31	July 4	77	77	8	Detroit, Frank Lary
32	July 5	78	78	7	Cleveland, Frank Funk
33	July 9	82	82	7	Boston, Bill Monbouquette
34	July 13 (n)	84	84	1	At Chicago, Early Wynn
35	July 15	86	86	3	At Chicago, Ray Herbert
36	July 21 (n)	92	92	1	At Boston, Bill Monbouquette
37	July 25 (n)	95	95	4	Chicago, Frank Bauman*
38	July 25 (n)	95	95	8	Chicago, Don Larsen
39	July 25 (n)	96	96	4	Chicago, Russ Kemmerer
40	July 25 (n)	96	96	6	Chicago, Warren Hacker
41	Aug. 4 (n)	106	105	1	Minnesota, Camilo Pascual
42	Aug. 11 (n)	114	113	5	At Washington, Pete Burnside*
43	Aug. 12	115	114	4	At Washington, Dick Donovan
44	Aug. 13	116	115	4	At Washington, Bennie Daniels
45	Aug. 13	117	116	1	At Washington, Marty Kutyna
46	Aug. 15 (n)	118	117	4	Chicago, Juan Pizzaro*
47	Aug. 16	119	118	1	Chicago, Billy Pierce*
48	Aug. 16	119	118	3	Chicago, Billy Pierce*
49	Aug. 20	123	122	3	At Cleveland, Jim Perry
50	Aug. 22 (n)	125	124	6	At Los Angeles, Ken McBride
51	Aug. 26	129	128	6	At Kansas City, Jerry Walker
52	Sept. 2	135	134	6	Detroit, Frank Lary
53	Sept. 2	135	134	8	Detroit, Hank Aguirre*
54	Sept. 6	140	139	4	Washington, Tom Cheney
55	Sept. 7 (n)	141	140	3	Cleveland, Dick Stigman*
56	Sept. 9	143	142	7	Cleveland, Jim (Mudcat) Grant
57	Sept. 16	151	150	3	At Detroit, Frank Lary
58	Sept. 17	152	151	12	At Detroit, Terry Fox
59	Sept. 20 (n)	155	154	3	At Baltimore, Milt Pappas
60	Sept. 26 (n)	159	158	3	Baltimore, Jack Fisher
61	Oct. 1	163	161	4	Boston, Tracy Stallard

At Yankee Stadium: 30 Apr.: 1
On the road: 31 May: 11
Off righthand pitchers: 49 June: 15
Off lefthand pitchers: 12 July: 13
Day: 36 Aug.: 11
Night: 25 Sept.: 9
Two-homer games: 7 Oct.: 1

*Lefthander.

Ron Guidry's 27-3 Record, 1978

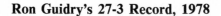

Date	Opposing Team	Score	IP	H	R	ER	BB	SO	Record	ERA
Apr. 8	At Texas	1–2	7	6	1	1	2	2		1.29
13	Chicago	4–2	9	10	2	2	2	4	1-0	1.69
18	Baltimore	4–3	6.2	7	3	3	2	4		2.38
24	At Baltimore	8–2	7	6	1	0	2	2	2-0	1.82
30	At Minn.	3–2	6.1	3	2	0	4	7		1.50
May 5	Texas	5–2	6.1	5	1	1	5	7	3-0	1.49
13	At Kansas City	5–2	8	8	2	2	2	6	4-0	1.61
18	At Cleveland	5–3	8.1	6	3	3	3	5	5-0	1.84
23	Cleveland	10–1	9	5	1	1	2	11	6-0	1.73
28	Toronto	5–3	9	6	3	3	0	6	7-0	1.88
June 2	At Oakland	3–1	8.1	6	1	1	2	11	8-0	1.80
7	At Seattle	9–1	9	6	1	1	2	10	9-0	1.72
12	Oakland	2–0	9	3	0	0	2	11	10-0	1.57
17	California	4–0	9	4	0	0	2	18	11-0	1.45
22	At Detroit	4–2	8	6	2	2	2	8	12-0	1.50
27	Boston	6–4	6	8	4	4	3	6		1.71
July 2	Detroit	3–2	8	6	2	2	2	6	13-0	1.75
7	At Milwaukee	0–6	6	8	5	5	1	3	13-1	1.99
14	Chicago	7–6	9	8	6	6	3	10		2.23
20	At Minnesota	4–0	9	4	0	0	3	8	14-1	2.11
25	At Kansas City	4–0	9	6	0	0	0	8	15-1	1.99
30	Minnesota	4–3	6.2	6	3	2	3	10		2.02
Aug. 4	Baltimore	1–2	9	5	2	1	0	10	15-2	1.97
10	Milwaukee	9–0	9	3	0	0	1	9	16-2	1.88
15	At Oakland	6–0	9	4	0	0	3	9	17-2	1.79
20	At Seattle	4–5	5	3	2	1	1	3		1.79
25	Oakland	7–1	8	5	1	1	4	5	18-2	1.77
30	At Baltimore	5–4	7	7	4	4	1	8	19-2	1.88
Sept. 4	Detroit	9–1	9	5	1	1	3	8	20-2	1.84
9	At Boston	7–0	9	2	0	0	4	5	21-2	1.77
15	Boston	4–0	9	2	0	0	3	5	22-2	1.71
20	At Toronto	1–8	1.2	6	5	3	0	1	22-3	1.81
24	At Cleveland	4–0	9	2	0	0	1	8	23-3	1.74
28	Toronto	3–1	9	4	1	1	1	9	24-3	1.72
Oct. 2	At Boston	5–4	6.1	6	2	2	1	5	25-3	1.74
	Total		273.2	187	61	53	72	248	25-3	1.74
American League Championship Series										
Oct. 7	Kansas City	2–1	8	7	1	1	1	7		
World Series										
13	Los Angeles	5–1	9	8	1	1	7	4		

All-Time Yankee Roster

Harry Ables   1911
Spencer Adams   1926
Doc Adkins   1903
Jack Aker   1969–72
Doyle Alexander   1976
Walt Alexander   1915–17
Bernie Allen   1972–73
Johnny Allen   1932–35
Sandy Alomar   1974–76
Felipe Alou   1971–73

Matty Alou   1973
Dell Alston   1977
Ruben Amaro   1966–68
John Anderson   1904–05
Rick Anderson   1979
Ivy Andrews   1931–32, 1937–38
Pete Appleton   1933
Angel Aragon   1914, 1916–17
Rugger Ardizoia   1947
Luis Arroyo   1960–63

Jimmy Austin   1909–10
Martin Autry   1924

Loren Babe   1952–53
Stan Bahnsen   1966, 1968–71
Bill Bailey   1911
Frank Baker   1916–19, 1921–22
Frank Baker   1970–71
Neal Ball   1907–09
Steve Barber   1967–68

Cy Barger   1906–07
Ray Barker   1965–67
Frank Barnes   1930
Honey Barnes   1926
Ed Barney   1915
George Batten   1912
Hank Bauer   1948–59
Paddy Baumann   1915–17
Walter Beall   1924–27
Jim Beattie   1978–79
Rich Beck   1965
Zinn Beck   1918
Fred Beene   1972–74
Joe Beggs   1938
Rudy Bell   1907
Zeke Bella   1957
Benny Bengough   1923–30
Juan Beniquez   1979
Lou Berberet   1954–55
Dave Bergman   1975, 1977
Juan Bernhardt   1976
Walter Bernhardt   1918
Yogi Berra   1946–63
Bill Bevens   1944–47
Monte Beville   1903–04
Harry Billiard   1908
Ewell Blackwell   1952–53
Rick Bladt   1975
Paul Blair   1977–79
Walter Blair   1907–11
Johnny Blanchard   1955, 1959–65
Gil Blanco   1965
Wade Blasingame   1972
Steve Blateric   1972
Gary Blaylock   1959
Curt Blefary   1970–71
Elmer Bliss   1903–04
Ron Blomberg   1969, 1971–77
Eddie Bockman   1946
Ping Bodie   1918–21
Len Boehmer   1969, 1971
Don Bollweg   1953
Bobby Bonds   1975
Ernie Bonham   1940–46
Luke Boone   1913–16
Frenchy Bordagaray   1941
Hank Borowy   1942–45
Babe Borton   1913
Jim Bouton   1962–68
Clete Boyer   1959–66
Neal Brady   1915
Ralph Branca   1954
Norm Branch   1941–42
Garland Braxton   1925–26
Don Brennan   1933
Jim Brenneman   1965
Ken Brett   1976
Marv Breuer   1939–43
Fritzie Brickell   1958–59
Jim Brideweser   1951–53
Marshall Bridges   1962–63

Harry Bright   1963–64
Ed Brinkman   1975
Johnny Broaca   1934–37
Lew Brockett   1907, 1909
Jim Bronstad   1959
Boardwalk Brown   1914–15
Bobby Brown   1946–52, 1954, 1979
Hal Brown   1962
Jumbo Brown   1932–33, 1935–36
Billy Bryan   1966–67
Jess Buckles   1916
Bill Burbach   1969–71
Lew Burdette   1950
George Burns   1928–29
Alex Burr   1914
Ray Burris   1979
Joe Bush   1922–24
Tom Buskey   1973–74
Ralph Buxton   1949
Joe Buzas   1945
Harry Byrd   1954
Sammy Byrd   1929–34
Tommy Byrne   1943, 1946–51, 1954–57

Charlie Caldwell   1925
Ray Caldwell   1910–18
Johnny Callison   1972–73
Howie Camp   1917
Archie Campbell   1928
Mike Cantwell   1916
Andy Carey   1952–60
Roy Carlyle   1926
Duke Carmel   1965
Dick Carroll   1909
Ownie Carroll   1930
Tommy Carroll   1955–56
Hugh Casey   1949
Roy Castleton   1907
Danny Cater   1970–71
Bob Cerv   1951–56, 1960–62
Chris Chambliss   1974–79
Frank Chance   1913–14
Spud Chandler   1937–47
Les Channell   1910
Ben Chapman   1930–36
Mike Chartak   1940
Hal Chase   1905–13
Jack Chesbro   1903–09
Al Cicotte   1957
Allie Clark   1947
George Clark   1913
Horace Clarke   1965–74
Walter Clarkson   1904–07
Ken Clay   1977–79
Tex Clevenger   1961–62
Lu Clinton   1966–67
Al Closter   1971–72
Andy Coakley   1911
Jim Coates   1956, 1959–62
Jim Cockman   1905
Rich Coggins   1975–76

Rocky Colavito   1968
King Cole   1914–15
Curt Coleman   1912
Jerry Coleman   1949–57
Rip Coleman   1955–56
Bob Collins   1944
Joe Collins   1948–57
Orth Collins   1904
Pat Collins   1926–28
Rip Collins   1920–21
Frank Colman   1946–47
Loyd Colson   1970
Earle Combs   1924–35
Tom Connelly   1920–21
Joe Connor   1905
Wid Conroy   1903–08
Doc Cook   1913–16
Dusty Cooke   1930–32
Johnny Cooney   1944
Phil Cooney   1905
Guy Cooper   1914
Dan Costello   1913
Ensign Cottrell   1915
Clint Courtney   1951
Ernie Courtney   1903
Stan Coveleski   1928
Billy Cowan   1969
Bobby Cox   1968–69
Casey Cox   1972–73
Birdie Cree   1908–15
Lou Criger   1910
Herb Crompton   1945
Frank Crosetti   1932–48
Jack Cullen   1962, 1965–66
Roy Cullenbine   1942
Nick Cullop   1916–17
Nick Cullop   1926
John Cumberland   1968–70
Jim Curry   1911
Fred Curtis   1905

Babe Dahlgren   1937–40
Buddy Daley   1961–64
Tom Daley   1914–15
Bert Daniels   1910–13
George Davis   1912
Kiddo Davis   1926
Lefty Davis   1903
Ron Davis   1978–79
John Deering   1903
Jim Deidel   1974
Frank Delahanty   1905–06, 1908
Bobby Del Greco   1957–58
Jim Delsing   1949–50
Joe DeMaestri   1960–61
Ray Demmitt   1909
Rick Dempsey   1973–76
Bucky Dent   1977–79
Claud Derrick   1913
Russ Derry   1944–45
Jimmie DeShong   1934–35
Charlie Devens   1932–34

Al DeVormer 1921–22
Bill Dickey 1928–43, 1946
Murry Dickson 1958
Jack DiLauro 1973
Joe DiMaggio 1936–42, 1946–51
Kerry Dineen 1975–76
Art Ditmar 1957–61
Sonny Dixon 1956
Pat Dobson 1973–75
Cozy Dolan 1911–12
Atley Donald 1938–45
Mike Donovan 1908
Wild Bill Donovan 1915–16
Patsy Dougherty 1904–06
Al Downing 1961–69
Brian Doyle 1978–79
Jack Doyle 1905
Slow Joe Doyle 1906–10
Bill Drescher 1944–46
Karl Drews 1946–48
Monk Dubiel 1944–45
Joe Dugan 1922–28
Ryne Duren 1958–61
Leo Durocher 1925, 1928–29
Cedric Durst 1927–30

Rawly Eastwick 1978
Doc Edwards 1965
Foster Edwards 1930
Kid Elberfeld 1903–09
Gene Elliott 1911
Dock Ellis 1976–77
John Ellis 1969–72
Red Embree 1948
Clyde Engle 1909–10
John Enright 1917
Nick Etten 1943–46

Dock Farrell 1932–33
Alex Ferguson 1918, 1921
Frank Fernandez 1967–69
Mike Ferraro 1966
Wes Ferrell 1938–39
Tom Ferrick 1950–51
Chick Fewster 1917–22
Ed Figueroa 1976–79
Happy Finneran 1918
Gus Fisher 1912
Ray Fisher 1910–17
Mike Fitzgerald 1911
Russ Ford 1909–13
Whitey Ford 1950, 1953–67
Eddie Foster 1910
Jack Fournier 1918
Ray Francis 1925
Mark Freeman 1959
Ray French 1920
Lonny Frey 1947–48
Bob Friend 1966
John Frill 1910
Dave Fultz 1903–05
Liz Funk 1929

John Gabler 1959–60
Joe Gallagher 1939
Oscar Gamble 1976, 1979
John Ganzel 1903–04
Mike Garbark 1944–45
Damaso Garcia 1978–79
Billy Gardner 1961–62
Earl Gardner 1908–12
Rob Gardner 1970–72
Ned Garvin 1904
Milt Gaston 1924
Mike Gazella 1923, 1926–28
Joe Gedeon 1916–17
Lou Gehrig 1923–39
Al Gettel 1945–46
Joe Giard 1927
Jake Gibbs 1962–71
Sam Gibson 1930
Frank Gilhooley 1913–18
Fred Glade 1908
Frank Gleich 1919–20
Joe Glenn 1932–33, 1935–38
Lefty Gomez 1930–42
Jesse Gonder 1960–61
Fernando Gonzalez 1974
Pedro Gonzalez 1963–65
Wilbur Good 1905
Art Goodwin 1905
Joe Gordon 1938–43, 1946
Tom Gorman 1952–54
Rich Gossage 1978–79
Dick Gossett 1913–14
Larry Gowell 1972
Johnny Grabowski 1927–29
Wayne Granger 1973
Ted Gray 1955
Eli Grba 1959–60
Willie Greene 1903
Mike Griffin 1979
Clark Griffith 1903–07
Bob Grim 1954–58
Burleigh Grimes 1934
Oscar Grimes 1943–46
Lee Grissom 1940
Ron Guidry 1975–79
Brad Gulden 1979
Don Gullett 1977–79
Randy Gumpert 1946–48
Larry Gura 1974–76

Bump Hadley 1936–40
Kent Hadley 1960
Ed Hahn 1905–06
Noodles Hahn 1906
Hinkey Haines 1923
George Halas 1919
Bob Hale 1961
Jimmie Hall 1969
Roger Hambright 1971
Steve Hamilton 1963–70
Mike Handiboe 1911

Jim Hanley 1913
Truck Hannah 1918–20
Ron Hansen 1970–71
Joe Hanson 1913
Jim Hardin 1971
Bubbles Hargrave 1930
Harry Harper 1921
Joe Harris 1914
Jim Hart 1973–74
Roy Hartzell 1911–16
Buddy Hassett 1942
Chicken Hawks 1921
Fran Healy 1976–78
Mike Heath 1978
Don Heffner 1934–37
Mike Hegan 1964, 1966–67, 1973–74
Fred Heimach 1928–29
Woodie Held 1954
Charlie Hemphill 1908–11
Rollie Hemsley 1942–44
Bill Henderson 1930
Harvey Hendrick 1923–24
Elrod Hendricks 1976–77
Tim Hendryx 1915–17
Tommy Henrich 1937–42, 1946–50
Bill Henry 1966
Ed Herrmann 1975
Hugh High 1915–18
Oral Hildebrand 1939–40
Jesse Hill 1935
Frank Hiller 1946, 1948–49
Mack Hillis 1924
Rich Hinton 1972
Myril Hoag 1931–32, 1934–38
Red Hoff 1911–13
Danny Hoffman 1906–07
Solly Hofman 1916
Fred Hofmann 1919–25
Bill Hogg 1905–08
Bobby Hogue 1951–52
Ken Holcombe 1945
Bill Holden 1913–14
Ken Holloway 1930
Fred Holmes 1903
Ken Holtzman 1976–78
Don Hood 1979
Wally Hood 1949
Johnny Hopp 1950–52
Shags Horan 1924
Ralph Houk 1947–54
Elston Howard 1955–67
Harry Howell 1903
Dick Howser 1967–68
Waite Hoyt 1921–30
Long Tom Hughes 1904
Tom Hughes 1906–07, 1909–10
John Hummel 1918
Ken Hunt 1959–60
Billy Hunter 1955–56
Catfish Hunter 1975–79
Ham Hyatt 1918

Fred Jacklitsch   1905
Grant Jackson   1976
Reggie Jackson   1977–79
Johnny James   1958, 1960–61
Jackie Jensen   1950–52
Elvio Jimenez   1964
Tommy John   1979
Alex Johnson   1974–75
Billy Johnson   1943, 1946–51
Cliff Johnson   1977–79
Darrell Johnson   1957–58
Deron Johnson   1960–61
Don Johnson   1947
Ernie Johnson   1923–25
Hank Johnson   1925–26, 1928–32
Johnny Johnson   1944
Ken Johnson   1969
Otis Johnson   1911
Roy Johnson   1936–37
Jay Johnstone   1978–79
Darryl Jones   1979
Gary Jones   1970–71
Sad Sam Jones   1922–26
Tim Jordan   1903
Art Jorgens   1929–39
Mike Jurewicz   1965

Jim Kaat   1979
Bob Kammeyer   1978–79
Frank Kane   1919
Bill Karlon   1930
Herb Karpel   1946
Benny Kauff   1912
Eddie Kearse   1942
Ray Keating   1912–16, 1918
Bob Keefe   1907
Willie Keeler   1903–09
Mike Kekich   1969–73
Charlie Keller   1939–43, 1945–49, 1952
John Kennedy   1967
Jerry Kenney   1967, 1969–72
Dave Kingman   1977
Harry Kingman   1914
Fred Kipp   1960
Frank Kitson   1907
Ted Kleinhans   1936
Red Kleinow   1904–10
Ed Klepfer   1911
Ron Klimkowski   1969–70, 1972
Steve Kline   1970–74
Mickey Klutts   1976–78
Bill Knickerbocker   1938–40
John Knight   1909–11, 1913
Mark Koenig   1925–30
Jim Konstanty   1954–56
Andy Kosco   1968
Steve Kraly   1953
Jack Kramer   1951
Ernie Krueger   1915
Dick Kryhoski   1949
Tony Kubek   1957–65

Johnny Kucks   1955–59
Bill Kunkel   1963
Bob Kuzava   1951–54

Joe Lake   1908–09
Bill Lamar   1917–19
Hal Lanier   1972–73
Frank LaPorte   1905–10
Don Larsen   1955–59
Lyn Lary   1929–34
Gene Layden   1915
Tony Lazzeri   1926–37
Frank Leja   1954–55
Jack Lelivelt   1912–13
Eddie Leon   1975
Louis LeRoy   1905–06
Ed Levy   1942
Duffy Lewis   1919–20
Terry Ley   1971
Paul Lindblad   1978
Johnny Lindell   1941–50
Phil Linz   1962–65
Jack Little   1912
Clem Llewellyn   1922
Gene Locklear   1976–77
Sherm Lollar   1947–48
Dale Long   1960, 1962–63
Herman Long   1903
Ed Lopat   1948–55
Art Lopez   1965
Hector Lopez   1959–66
Baldy Louden   1907
Slim Love   1916–18
Johnny Lucadello   1947
Joe Lucey   1920
Roy Luebbe   1925
Jerry Lumpe   1956–59
Sparky Lyle   1972–78
Al Lyons   1944, 1946–47
Jim Lyttle   1969–71

Duke Maas   1958–61
Danny MacFayden   1932–34
Ray Mack   1947
Bunny Madden   1910
Elliott Maddox   1974–76
Dave Madison   1950
Lee Magee   1916–17
Sal Maglie   1957–58
Stubby Magner   1911
Jim Magnuson   1973
Fritz Maisel   1913–17
Hank Majeski   1946
Frank Makosky   1937
Pat Malone   1935–37
Pat Maloney   1912
Al Mamaux   1924
Rube Manning   1907–10
Mickey Mantle   1951–68
Cliff Mapes   1948–51
Roger Maris   1960–66
Cliff Markle   1915–16, 1924

Jim Marquis   1925
Armando Marsans   1917–18
Cuddles Marshall   1946, 1948–49
Billy Martin   1950–53, 1955–57
Hersh Martin   1944–45
Jack Martin   1912
Tippy Martinez   1974–76
Jim Mason   1974–76
Carlos May   1976–77
Rudy May   1974–76
Carl Mays   1919–23
Larry McCall   1977–78
Joe McCarthy   1905
Pat McCauley   1903
Larry McClure   1910
George McConnell   1909, 1912
Mike McCormick   1970
Lindy McDaniel   1968–73
Mickey McDermott   1956
Danny McDevitt   1961
Dave McDonald   1969
Jim McDonald   1952–54
Gil McDougald   1951–60
Sam McDowell   1973–74
Lou McEvoy   1930–31
Herm McFarland   1903
Bob McGraw   1917–20
Deacon McGuire   1904–07
Marty McHale   1913–15
Irish McIlveen   1908–09
Bill McKechnie   1913
Rich McKinney   1972
Frank McManus   1904
Norm McMillan   1922
Tommy McMillan   1912
Mike McNally   1921–24
Herb McQuaid   1926
George McQuinn   1947–48
Charlie Meara   1914
George Medich   1972–75
Fred Merkle   1925–26
Andy Messersmith   1978
Tom Metcalf   1963
Bud Metheny   1943–46
Bob Meusel   1920–29
Bob Meyer   1964
Gene Michael   1968–74
Ezra Midkiff   1912–13
Pete Mikkelsen   1964–65
Bill Miller   1952–54
Elmer Miller   1915–18, 1921
John Miller   1966
Buster Mills   1940
Mike Milosevich   1944–45
Paul Mirabella   1979
Willie Miranda   1953–54
Bobby Mitchell   1970
Fred Mitchell   1910
Johnny Mitchell   1921–22
Johnny Mize   1949–53
George Mogridge   1915–20

Fenton Mole   1949
Bill Monbouquette   1967–68
Ed Monroe   1917–18
Zack Monroe   1958–59
Archie Moore   1964–65
Earl Moore   1907
Wilcy Moore   1927–29, 1932–33
Ray Morehart   1927
Tom Morgan   1951–52, 1954–56
George Moriarty   1906–08
Ross Moschitto   1965
Gerry Moses   1973
Charlie Mullen   1914–16
Bob Muncrief   1951
Thurman Munson   1969–79
Bobby Murcer   1965–66, 1969–74, 1979
Johnny Murphy   1932, 1934–43, 1946
George Murray   1922
Larry Murray   1974–76

Jerry Narron   1978–79
Bots Nekola   1929
Luke Nelson   1919
Graig Nettles   1973–79
Tacks Neuer   1907
Ernie Nevel   1950–51
Floyd Newkirk   1934
Bobo Newsom   1947
Doc Newton   1905–09
Gus Niarhos   1946, 1948–50
Harry Niles   1908
Irv Noren   1952–56
Don Nottebart   1969
Les Nunamaker   1914–17

Andy O'Connor   1908
Jack O'Connor   1903
Paddy O'Connor   1918
Heinie Odom   1925
Lefty O'Doul   1919–20, 1922
John O'Dowd   1912
Rube Oldring   1905
Bob Oliver   1975
Nate Oliver   1969
Steve O'Neill   1925
Queenie O'Rourke   1908
Al Orth   1904–09
Champ Osteen   1904
Joe Ostrowski   1950–52
Bill Otis   1912
Stubby Overmire   1951

Del Paddock   1912
Dave Pagan   1973–76
Joe Page   1944–50
Ben Paschal   1924–29
Gil Patterson   1977
Monte Pearson   1936–40
Roger Peckinpaugh   1913–21
Steve Peek   1941
Herb Pennock   1923–33
Joe Pepitone   1962–69

Marty Perez   1977
Cecil Perkins   1967
Cy Perkins   1931
Fritz Peterson   1966–74
Eddie Phillips   1932
Jack Phillips   1947–49
Cy Pieh   1913–15
Bill Piercy   1917
Duane Pillette   1949–50
Lou Piniella   1974–79
George Pipgras   1923–24, 1927–33
Wally Pipp   1915–25
Jim Pisoni   1959–60
Bob Porterfield   1948–51
Jack Powell   1904–05
Jake Powell   1936–40
Mike Powers   1905
Del Pratt   1918–20
Jerry Priddy   1941–42
Johnnie Priest   1911–12
Ambrose Puttman   1903–05

Mel Queen   1942, 1944, 1946–47
Ed Quick   1903
Jack Quinn   1909–12, 1919–21

Dave Rajsich   1978
Domingo Ramos   1978
Pedro Ramos   1964–66
Lenny Randle   1979
Willie Randolph   1976–79
Vic Raschi   1946–53
Jack Reed   1961–63
Jimmy Reese   1930–31
Hal Reniff   1961–67
Bill Renna   1953
Tony Rensa   1933
Roger Repoz   1964–66
Allie Reynolds   1947–54
Bill Reynolds   1913–14
Gordon Rhodes   1929–32
Harry Rice   1930
Bobby Richardson   1955–66
Nolan Richardson   1935
Branch Rickey   1907
Ed Ricks   1977
Dave Righetti   1979
Mickey Rivers   1976–79
Phil Rizzuto   1941–42, 1946–56
Roxy Roach   1910–11
Dale Roberts   1967
Gene Robertson   1928–29
Aaron Robinson   1943, 1945–47
Bill Robinson   1967–69
Bruce Robinson   1979
Eddie Robinson   1954–56
Hank Robinson   1918
Ellie Rodriguez   1968
Oscar Roettger   1923–24
Jay Rogers   1914
Tom Rogers   1921
Jim Roland   1972

Red Rolfe   1931, 1934–42
Buddy Rosar   1939–42
Larry Rosenthal   1944
Steve Roser   1944–46
Braggo Roth   1921
Muddy Ruel   1917–20
Dutch Ruether   1926–27
Red Ruffing   1930–42, 1945–46
Allan Russell   1915–19
Marius Russo   1939–43, 1946
Babe Ruth   1920–34
Blondy Ryan   1935
Rosy Ryan   1928

Johnny Sain   1951–55
Jack Saltzgaver   1932, 1934–37
Celerino Sanchez   1972–73
Roy Sanders   1918
Charlie Sands   1967
Fred Sanford   1949–51
Don Savage   1944–45
Rick Sawyer   1974–75
Ray Scarborough   1952–53
Germany Schaefer   1916
Harry Schaeffer   1952
Roy Schalk   1932
Art Schallock   1951–55
Wally Schang   1921–25
Bob Schmidt   1965
Butch Schmidt   1909
Johnny Schmitz   1952–53
Pete Schneider   1919
Dick Schofield   1966
Paul Schreiber   1945
Art Schult   1953
Al Schulz   1912–14
Bill Schwartz   1914
Pius Schwert   1914–15
Everett Scott   1922–25
George Scott   1979
Ken Sears   1943
Bob Seeds   1936
Kal Segrist   1952
George Selkirk   1934–42
Ted Sepkowski   1947
Hank Severeid   1926
Joe Sewell   1931–33
Howard Shanks   1925
Billy Shantz   1960
Bobby Shantz   1957–60
Bob Shawkey   *1915–27
Spec Shea   1947–49, 1951
Al Shealy   1928
George Shears   1912
Tom Sheehan   1921
Rollie Sheldon   1961–62, 1964–65
Skeeter Shelton   1915
Roy Sherid   1929–31
Dennis Sherrill   1978
Ben Shields   1924–25
Urban Shocker   1916–17, 1925–28
Tom Shopay   1967

Ernie Shore   1919–20
Bill Short   1960
Norm Siebern   1956, 1958–59
Charlie Silvera   1948–56
Ken Silvestri   1941, 1946–47
Hack Simmons   1912
Dick Simpson   1969
Harry Simpson   1957–58
Duke Sims   1973–74
Bill Skiff   1926
Camp Skinner   1922
Lou Skizas   1956
Bill Skowron   1954–62
Roger Slagle   1979
Enos Slaughter   1954–59
Walt Smallwood   1917
Charley Smith   1967–68
Elmer Smith   1922–23
Joe Smith   1913
Klondike Smith   1912
Harry Smythe   1934
Tony Solaita   1968
Steve Souchock   1946
Jim Spencer   1978–79
Charlie Spikes   1972
Bill Stafford   1960–65
Jake Stahl   1908
Roy Staiger   1979
Tuck Stainback   1942–45
Gerry Staley   1955–56
Charley Stanceu   1941
Fred Stanley   1973–79
Dick Starr   1947–48
Rick Stelmaszek   1976
Dutch Sterrett   1912–13
Bud Stewart   1948
Lee Stine   1938
Snuffy Stirnweiss   1943–50
Mel Stottlemyre   1964–74
Hal Stowe   1960
Gabby Street   1912
Marlin Stuart   1954
Bill Stumpf   1912–13
Tom Sturdivant   1955–59
Johnny Sturm   1941
Bill Sudakis   1974
Steve Sundra   1936, 1938–40
Ed Sweeney   1908–15
Ron Swoboda   1971–73

Fred Talbot   1966–69
Vito Tamulis   1934–35
Jesse Tannehill   1903
Zack Taylor   1934
Frank Tepedino   1967, 1969–72
Ralph Terry   1956–57, 1959–64
Dick Tettelbach   1955
Ira Thomas   1906–07
Lee Thomas   1961
Myles Thomas   1926–29
Stan Thomas   1977

Gary Thomasson   1978
Homer Thompson   1912
Tommy Thompson   1912
Jack Thoney   1904
Hank Thormahlen   1917–20
Marv Throneberry   1955, 1958–59
Luis Tiant   1979
Dick Tidrow   1974–79
Bobby Tiefenauer   1965
Eddie Tiemeyer   1909
Ray Tift   1907
Bob Tillman   1967
Thad Tillotson   1967–68
Dan Tipple   1915
Earl Torgeson   1961
Rusty Torres   1971–72
Mike Torrez   1977
Cesar Tovar   1976
Tom Tresh   1961–69
Gus Triandos   1953–54
Virgil Trucks   1958
Frank Truesdale   1914
Bob Turley   1955–62
Jim Turner   1942–45

George Uhle   1933–34
Bob Unglaub   1904
Cecil Upshaw   1974

Elmer Valo   1960
Russ Van Atta   1933–35
Dazzy Vance   1915
Joe Vance   1937–38
Bobby Vaughn   1909
Hippo Vaughn   1908, 1910–12
Bobby Veach   1925
Otto Velez   1973–76
Joe Verbanic   1967–68, 1970
Frank Verdi   1953
Sammy Vick   1917–20

Jake Wade   1946
Dick Wakefield   1950
Curt Walker   1919
Dixie Walker   1931, 1933–36
Mike Wallace   1974–75
Jimmy Walsh   1914
Joe Walsh   1910–11
Roxy Walters   1915–18
Danny Walton   1971
Paul Waner   1944–45
Jack Wanner   1909
Pee Wee Wanninger   1925
Aaron Ward   1917–26
Joe Ward   1909
Pete Ward   1970
Jack Warhop   1908–15
George Wasburn   1941
Gary Waslewski   1970–71
Roy Weatherly   1943
Jim Weaver   1931
Lefty Weinert   1931

Ed Wells   1929–32
Butch Wensloff   1943
Julie Wera   1927
Bill Werber   1930
Dennis Werth   1979
Steve Whitaker   1966–68
Roy White   1965–79
George Whiteman   1913
Terry Whitfield   1974–76
Kemp Wicker   1936–38
Al Wickland   1919
Bob Wiesler   1951, 1954–55
Bill Wight   1946–47
Ed Wilkinson   1911
Bob Williams   1911–14
Harry Williams   1913
Jimmy Williams   1903–07
Stan Williams   1963–64
Walt Williams   1974–75
Archie Wilson   1951–52
Pete Wilson   1908–09
Ted Wilson   1956
Snake Wiltse   1903
Gordie Windhorn   1959
Mickey Witek   1949
Whitey Witt   1922–25
Bill Wolfe   1903–04
Harry Wolter   1910–13
Harry Wolverton   1912
Dooley Womack   1966–68
Gene Woodling   1949–54
Ron Woods   1969–71
Dick Woodson   1974
Hank Workman   1950
Ken Wright   1974
Yats Wuestling   1930
John Wyatt   1968
Jim Wynn   1977

Joe Yeager   1905–06
Jim York   1976
Ralph Young   1913

Tom Zachary   1928–30
Jack Zalusky   1903
George Zeber   1977–78
Rollie Zeider   1913
Guy Zinn   1911–12
Bill Zuber   1943–46

YANKEE STADIUM DIMENSIONS

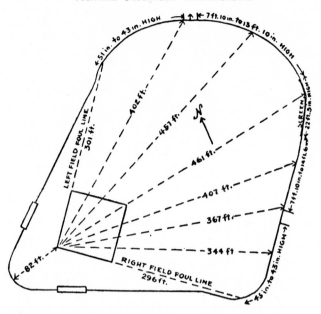

The House That Ruth Built (1923)

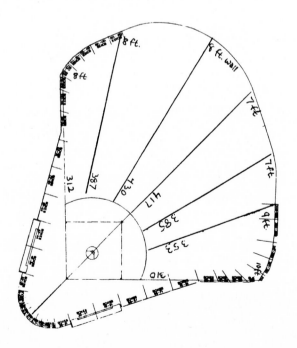

The remodeled stadium (1976)

About the Authors

ROBERT CREAMER, a senior editor at *Sports Illustrated* magazine, is the author of *Babe—The Legend Comes to Life,* a biography of Babe Ruth. He has been with *SI* since its inception in 1954 and has published four other books.

DAVE ANDERSON, a sports columnist for *The New York Times,* is the author of ten books and nearly 250 magazine articles. His books include *Always on the Run,* with Larry Csonka and Jim Kiick, and most recently *Sports of Our Times.*

HAROLD ROSENTHAL covered the Yankees for the New York *Herald Tribune* for virtually all of the Mantle era. He is the author of four books, including *Baseball Is Their Business, Baseball's Best Managers* and *Playing Pro Football to Win* with John Unitas.

MURRAY CHASS, a sportswriter for *The New York Times,* has covered the Yankees throughout the Reggie Jackson years. He joined the *Times* sports staff in 1969 after nearly ten years with the Associated Press. He is recognized as an authority on baseball's legal and labor problems. His reporting of Billy Martin's statements about George Steinbrenner and Reggie Jackson led to Martin's resignation as Yankee manager in July 1978.